The Salome Project

The Salome Project

SALOME AND HER AFTERLIVES

Gail P. Streete

CASCADE *Books* • Eugene, Oregon

THE SALOME PROJECT
Salome and Her Afterlives

Copyright © 2018 Gail P. Streete. All rights reserved. Except for brief quotations in critical publications or reviews, no part of this book may be reproduced in any manner without prior written permission from the publisher. Write: Permissions, Wipf and Stock Publishers, 199 W. 8th Ave., Suite 3, Eugene, OR 97401.

Cascade Books
An Imprint of Wipf and Stock Publishers
199 W. 8th Ave., Suite 3
Eugene, OR 97401

www.wipfandstock.com

PAPERBACK ISBN: 978-1-5326-1887-1
HARDCOVER ISBN: 978-1-4982-4472-5
EBOOK ISBN: 978-1-4982-4471-8

Cataloging-in-Publication data:

Names: Streete, Gail Paterson, 1949–, author.

Title: The Salome project : Salome and her afterlives / Gail P. Streete.

Description: Eugene, OR: Cascade Books, 2018. | Includes bibliographical references and index.

Identifiers: ISBN: 978-1-5326-1887-1 (paperback). | ISBN: 978-1-4982-4472-5 (hardcover). | ISBN: 978-1-4982-4471-8 (ebook).

Subjects: LCSH: Salome (Biblical figure).

Classification: BS2520.S6 S77 2018 (print). | BS2520 (ebook).

Manufactured in the U.S.A.

The Scripture quotations contained herein are from the New Revised Standard Version Bible copyright © 1989 by the Division of Christian Education of the National Council of Churches of Christ in the U. S. A., and are used by permission. All rights reserved.

To Mom: A veteran of many an Easter pageant

Contents

Preface | *ix*

Acknowledgments | *xi*

Abbreviations | *xiii*

Introduction: The Salome Project | 1

1. The Daughter of Herodias | 13

2. Salome and the Head of John the Baptist | 37

3. Salome Counter Salome | 62

4. Reviving Salome | 96

Bibliography | 127

Index | 139

Preface

This book represents a departure for me as a scholar and writer. My main field of expertise is Late Antiquity and Early Christianity, although I can venture and have ventured into the Middle Ages and dipped a toe into the Renaissance and Reformation, albeit with trepidation. My explorations into the story of Salome (if there was a Salome) and her dance (if there was a dance) have led me into some wild and strange places where, though fascinated, I have not felt exactly at home. As a faculty member at a liberal arts college for twenty-three years, I became used to venturing outside of my comfort zone in my teaching, and, although I had no desire to reinvent myself, I did enjoy forays into places other than where my previous training led me. This book is an extension and perhaps an inevitable outcome of these expeditions.

Although it is obvious from the introduction that I have a long-standing interest in Salome's dance, my curiosity about it resurfaced about six years ago, when I was in my office, musing about possibilities for another book, when I suddenly thought, "What was that darned dance of Salome, anyway?" A flurry of Google searches and an avalanche of Post-It notes (my favored form of note-taking) later, I still had no answer. But I had a lot of questions, and a lot of avenues for research.

It turned out that one avenue led to another, and that led to several more alleys, and so on. The search was endless. I grew to realize that I could never determine what The Dance was, nor could I completely explore all the numerous byways and intersections in the "Salome narrative." That is why I decided to call this work, *The Salome Project*. It represents years of this kind of exploration, conversations with friends and colleagues, eventually stepping into the deep end of areas I was unfamiliar with. Hence, a highly personal and possibly quirky exploration of the topic of Salome and

Preface

her dance. I do not pretend to have explored or covered everything. Many others have done in-depth scholarship on various pieces of the Salome puzzle. What I do want is to share my sense of astonishment and at times incredulity at the places my search has led. I have singled out some of the treatments of the Salome legend, and probably have neglected or dismissed others, not for lack of interest, but for lack of space. The bibliography supplies not only the texts I have cited, but others about Salome, so the readers may do their own explorations. I have found that Salome is infinite. This is the idea I hope to convey.

Memphis, November 2017

Acknowledgments

In a project of this duration (six years and counting!), there are many people who have been involved, whether they wanted to be or not. And thanks are due to them all, in many ways, for taking an interest in what is admittedly a very idiosyncratic venture.

First, and foremost, to the Salome hunters and gatherers, especially Sally Dormer, of the Victoria and Albert Museum. She was an indefatigable expert at uncovering the most unusual and provocative of the medieval depictions of Salome. Thanks also to members of the Women in the Biblical World Section of the Society of Biblical Literature: Amy Easton-Flake, of Brigham Young University, for her contribution of Harriet Beecher Stowe's work on biblical women, and Nancy Heisey, of Eastern Mennonite University, for pointing me to Pier Paolo Pasolini's Salome. Thanks also to the Shakespeare Theatre Company for inviting me to write a brief history of Salome and acquainting me with Yaël Farber's work. (And to Amy-Jill Levine, for putting them in touch with me.)

Early versions of this work had assistance from (as ever) my friend of fifty years (and no mean wordsmith herself), Linda Laufer, who talked me through the story of Salome, and asked a storyteller's questions. Stevens Anderson helped with the essential question: "What do you want to do with this?" John Loudon, of Yale University Press, provided invaluable help with critique in the early stages of writing.

Colleagues at Rhodes College provided me with information and steered me in new directions. My thanks to Shira Malkin and Jonathan Judaken, who acquainted me with *la belle juive* and her role in European literature. Thanks also to Scott Newstok, who sent me information on "Spotlight: Salome."

Acknowledgments

To the editors and staff at Cascade Books, my most heartfelt thanks—especially to K. C. Hanson for his enthusiasm and support, to Matthew Wimer for his understanding and encouragement, and to Jeremy Funk for his meticulous copyediting.

To Jack Streete, who always believes in me more than I believe in myself. And to Delta, for sitting patiently so often outside my office door and whimpering only a little. Love you two.

To the late Walter and Betty Aures, composers of many an Easter pageant. Thanks for my first taste of acting. And to Marlene, wherever you are—you started it all.

Abbreviations

ALUOS	*Annual of Leeds University Oriental Society*
BBR	*Bulletin for Biblical Research*
BibInt	*Biblical Interpretation*
CCEL	Christian Classics Ethereal Library
ExpT	*Expository Times*
JAAR	*Journal of the American Academy of Religion*
JBL	*Journal of Biblical Literature*
JSNT	*Journal for the Study of the New Testament*
JSOT	*Journal for the Study of the Old Testament*
LCL	Loeb Classical Library
LS	*Louvain Studies*
LW	*Luther's Works*
NovT	*Novum Testamentum*
NPNF1	Nicene and Post-Nicene Fathers, Series 1
NPNF2	Nicene and Post-Nicene Fathers, Series 2
NTS	*New Testament Studies*
PG	Patrologia Graeca
PL	Patrologia Latina

Introduction

THE DANCE

When I was a girl in First United Methodist Church in Buffalo, New York, we did not have the usual church Christmas pageants. For some reason, we had Easter pageants instead. These took place, not in the church basement auditorium like the usual Sunday school dramas, but on the altar platform in the main sanctuary. The pageants were major productions, and almost always were about the events of Passion Week. With one exception, Easter in Camelot, they took place in Jesus's day and were loosely based on the canonical gospel accounts, with the dialogue in King James English, of course. The plays were staged by an older couple who were the writers, directors, and producers, and who had illusions about someday having their dramas performed in a venue other than church, aspirations that were sadly but understandably defeated. But in church everyone took the pageants seriously. There were auditions and costumes. I always got a part, sometimes a very minor one that required me to say things like, "Look, father!" or "Lo!" or to wave a palm branch and shout, "Hosanna!"

My clearest memories are of an Easter pageant when I was about twelve years old because it was somewhat controversial, and I was more envious than usual of someone with a bigger part. The controversy was caused by the fact that our playwrights had chosen to represent Salome's[1] dance before Herod and the subsequent beheading of John the Baptist. Ironically, this episode, which occurs only in the Gospels of Mark (6:22–29) and Matthew (14:1–12), is not strictly speaking a part of the Passion narrative in

---

1. The spelling of *Salome* varies. It is sometimes spelled with an acute accent on the last syllable: "Salomé." I will normally spell it without the accent, except as it occurs in excerpts or titles from other authors: for example, Oscar Wilde's *Salomé*.

either. The episode does in a sense foreshadow the death of Jesus, since in both Mark 6:14–16 and Matt 14:1–2, a guilty Herod believes that Jesus may be John risen from the dead. While the part of Herod in the pageant was readily sewn up by my very hammy Sunday school teacher and that of John was relatively easy—he appeared only as a papier-mâché head on an ersatz silver platter—that of Salome was more difficult. It definitely required a dance. In popular imagination, it required a sexy dance, unquestionably the "Dance of the Seven Veils," virtually a striptease. And for the older members of the congregation, including women who still belonged to the Women's Christian Temperance Union, any dancing was out of the question. One stalwart pillar of church and Sunday school expressed the opinion that "dancing is vile!" and boycotted the performance. Even though the pageant would go forward as planned, questions remained: Who would do the Dance? What would it be like? And what would she *wear*?

As it turned out, the playwrights eschewed what everyone thought would be the "Dance of the Seven Veils" and opted for a more acrobatic, gymnastic Salome. Probably without knowing it, they were following in the footsteps of several Romanesque and medieval depictions of an athletic Salome.[2] Veils did not enter into it. One of my fellow junior choir members, a tall girl about my age named Marlene, who was an accomplished gymnast, got the part. I was pea-green with envy. The costume was a great compromise: it consisted of a long, swirling skirt that left only her feet bare (she danced barefoot) and had a bodice that would have bared her midriff, except that a swathe of heavy netting left no skin showing. I remember that the whole costume was heavily studded with sequins in a nod to Hollywood Salomes. I don't know who choreographed the dance, perhaps Marlene herself, but it owed a lot to fabric and gymnastics. The most breathtaking part of it was the end, when Salome sank into a graceful split right in front of Herod. The audience gasped.

Looking back recently on that dance, I began wondering, not why Marlene couldn't do the Dance of the Seven Veils in church, but what Salome's dance was supposed to be. Clearly it was persuasive. Clearly it had fatal consequences. Herod Antipas was enthralled by it. And for centuries, so have we been. We are drawn and drawn again, with admiration, with envy, with desire—sometimes with loathing—to a spectacle that is

---

2. For example, on an eleventh-century bronze plate from the Veronese church of San Zeno, she is bent backwards in an improbable circle, as in a fourteenth-century illustration in a festal missal from the Abbey of St.-Jean-sur-la-Celle, Amiens. See chapter 2 for other examples.

Introduction

described with such tantalizing brevity in only two of the gospels—eight verses in Mark, six in Matthew—that each age inevitably supplies its own details and versions of the event. I started out trying to find what the dance itself was, only to be stymied by the fact that the "Dance of the Seven Veils" was a parenthetical stage direction by Oscar Wilde in his 1891 play, *Salomé*.[3] I then wanted to know what the first-century form of that dance might have been, only to find that it is probably the most famous dance that never took place, just as its unnamed performer, for centuries known as Salome, is "a woman who never was."[4]

THE SALOME PROJECT

Trying to discover (or uncover) the myriad versions both of dancer and dance has been a search that has led me down many interesting, frustrating, and occasionally exhilarating byways. I even thought at one point that I could rehabilitate the image of Salome by seeing her as a child, innocently and unconsciously pushed by her mother into a performance with fatal consequences and subsequently eroticized,[5] the JonBenét Ramsey of the first century, a sexualized miniature woman, substituting for a mother who is no longer sure of her powers of physical attraction. American novelist Joyce Carol Oates writes of the simultaneous fascination and revulsion many observers felt on seeing photos and videos of the murdered child beauty queen:

> Imposed upon her childish innocence like a lurid mask is a look of sexual precocity . . . The expensive, ludicrous costumes the child has been made to wear are as much a part of the display as the child herself. Perhaps, for the mother who obsessively displayed her, a former Miss West Virginia, the costumes were more important than the child for the signals they sent of an exhibitionist, aggressive "femininity." (. . . One of her routines was a mock striptease, the removal of a see-through skirt.) Part of the power of JonBenét Ramsey as a symbolic presence in contemporary American consciousness is the paradox of what she, or her image, might mean. Is she Mommy's little girl dolled up to attract the male gaze as Mommy no longer can? Is she a defiant image, provoking male

---

3. According to Becker-Leckrone, "Fetishization of a Textual Corpus," 255–56, the "Dance of the Seven Veils" is Wilde's own invention.
4. Neginsky, *Salome*, front cover, subtitle.
5. Kraemer, "Implicating Herodias," 349.

desire even as, with her undeveloped, seemingly asexual body, she can have no intention of satisfying it? Or is she a mockery of female sexiness, all makeup and costumes? Is she purely for show, thus pure? Is the perversity of her image exclusively in the eye of the beholder?[6]

Many of these questions could be and have been asked about Salome. Often, they reveal more about the questioner than about the image: Oates, for example, cannot hide her distaste for the very idea of a child beauty pageant. In the end, however, just as JonBenét's life and death remain a mystery in which the erotic, the fatal, and a grisly kind of fascination with both are inextricably entwined, so with Salome. I found that I could not rehabilitate, reconstruct, or even conversely deconstruct Salome; I could not make a complete catalog of "all things Salome."[7] The project continually mushroomed. I found that, as Laurie Colwin sagely observes in quite another context, "Like most heroic quests, this search has not turned up any ultimates, but the adventure has definitely been worthwhile."[8] Salome is an ongoing project, a personal and somewhat idiosyncratic study of responses over time to the tantalizing nexus of sexuality, desire, death, religion, and the politics of gender that her tale offers. We seem to be always constructing Salome, building on or rejecting what went before. According to Carmen Trammell Skaggs, "While the basic elements of the [Salome] narrative remain in each interpretation, the individual interpreter reacts and responds to the cultural and artistic ideologies of his [sic] own time."[9] The literary and artistic "afterlives" of Salome are basically *midrashim*—interpretive retellings—of the bare yet allusive bones of the story as we find it in Mark and Matthew. Like all midrashim, they expand and alter the narrative to fit changing cultural and spiritual needs.

Since this project began as, and to some extent remains, a highly personal venture, I am not especially interested in advancing or advocating a theory that fits or explains all representations of Salome. I do not think it is possible, even if we could track them down and gather them into a single volume. But if, on the other hand, there were to be a unifying theme, it

---

6. Oates, "Mystery of JonBenét Ramsey," 2.

7. The closest that I have found to this all-inclusive catalog is an entry by Gabriele Boccaccini in material on 4 Enoch within the *Online Encyclopedia of Second Temple Judaism and Christian Origins*. See Boccaccini, ed., "Category: Salome."

8. Colwin, *More Home Cooking*, 66.

9. Skaggs, "Modernity's Revision," 125.

INTRODUCTION

would be the way Salome and her mother and frequent alter ego, Herodias, are used to "think with," as women frequently are, by writers, artists, and theologians who have historically been overwhelmingly men; therefore Salome and Herodias become images that reflect male anxieties, desires, and ideals. Even the stories of female historical figures with well-known factual backgrounds have been subject to legendary embellishments and downright mythologizing. How much more the Herodian Salome, about whom we know so little historically, and who appears so tangentially in the biblical narratives. The figure of Salome has been made to "work" in various representations and transfigurations, as both subject and object of desire, from the very moment she is made to dance before Herod Antipas at his birthday dinner. My aim in this book, therefore, is not to follow the arc of a Salome narrative (if there even is such a thing) in every detail from the first century to the twenty-first. I want rather to show how several "afterlives" of Salome contribute to a persistent image of her, one that later interpreters accept, even as they resist or revise it.

THE SALOME NARRATIVE

We might begin with a brief outline of the story as it appears in the Gospels of Mark (about 70 CE) and Matthew (85–95 CE), who used Mark as a source. There is no such story in the Gospel of Luke or John, for reasons that will be suggested in chapter 1. Herod Antipas, one of the sons of Herod the Great, and himself the ruler of Galilee with the support of the Roman occupiers of Judea, has arrested the apocalyptic prophet and preacher of repentance, John the Baptist.[10] John has dared to criticize what he believes is a sinful marriage between Herod Antipas and his second wife, Herodias, who has divorced Herod's brother Philip. The issue is not one of divorce per se, but that Herod has married his brother's wife while that brother is still alive, thus violating the religious law cited in Leviticus 18:16. Herod wants to execute John but is afraid to do so because of John's popularity. Herodias also desires John's death, and finds the opportunity to contrive it at a birthday banquet for Herod, to which he has invited his courtiers and the leaders of Galilee. Herodias sends her daughter to dance for the company, and the dance—or the dancer—pleases Herod so much that he

---

10. He is also referred to in some translations as John the Baptizer, emphasizing the practice rather than the title.

vows he will give the girl whatever she asks, "even half of my kingdom."[11] Prompted by her mother, the girl asks for the head of John the Baptist on a platter. Because Herod has sworn an oath before the entire company that he considers irrevocable, he regretfully orders her request to be carried out. The girl gives the head on the platter to her mother. John's disciples come, take the body, and put it in a tomb. We are not told here what became of the head. There is no further word in either gospel about Herodias or her daughter. Herod has a brief mention again in Mark, in a warning by Jesus to his disciples: "Beware the yeast of the Pharisees and of Herod (Mark 8:15)," perhaps a reference to the earlier conspiracy between the Pharisees and "Herodians" to kill Jesus (Mark 3:6). Herod does appear briefly in the passion narrative in Luke 23:6–12, but has no further role to play in Mark or Matthew, and plays none in the Gospel of John.

The dancer who asks for the head of John the Baptist in the Gospels of Mark and Matthew is not named, although she is called Herodias in some manuscript traditions. She has only a cursory appearance, and so has provided a virtual blank slate for conjecture. In fact, it could be said that the "daughter of Herodias" who so briefly enters the gospels is herself a construction of the writers, serving their own anti-Herodian bias[12] as they offer up what become the classic threads of the story: an adulterous couple—a corrupt, foolish king and his scheming queen—and a dance as entertainment at a formal banquet, with fatal consequences for a righteous prophet. The girl who dances in the gospels is called a *korasion*, a "little girl," probably under twelve years old.[13] On the mere surface of it, as I have previously claimed, there is nothing in either text to suggest that the dance is erotic in nature.[14] Throughout both gospel narratives, the power behind the scenes is Herodias, with her desire to manipulate her husband into getting rid of an influential and critical prophet whom she hates. Yet even here we must assume, not being specifically told, that Herodias put her daughter up to the dance, knowing what its effect would be. As any interpreter understands, the surface does not carry the whole meaning of the text: there are contexts and nuances, together with echoes from biblical and classical literature, within the brief narrative, that will be discussed in chapter 1,

---

11. All English quotations from the Bible, unless otherwise noted, are taken from the New Revised Standard Version (NRSV).
12. Kraemer, "Implicating Herodias," 321–49.
13. Her age and its implications for the narrative will be discussed in chapter 1.
14. Streete, *Strange Woman*, 149.

which I initially and perhaps willfully missed in my desire to see Salome and her dance as unconsciously innocent.

SALOME'S AFTERLIVES

Even so, based on my reading of the story in the gospel texts, I became more and more puzzled about the afterlives of Salome, if we can indeed call her by the name first given to Herodias's daughter by the first-century historian Josephus,[15] and how she went from a little girl who danced at her stepfather's birthday party to entertain him and his guests to the "idol of perversity," in Bram Dijkstra's pungent phrase, the epitome of self-absorbed feminine evil.[16] By the nineteenth century, a kind of master narrative of Salome had developed, to the extent that, as Anthony Pym observes, 82 percent of the art and literature in the "Salome corpus" is produced between 1860 and 1920.[17]

Oscar Wilde's one-act play *Salomé* (1891) is probably the most influential moment in the modern afterlife of Salome. It is a culmination of several centuries of art and literature that spotlight the dancing daughter and her role in the gruesome death of John the Baptist, with his severed head as her trophy. It is this play that contains the brief yet enormously influential direction, "Salomé dances the Dance of the Seven Veils." Richard Strauss's opera *Salomé* based on Wilde's play, premiered in 1905, with his protagonist also performing the Dance of the Seven Veils. A recent controversial production of Strauss's opera at Belfast's Grand Opera House in February of 2015 left Salome nude after the removal of the seventh veil, leading to protests that the stage production had "sexualized" the biblical narrative. Such protests quite forgot or ignored the fact that both Wilde's play and Strauss's opera had done exactly that, following a host of late nineteenth-century depictions of a highly eroticized Salome—also somewhat confusingly called Herodias—including Heinrich Heine's *Atta Troll*, Gustave Flaubert's "Hérodiade," several paintings by Gustave Moreau, and Joris-Karl Huysmans's *À Rebours* (*Against the Grain*), among other portrayals characterized as

---

15. After Josephus, the name Salome is applied to Herodias's dancing daughter as early as the fifth century, but the name is not applied consistently until the latter part of the nineteenth century. See Wikipedia, "Salome."

16. Dijkstra, *Idols of Perversity*, 380–401.

17. Pym, "Importance of Salome," 312. See also Bach, *Women, Seduction, and Betrayal*, 210–62.

Decadent and Symbolist. Wilde's play and Strauss's opera gave birth to—or perhaps rode the crest of—a wave of dancers in the early twentieth century eager to present Salome's fatal dance on the stage, characterized at the time as "the Salome dance," in a phenomenon so well known that it was called "Salomania."[18] Wilde's portrayal of Salome, as it gathers in these representations and adapts them, has influenced and dominated most subsequent portrayals, right up to the present. American actor Al Pacino's fascination with Wilde's play led him to direct, and to play King Herod in no fewer than three versions. The first stage version (2006) was the basis for a documentary drama, *Wilde Salomé* (2011), which later appeared, minus the documentary, simply as a staging of *Salomé* (2013). Most recently, South African playwright Yaël Farber adapted Wilde's *Salomé* for the Women's Voices in Theatre Festival (2015), presenting it as a political play that takes back the story and retells it in Salome's voice, as an ally of John the Baptist. Farber portrays her Salome as acting against the patriarchal grain, but the power of her adaptation derives in part from deliberately countering the decadent feminine sensuality of Wilde's character.[19]

If Wilde's virginal femme fatale has become the dominant image of Salome, there are nonetheless other, albeit minor, strains of the Salome legend that attempt to complete her story, including her death (a different one than Wilde constructed for her) or to rehabilitate her image. Nineteenth-century American writers produced literature on Salome that is largely apologetic. Christian themes of fall and redemption are reflected in J. C. Heywood's florid trilogy of dramatic poems, *Herodias* (1867), *Salome* (1862, revised in 1867), and *Antoninus* (1867), all of which feature Salome as an ally of John the Baptist, whom she calls her "Good Master," and as an innocent victim of her scheming mother, Herodias. Heywood's Salome eventually becomes a Christian and a virtual martyr. Heywood's poem *Salome* was deemed inspiring by Ralph Waldo Emerson, but less so by Oscar Wilde, who nevertheless transferred Heywood's image of Herodias abusing the Baptist's head to Salome in his own drama.[20] Harriet Beecher Stowe also portrayed Salome in her chapter "The Daughter of Herodias" in her *Woman in Sacred*

---

18. Medieval dancers also produced a "Dance of Salome," as will be shown in chapter 2.

19. Streete, "Salomé as History and Fetish," 14–17.

20. Wilde reviewed Heywood's *Salome* in The Poet's Corner of the *Pall Mall Gazette* (February 19, 1888) with less than enthusiasm. See a fuller discussion by Neginsky, *Salome*, 169.

Introduction

History (1873),[21] acknowledging the story as "a favorite subject among artists as giving an opportunity of painting female beauty and fascination in affinity with the deepest and most dreadful tragedy."[22] She castigates Herod for being "licentious," and Herodias as a "bad woman," but exempts her daughter, because of her childlike innocence, from moral culpability for the Baptist's death.

The English poet Michael Field—the pseudonym of Katherine Bradley and Edith Cooper—used a little-known legend of the death of Salome, when she was decapitated by falling through the ice on which she was dancing, in "A Dance of Death," which appears in a volume of devotional poetry, *Poems of Adoration* (1912), written after their conversion to Catholicism. Previously, in the seventeenth century, the Welsh metaphysical poet Henry Vaughan had used the same story in his poem, "The Daughter of Herodias," but referred to Salome as a "yong [sic] Sorceress," speaking of the "vain, sinful Art" of her dancing, with its "lewd loath'd Motions."[23] Field, on the other hand, neither exonerates nor condemns the dancer, but simply marvels at the "lovely dancing-girl" whose "spell" is joined by "Winter, in a rapture of delight." Her death is not described as a retribution—the mention of John the Baptist at the end of the poem simply acknowledges the stillness of his head, in contrast to Salome's still-dancing one, after he had "done God's will."[24]

Anzia Yezierska's romantic, radical "immigrant novel," *Salome of the Tenements* (1923), revived the idea of an unsustainable love between Salome and John the Baptist, setting it in the conflict between "Oriental" (Jewish) immigrants and Anglo-Saxon (Protestant) Brahmins. When the passionate Eastern European Jewish immigrant, the working-class Sonya Vrunsky, achieves marriage to the upright WASP John Manning, he initially repulses her overt sexual need, only to become "the cross on which he bled" in his own aroused need for her,[25] an interesting twist on the rejection of Salome by John the Baptist in Wilde's play, a rejection that can only be resolved by John's death.

---

21. My thanks to Amy Easton-Flake, "Harriet Beecher Stowe's Popular Exegesis," for her analysis of Stowe's work.
22. Stowe, *Women in Sacred History*, 321–23.
23. Vaughan, "The Daughter of Herodias," stanza 3.
24. Field, " A Dance of Death," stanza 8.
25. Yezierska, *Salome of the Tenements*, 108, 182.

A FEMINIST SALOME?

Given the multiplicity of reinventions and reinterpretations of the Salome narrative, there is surprisingly little feminist commentary that interprets Herodias's daughter's dance positively, or attributes any kind of agency to Salome herself. Most interpreters point out the inherent misogyny of the gospel texts, with Herodias, rather than Salome, as the object of sexual suspicion, or they point out the objectification of the dancer as an object of the male gaze.[26] Joanna Dewey's feminist analysis of Herod's banquet in Mark 6:7–29 merely remarks that while "Christian interpreters have used the . . . story to blame female behavior for male lust," a "more feminist interpretation" would make Herodias's use of her daughter regrettably necessary because of the patriarchal nature of the culture, in which women can only achieve their ends by manipulating men in power, even if it means using other women to do so.[27] Jennifer Glancy agrees that "the women in the scene have no power that Herod has not given them," but concentrates largely on the ways that late nineteenth- and twentieth-century interpreters read the Markan text, noting only that "the familiar, iconic Salome is an invention of men's imagination."[28] Janice Capel Anderson, who is among the few commentators to attribute a possible innocence to the dance, agrees that the story in Mark reflects assumptions both of the writer and of his interpreters.[29] Similarly, Alice Bach prefers a "cool" reading of the dance, based on an interpretation that "the kind of pleasure the daughter's dance evokes (Mark 6:22) . . . refers not to erotic pleasure but rather to 'accommodating' someone."[30] Ross S. Kraemer's analysis of the narrative, which refers to Glancy and Anderson, tries to "rehabilitate both the historical Salome, who is likely to have played no role in the death of John, and probably her mother Herodias, who, if she played any role, is unlikely to have played the particularly craven role assigned to her," but Kraemer focuses on the story as feeding a Christian apologetic need to prove that Jesus cannot be John risen from the dead, as Herod fears.[31]

---

26. Streete, *Strange Woman*, 150. See also Maureen Mara's reimaging the story from Herodias's point of view in Schüssler Fiorenza, *But She Said*, 48–50.
27. Dewey, "Gospel of Mark," 482–84.
28. Glancy, "Unveiling Masculinity," 34–50.
29. Anderson, "Feminist Criticism," 111–43.
30. Bach, "Calling the Shots," 109.
31. Kraemer, "Implicating Herodias," 348–49. Adela Yarbro Collins's commentary on Mark also contends that his account "seeks to exonerate Antipas for the execution of

INTRODUCTION

There are two rare exceptions in this feminist criticism. One is Ella Ferris Pell's painting of Salome (1890). According to Bram Dijkstra and Elaine Showalter, this American painter's Salome is a "feminist" Salome, although one widely ignored by the critics.[32] Pensively, she carries the charger on which John the Baptist's head will either be carried or has already been presented. Pell makes a "revolutionary feminist statement for its period," a Salome that is without "crazed sexual hunger."[33] As Dijkstra observes, Pell's painting "makes a revolutionary statement" by depicting "a real-life woman, independent, confident, and assertive."[34] (Nevertheless, it must be noted that she is standing with the plate on which the severed head of John the Baptist will soon rest.) The second feminist exception is recounted in Toni Bentley's *Sisters of Salome* (2002). Bentley, a dancer herself, highlights the seminude exotic dancers who followed "the way of Salome" in performances that claimed the female body as sensual and powerful, but beyond guilt. For Bentley, these women demonstrated "the triumph of a woman's erotic power" found in Salome's dance, a power that elicits and then thwarts male desire.[35] The problem with Bentley's argument is that Salome's dance cannot be recovered for triumphant female eroticism by divorcing it from its inevitable consequence, the death of John by beheading. As Helen Grace Zagona's history of the Salome legend points out, the rise of veneration of the Baptist and for his relics increasingly spotlights the fatal dance and the dancer's seductive culpability in the prophet's grisly end.[36] Legends from the sixth century onward have created a retributive end for Salome: she falls through the ice and drowns, or her own head is cut off by jagged shards of ice after it breaks. In Wilde's play, she is crushed to death beneath the shields of Herod's soldiers at his command; Jules Massenet's opera *Hérodiade* (1881) has her stab herself after seducing the Baptist; Jules Laforgue's *Moralités Légendaires* (1887) fantastically depicts her falling into the sea while attempting to throw the Baptist's head into it; Constantine Cavafy, in his poem "Salome (1896)" has Salome cut off first John's head, and then have her own head cut off as a gift to her heedless sophist lover; Carlos Saura's 2002 film has Salome hang herself. All these accretions are a far cry

John and to place the blame on Herodias" (Collins, *Mark*, 19–20).
32. Showalter, *Sexual Anarchy*, 158–59. Dijkstra, *Idols of Perversity*, 392–93.
33. Dijkstra, *Idols of Perversity*, 392.
34. Ibid.
35. Bentley, *Sisters of Salome*, 16.
36. Zagona, *Legend of Salome*, 20.

from the stark scenario presented in the Gospels of Mark and Matthew, but even their accounts are constructed upon and echo previous stories of foolish leaders, dangerous and drunken banquets, manipulative women, and ill-considered vows, as we shall see in chapter 1.

1

The Daughter of Herodias

WHO WAS HERODIAS'S DAUGHTER?

The Evidence of Josephus

Before we can consider the afterlives of Salome, if that is indeed her name, we need to look at her original life. Like all stories of legendary and mythic characters, hers begins even before her birth. The dancing daughter of Herodias in the Gospels of Mark and Matthew is either unnamed in some manuscripts, or named Herodias in others; so how does she come down to us by the name of Salome? The daughter of Herodias long continued to be referred to as "Herodias," "Herodias's daughter," "the woman who danced" or the "dancing girl."[1] The answer ultimately comes from the Jewish historian Flavius Josephus (37–100 CE), who wrote a multivolume history, *The Antiquities of the Jews*, an apologetic attempt to explain Jewish history to Gentiles, particularly the conquering Romans. In his history, he emphasizes the ancient origin of the Jewish religion and the Jews' deep respect for the law, two areas likely to impress the Romans, who valued antiquity and law highly. The probable need for such a work came from Josephus's own rather checkered history of relations with the Romans. Josephus was born Yosef ben Matityahu, of priestly and possibly royal descent. He led the Galilean forces against the Romans in the First Jewish War, an uprising against Roman domination (66–70 CE), but was forced to surrender his forces at Jotapata in 67, probably saving his life by deftly interpreting Jewish messianic prophecies to mean that the commander of the Roman forces,

1. Poplin, "Post-Biblical Traditions on John the Baptizer."

Vespasian, would become emperor of Rome, a prophecy that fortunately for Josephus came true. Yosef Latinized his name to Josephus and took his patron's family name, Flavius.

It is from Josephus's *Antiquities* that we find what little extrabiblical evidence there is of a connection between Herod Antipas, his (second) wife Herodias, and her daughter, to whom Josephus gives the name Salome, a Hellenized version of the Hebrew Shlomit (Josephus, *Antiquities of the Jews* 18.5.3). Josephus says that shortly after her daughter was born, "Herodias took it upon her to confound the laws of our country and divorced herself from her husband while he was still alive, and was married to Herod [Antipas], her husband's brother by the father's side" (*Ant.* 18.5.4.). The daughter of Herodias's first marriage, Salome, married her paternal uncle Philip and later her cousin Aristobulus, eventually becoming queen of Lesser Armenia, a fairly typical dynastic career for a Hellenistic princess.[2]

All this confusing family history is tangential to Josephus's main narrative, which relates Herod Antipas's war with Aretas IV, king of the Nabataeans, a war Josephus believes is occasioned by Herod's plan to divorce his wife, Aretas's daughter, to marry Herodias, his half-brother's wife, with whom he fell in love while staying with them on his way to Rome (*Ant.*18.5.1). Aretas's army easily annihilates that of Herod "through the treachery of some fugitives." When Herod complains to his superior, the Roman emperor Tiberius, the latter dispatches the governor of Syria, Vitellius, later to become a contender for the imperial throne himself, to defeat and capture Aretas. If that is not possible, Vitellius is to kill Aretas and send the emperor his head. Ross Kraemer suggests a possible link between Aretas's threatened death by decapitation and the death of John as reported in the Gospels of Mark and Matthew, seeing that no other author tells us how John died.[3] Tiberius's plan, however, was foiled by his own death. Nonetheless, "some of the Jews thought that the destruction of Herod's army came from God, and that very justly, as a punishment of what he [Herod] did against John, that was called the Baptist" (*Ant.* 18.5.2). Josephus goes on to describe John as "a good man [who] commanded the Jews to exercise virtue, both as to righteousness towards one another, and piety towards God." As Josephus relates it, John was such a popular preacher that Herod, being "of a suspicious temper," feared he would "raise a rebellion" and so

---

2. For endogamous marriage among the Herodians, see Hanson, "Herodians and Mediterranean Kinship," parts 1 and 2. My thanks to K.C. Hanson for these references.

3. Kraemer, "Implicating Herodias," 325.

The Daughter of Herodias

had him imprisoned at the fortress of Machaerus and subsequently put to death. Josephus does not specify the manner of John's' death.

From Josephus, then, we have the following story: Herod Antipas, tetrarch of Galilee and Perea thanks to Roman support, marries his (living) brother's (ex-)wife, Herodias. Josephus expresses his own view that this marriage is against "the laws of this country," presumably meaning the religious law of Leviticus 18:16. According to Josephus, Herodias has a daughter from her first marriage, here called Salome. Herod Antipas fears the preacher John the Baptist and has him put to death. By mentioning the belief of the Jews that Aretas's victory over Herod is the result of divine retribution, Josephus registers his own disapproval of Herod's self-interested political moves. What we do not have in this account is a banquet, a dance, a beheading, or even a definite age for Herodias's daughter. All we have is a name, that of her mother. If the events narrated in the gospels indeed took place and were known or even rumored, we may be sure that Josephus, who always loved gossip and a good scandal, especially if it was about elite women and their associations with foreign male religious leaders, certainly would not have hesitated to mention it.[4]

The Evidence of Mark and Matthew

Two gospels in the New Testament, Mark and Matthew, have a narrative that links Herod, Herodias, her daughter, and the death of John the Baptist. Of the other two canonical gospels, the Gospel of Luke assigns sole responsibility for John's death by beheading to Herod, who also fears that Jesus may be John raised from the dead (Luke 9:7-9). The Gospel of John features the Baptist prominently in chapters 1-3, both as a prophet ("a man sent by God") and a forerunner of Jesus ("a witness to the light"), but has no account of John's death. He simply disappears from the narrative when Jesus takes over. It is only in Mark and Matthew that we have any account at all of Herodias's and her daughter's involvement in John's death, which is opposed to Herod's reluctance to kill him, and the details of the dance and the outré demand for John's head on a serving dish.

---

4. In *Ant.* 18.3-5, for example, Josephus mentions the deception of the aristocratic Paulina by corrupt adherents of Isis, causing the priests of the religion to be crucified and the statue of the goddess thrown into the river Tiber. In the same chapters, he attributes the expulsion of Jews from Rome in that same year (19 CE) to the deception of an aristocratic Roman convert to Judaism, Fulvia, by Jews who persuaded her to donate purple and gold to the Temple in Jerusalem, then keeping it for themselves.

Nearly all biblical scholars assume that the Gospel of Mark, written around 70 CE, is the first of the canonical gospels, and that Mark's narrative of the Baptist's death has been used, with little alteration, by Matthew. As Mark tells the story, Herod Antipas has heard of Jesus's preaching about repentance, along with his exorcisms and healings, together with the speculation about who Jesus might be (Mark 6:14–15). As in Luke's narrative, so in Mark's Herod believes, "John, whom I beheaded, has been raised" (6:16). Mark's account reads as follows:

> For Herod himself had sent men who arrested John, bound him, and put him in prison on account of Herodias, his brother Philip's wife, because Herod had married her. For John had been telling Herod, "It is not lawful for you to have your brother's wife." And Herodias had a grudge against him, and wanted to kill him. But she could not, for Herod feared John, knowing he was a righteous and holy man, and protected him. When he heard him, he was greatly perplexed; and yet he liked to listen to him. But an opportunity came when Herod on his birthday gave a banquet for his courtiers and officers and for the leaders of Galilee. When his daughter Herodias came in and danced, she pleased Herod and his guests; and the king said to the girl, "Ask me for whatever you wish, and I will give it." And he solemnly swore to her, "Whatever you ask me, I will give you, even half of my kingdom." She went out and said to her mother, "What should I ask for?" She replied, "The head of John the baptizer." Immediately she rushed back to the king and requested, "I want you to give me at once the head of John the Baptist on a platter." The king was deeply grieved; yet out of regard for his oaths and for the guests, he did not want to refuse her. Immediately the king sent a soldier of the guard with orders to bring John's head. He went and beheaded him in the prison, brought his head on a platter, and gave it to the girl. Then the girl gave it to her mother. When his disciples heard about it, they came and took his body, and laid it in a tomb. (Mark 6:17–29)

This account moves quickly, as is characteristic of Mark's narrative style, assisted by the regular use of the adverb "immediately": once, when the daughter "rushed back" to the king with her mother's request for the head, which she wants "at once," and again, when Herod sends a guard to bring back the head. There is little time for reflection or description of motive on the girl's part, but there is nevertheless quite a bit about the motivation and emotions of Herod and Herodias. Josephus assigns a political motive to Herod's fear of John and his desire to get rid of him; Mark, however, states that the reason for John's arrest and imprisonment is "on account

The Daughter of Herodias

of Herodias, his brother Philip's wife." Mark also implies that Herod's fear of John may be a form of awe, since he listens to the Baptist with a kind of pleasure. Herodias's emotions are quite simply stated: she wants John dead. In Matthew's version of the story, Herod himself "wanted to put him [John] to death" (Matt 14:5) but is afraid of "the crowd" because of their regard for the righteous prophet. In both gospels, Herod is described as "pleased" with the dancer and her dance, but he is later "grieved" at her request because he has unthinkingly sworn an oath he feels he cannot retract. The emotions of the daughter do not enter the narrative, although in Mark she makes one curious addition to her mother's request for John's head: she wants it "on a platter." Why, we are not told. In Matthew, the manner of delivery as well as the request come from the girl's mother, Herodias.

In both gospels, then, the emotional motivations and reactions of the daughter remain unexplained. Because of variant manuscript readings, we are not even sure of her name or of her relationship to Herod in Mark's gospel: is Herod her father or her stepfather? Matthew characteristically smooths out this difficulty by saying merely that she is "the daughter of Herodias," and adds nothing about her father (Matt 14:6). We might assume, as do many readers who follow Josephus's account, that Herodias brought her daughter from her previous husband into her marriage with Herod Antipas, but there is actually no reason to assume that fact from the scant information provided by Mark. As I previously noted, some manuscripts of Mark call her "the daughter of Herodias herself" (or, "the daughter of the same Herodias"); other readings, like that preferred by the translators of the NRSV, call her "his [i.e., Herod's] daughter Herodias," implying that Herod has both a wife and a daughter called Herodias.[5]

Herodias's Daughter's Dance Recital?

While Mark does not give us the daughter's name or exact parentage, there is one detail he emphasizes: her age. Followed by Matthew, he calls her by the Greek term *korasion*, the diminutive of *korē*, "girl" or "maid(en)": hence, a little girl.[6] Mark makes it fairly clear what he himself means by the term

---

5. See Kraemer's excellent discussions of these manuscript and translation difficulties in "Implicating Herodias," 332–33. Lilie, "Salome or Herodias?," 251, asserts that the dancer was Herod Antipas's daughter, Herodias, a claim that he buttresses by reference to the apocryphal sixth-century *Letter of Herod to Pilate*, which will be discussed in chapter 2. In it, Herod refers to "my daughter, Herodias."

6. In Greek, the addition of the suffix *-ion* makes it a diminutive, meaning "little."

korasion by using it in the previous chapter to describe Jairus's daughter, the girl whom Jesus raises from the dead (Mark 5:35–45).[7] He uses a number of synonyms for the other girl, all of which point to her youth: other Greek diminutives like *thygaterion* ("little daughter") and *paidion* ("little child"). He even helpfully translates Jesus's Aramaic address to the daughter, *talitha*, by the Greek *korasion* ("little girl"), and adds the further parenthetical detail that this particular little girl was twelve years old (Mark 5:42), which could also be the age of Herodias's daughter. In fact, one of the earliest commentators on Matthew's version of the story, John Chrysostom (347–407), calls "Herodias' daughter" a *paidion* (*Homilies on Matthew* 48).[8] The term *korasion*, moreover, is also used in the Greek Bible, the Septuagint, for Esther and the other candidates who are being groomed as Ahasuerus's potential next queen (Esth 2:3):[9] here, the term is translated by the NRSV as "young virgin," and probably denotes a girl prior to the age of marriage.[10]

All this commentary is by way of speculation why Mark, whose prose is usually so grudging with detail, is so emphatic about the age correlation between Herodias's daughter and Jairus's daughter, who is also unnamed. It seems a deliberate way to draw both a comparison and a contrast between them. Jairus's daughter, the object of her desperate father's request to Jesus to keep her from dying, and Herod's daughter, whose dancing pleases him so much that he indulgently and extravagantly promises her half his kingdom—a promise that results in someone else's dying—might be seen here as cherished offspring, the apples of their respective fathers' eyes (in the alternative meaning of *korasion*). The age connection between the two girls could emphasize their passivity under their parents' control: they have no agency in the events related to them. It might also underscore the unconscious innocence of Herod's daughter's dance: obediently, she does what

---

Although Collins claims that Greek diminutives have lost their significance in the New Testament (Collins, *Mark*, 308n111), the diminutive is used to strike a patronizing note—as in the *gynaikaria* or "(silly) little women" of 2 Tim 3:6—and may also be an endearment. *Korasion* can also mean "the apple of one's eye." For discussions of possible ranges of meaning of this term in the context of Herod's feast, see Anderson, "Feminist Criticism," 129; and Bach, *Women, Seduction, and Betrayal*, 228–29.

7. Bach, *Women, Seduction, and Betrayal*, 229.
8. Collins, *Mark*, 295.
9. Bach, *Women, Seduction, and Betrayal*, 229; Bach, "Calling the Shots," 108n3.
10. The connection between the story of Esther and that of Herodias's daughter, including a banquet (or two) with disastrous consequences, together with a rash vow by a foolish king, will be treated more fully later in this chapter.

her mother tells her to do.¹¹ In this respect, it is difficult not to "construct the ancient world in our own image,"¹² assuming that because the dancing daughter is characterized as a child, her performance, as briefly and drily described by Mark, is devoid of erotic overtones: "There is neither a suggestion nor an assumption that Herodias' daughter dances before an exclusively male audience . . . or that the dance was erotic in nature, only that it was pleasing to Herod . . . A.-J. Levine connects her 'ill-fated dance' with the wisdom sayings in Matt 11:17 about the children who refused to dance, a link that further de-eroticizes Salome's dancing."¹³

On the other hand, is it too much of a deconstruction of the inherited image of the sexualized Salome, daughter of Herodias, to understand her dance at Herod's banquet to have been innocent, at least on her part, a kind of game playing, like that of the children in the marketplace, or an unconscious imitation of older dancers, like the performances of JonBenét Ramsey? The parable of the children in the marketplace occurs in Matt 11:16-18 (with a parallel in Luke) as imitation of their elders, calling to one another: "We played the flute for you, and you did not dance; we wailed, and you did not mourn." The extended metaphor applies to the nonresponse of the crowd both to the ascetic John the Baptist and to Jesus, "the friend of tax collectors and sinners." Kathleen Corley asserts that the term translated "children"—*paides*—can also refer to "slaves hired for funerals and banquets," and not to children's activities at all.¹⁴ Interestingly, in contrast to in other films, which feature hypersexual portrayals of Salome's dance, Pier Paolo Pasolini's *The Gospel according to Matthew* (1964) depicts a sweetly adolescent Salome dancing a rather restrained dance in a white slip, perhaps a nod to her innocence.¹⁵ F. F. Bruce dismisses "the objection that a princess of the blood royal would not have danced at Antipas's birthday party," claiming that "the ladies of Herod's family" may have acted unconventionally at times, but there is no suggestion of impropriety in the dance.¹⁶ Alice Bach also argues for a "cool" reading of the pleasure the dance gave Herod

---

11. Collins, *Mark*, 308, also notes the age connection between Jairus's daughter and Herodias's daughter.

12. Vander Stichele and Penner, *Contextualizing Gender*, 51.

13. Streete, *Strange Woman*, 149-50; Levine, "Matthew," 345.

14. Corley, *Private Women*, 128, as opposed to the interpretation of Cotter, "Parable of the Children in the Market-Place."

15. Pasolini's film, among others, is discussed in chapter 4. My thanks to Nancy Heisey of Eastern Mennonite University for this reference.

16. Bruce, "Herod Antipas," 13.

(Mark 6:22), substantially agreeing with Anderson.[17] Jennifer Glancy also refers to the dancer as a "child," and "a girl on the cusp of adulthood," but she does not find it "plausible to interpret the dance as innocent," because it is deliberately designed to attract the male gaze, to please Herod so that the dancer can make her outrageous request.[18]

THE DANCE

I thought that I could possibly answer the question of Herodias's daughter's innocence by discovering what the ill-fated dance might have been. Even if it is totally fictional, the idea of a dance performance would have carried with it an image. Though not the Dance of the Seven Veils, a nineteenth-century Orientalizing invention,[19] it is presumably related to a dance so well known to its hearers (or readers) that it did not need to be described and could easily be visualized. Modern readers are thrown back on what little exists in the contemporary historical records, and after that—conjecture.

The best-known dance performed by biblical women is the victory dance. The first mention of this dance is in Exodus 15:20–22, when Moses's sister, the prophet Miriam, leads the Israelite women in it after the successful passage through the Sea of Reeds and the drowning of Pharaoh's chariots. A victory dance is also performed by Jephthah's daughter, with fatal results (Judg 11:34). She does not know that as the first to greet her father with what she thinks is a celebratory dance, she has condemned herself because of an oath that he has rashly sworn and cannot take back, that the first being out of his house to greet him on his return would be sacrificed as a holocaust of thanksgiving for his victory. It is possible that Herodias's daughter's dance, resulting in her (step)father's unbreakable oath, recalls this earlier fatal dance, with John rather than Salome as the sacrificial victim. Like Jairus's daughter, Jephthah's daughter, who is a virgin (*parthenos* in the Greek Bible, a step closer to marriage than a *korasion*), can be compared to the daughter of Herodias, but whether this comparison intends to point to Salome's innocence is hard to say. It is equally hard to imagine that Salome's dance would have been a victory dance, as Herod's banquet is celebrating his birthday, not a military victory; indeed the historian Josephus

---

17. Bach, "Calling the Shots," 103; Anderson, "Feminist Criticism," 122.

18. Glancy, "Unveiling Masculinity," 39.

19. Much of this section is taken from my unpublished paper "Herodias' Daughter's Dance Recital."

suggests the exact opposite: Herod had experienced a humiliating defeat at the hands of Aretas's army precisely because of Herod's adulterous marriage (*Ant.* 18.5.1).

There is also a kind of ancient ring dance called the victim dance, which survived in children's games. (Perhaps the children from Jesus's parable, playing in the marketplace, would have known such a dance.) The victim dance may be related to the circle dance that Jesus dances with his disciples in the *Apocryphal Acts of John*, before he is "taken up."[20] Such a suggestion seems far-fetched, however, since Salome's dance results in the death of a victim, but not of the dancer (at least, not in the gospels). In the Song of Songs, the female lover/beloved, the Shulammite, is likened to a war dance, a "dance between two armies (6:13b)," suggesting an attractive but potentially lethal sensuality: this is a dance in which the dancer is a woman armed with a sword.[21] But in the context of Herod's dinner party, a war dance seems unlikely. Nonetheless, the connection between these dances and the hovering possibility of being lured into warfare and death could contribute in some measure to the overall impression of Salome's dance as fatal.

Another dance, mentioned in the book of Judges, is performed by young women of an age before marriage "in the vineyards" (Judg 21:19–21). It is also mentioned in Babylonian and Palestinian rabbinic commentary as occurring in midsummer as a form of courtship.[22] The connection in this dance between sexual availability and sexual arousal, particularly at the time of the grape harvest, is a probable given. Yet these dances, however intentionally erotic, are not performed solo. We would have to use a good deal of conjecture to think of Salome performing this kind of dance, unless she did it in imitation of other girls, or perhaps was taught it by her mother.[23]

A dance from the Hellenistic period that involved veiling and unveiling by the dancer is known as the mantle dance. According to Elisabet Friesländer, this dance, in contrast to the "female frenetic dancing" associated

20. Murray, "Ancient and Modern Ritual Dances," 403.

21. Ibid, 404. We do find a depiction of Salome doing an acrobatic sword dance in a twelfth-century manuscript illustration, but this may be a dance derived from Western contact with Muslim Spain. This dance will be discussed in chapter 2.

22. Ilan, "Dance and Gender," 135–36.

23. Webb, "Dance in the Ancient Mediterranean," 1, suggests exactly that. J. C. Heywood's dramatic poem *Herodias* (1862) assumes that Herodias taught her daughter to dance to seduce men and have power over them. See also Bach, "Calling the Shots," 112n6.

with the cults of Dionysus and Adonis, is performed by a dancer enveloped in a mantle or himation that covers the head, face, and hands, in a nod to "traditional rules of purity."[24] The mantle, however, is transparent, so that it reveals while it conceals. Although we cannot know the "function and meaning" of the mantle dancers frequently depicted in Hellenistic sculpture and pottery, the thin covering of the female body in the dance may have conveyed a nascent or barely veiled sexuality.[25] While we also have no way of knowing that Herodias's daughter's dance was a mantle dance (and it would be a stretch from this dance to the later Seven Veils), it is plausible that such a dance might have been known to a court remarkable for its adoption of Greco-Roman culture, and likewise vilified for it by more conservative Judean leaders and writers. We cannot determine with any certainty, therefore, what Herodias's daughter's dance was, or whether it was sexy or seductive, but we can make some judgments from the setting about how such a dance was likely to have been understood and interpreted.

BANQUETS AND BAD BEHAVIOR

Something in the context of this dance, in the world of the original text, would have led an audience to suspect a dangerous behavioral irregularity on the part of the child dancer. The context—a formal banquet, given by Herod Antipas for the crème de la crème of Galilee—is a setting that, given both its classical and biblical connections, is fraught with possibilities of loss of control and sexual arousal.

According to Mark, Herod gives a dinner (*deipnon* in Greek) to which his "greatest" citizens, his "commanders," and the "first in Galilee" are invited (6:21). At this dinner, Herodias's daughter comes in to dance. Matthew lacks Mark's specificity about the company and details about the setting, saying simply that the girl danced "in their midst" (14:6). Nonetheless, this dance is a solo performance before an audience that has been and still may be drinking as they are dining, a detail that lends a kind of grisly poignancy to the dancer's reward, a head served on a platter. In Mark's gospel, moreover, Herod's birthday celebration appears to be an all-male affair, while the presence of Herodias in the room at Matthew's version of the dinner indicates that it may have been mixed: Roman custom permitted married women to dine with their husbands at public meals, although unmarried

---

24. Friesländer, "Mantle Dancer," 4.
25. Ibid., 23.

The Daughter of Herodias

free women (and, presumably minor children such as Herodias's daughter) would still have been excluded.[26] Archaeological evidence at Herod's palace at Machaerus (where John the Baptist, according to Josephus and others, was confined) indicates separate male and female dining facilities,[27] supporting Mark's version of the banquet, which separates the sexes: first the daughter must "come in" to dance, then "go out" after her dance pleases Herod to ask her mother (presumably in another room) what to request; finally the girl "rushed back" with her demand. Matthew's account does not focus on the spectacle of the dance or on the wording of the request:

> But when Herod's birthday came, the daughter of Herodias danced before the company, and she pleased Herod so much that he promised on oath to grant her whatever she might ask. Prompted by her mother, she said, "Give me the head of John the Baptist here on a platter." (Matt 14:8)

Both gospels, however, depict a dance performed by a young girl in front of either an all-male or (possibly) mixed adult group of elites at a public dinner. In the course of trying to discover exactly what this dance may have been, and whether it would have been salacious (as several early Christian commentators suggested), I could not find any evidence of accounts of entertainment at either an aristocratic dinner party (*deipnon*) or a dinner followed by drinking (an all-male *symposion*) that would not have been performed by slave women who were also "sexual accompaniments," whatever their other talents may have been.[28] So, while the "motif of sexual entertainment" has been "relatively restrained" in the gospel texts, it is nonetheless a probable subtext.[29]

Several studies of the episode in Matthew and Mark have also found a parallel for the request for beheading at a banquet.[30] The story of this request is related by several ancient writers—Cicero, Livy, and Plutarch—and relates to a general and consul from a noteworthy Roman family, Lucius Quinctius Flamininus (d. 171 BCE). In Cicero's *De senectute* (*On Old Age*),

26. Corley, *Private Women*, 93. See also Kraemer, "Implicating Herodias," 331.
27. Corley, *Private Women*, 61.
28. Ibid., 49–54. Some female slaves called *saltatriculae*, or "little leaping dancers," performed acrobatic dances on public stages and could be as young as nine years old, as an epitaph for one of them (*Corpus Inscriptionum Latinarum* 6.10143) shows; see Hall and Wylos, *New Directions in Ancient Pantomime*, 117. These dancers will be discussed further in chapter 2.
29. Collins, *Mark*, 308–9.
30. Ibid, 313; Corley, *Private Women*, 94.

the main speaker, Cato the censor, whose role was to expel from the Senate those who had not upheld Roman virtues and values, recalls his having to expel Flamininus: "For, when in Gaul during his consulship, at the solicitation of the courtesan at a banquet, he beheaded a prisoner then under condemnation for some capital offense" (Cicero, *De senectute* 42). In his massive moralizing history of Rome, *From the Founding of the City*, Livy expands upon this story, offering two different versions: "On the request of his lover, the well-known prostitute Philip of Carthage, [Flamininus] personally killed a certain Gaul: or, as some say, had beheaded a condemned criminal to please the courtesan Placentina, for whom he was deadly in love" (Livy, *Ab urbe condita* 39.184). The Greek historian and biographer Plutarch takes account of all differing versions in his appraisal of the Roman statesman:

> Titus had a brother, Lucius, who was unlike him in all other ways, and especially in his shameful addiction to pleasure and his utter contempt of decency. This brother had as a companion a young boy whom he loved, and took him about and kept him always in his train, whether he was commanding an army or administering a province. At some drinking party, then, this boy was playing the coquet with Lucius, and said he loved him so ardently that he had come away from a show of gladiators in order to be with him, although he had never in all his life seen a man killed; he said; "Don't worry about that! I will give thee thy heart's desire." Then ordering a man who had been condemned to death to be brought forth from his prison, and sending for a lictor, he commanded him to strike off the man's head there in the banquet-hall. Valerius Antias, however, says it was not a lover, but a mistress whom Lucius thus sought to gratify. And Livy says that in a speech of Cato himself it is written that a Gaulish deserter had come to the door with his wife and children, and that Lucius admitted him into the banquet-hall and slew him with his own hand to gratify his lover. (Plutarch, *Titus Flamininus* 18.2–5)

While it is neither clear nor provable that either Mark or Matthew knew of the Flamininus story, some members of their respective audiences may have known it, and it is likely that later Christian interpreters, especially the church fathers, who were schooled in pagan culture, did. And although this beheading story is hardly "stereotypical,"[31] there seems to have

---

31. As suggested in Corley, *Private Women*, 94.

been widespread interest in it, at least on the part of several writers,[32] and it may thus have contributed to the overall impression of a decadent banquet in the Greco-Roman style at Herod's palace in Machaerus, whose result is the death of an innocent man to grant the request of a cunning seductress. Joanna Dewey notes that this story "is the only instance in Mark of a narrative with sexual overtones," one that she believes contributes to the overall indictment of the "debauchery of rulers."[33] This statement still begs the question of Herodias's and her daughter's presence in such a setting.

Biblical Bad Behavior at Banquets

But Mark and Matthew and their audiences need not have looked to the Greco-Roman world for instances of banquets as sites of risk, disturbance, debauchery, and danger. Banquets in the biblical world, as formal occasions of celebration, are assumed to include drinking to intoxication; the Hebrew word for "banquet" comes from the word "to drink." A diner at such a banquet might act foolishly or rashly, becoming emboldened to do what one otherwise might not, or to take advantage of another's being "merry with wine" to accomplish a nefarious purpose.[34]

For example, the "trouble" in King David's house that pursues him after his rape of Bathsheba and the assassination of her husband comes in the form of two episodes of disastrous meals, one private and one public. Amnon, David's son and heir, rapes his half sister Tamar after he contrives to get his father to order her to feed him a meal of some special cakes in his chamber (2 Sam 13:7-19). Tamar's full brother, Absalom, bides his time until he can "make a feast like a king's feast," inviting all of David's sons. Absalom instructs his servants that "when Amnon's heart is merry with wine," they should kill him. The apparent coup sets up trouble between Absalom and his father that ends in Absalom's rebellion and eventual death. In this narrative we have the persistent note that occurs in other banquet settings: drinking makes a person in authority, who ought to be vigilant, too relaxed and less than aware of potential danger.[35] Absalom does have his revenge,

---

32. Kraemer, "Implicating Herodias," 344-45n64.
33. Dewey, "Gospel of Mark," 482-83.
34. Walsh, "Under the Influence," 15-17.
35. Among the many warnings about excessive drinking in the book of Proverbs is the oracle of "King Lemuel's mother" in Prov 31:4-5: "It is not for kings, O Lemuel, / It is not for kings to drink wine, / or for rulers to desire strong drink," lest they forget laws and the rights of the afflicted. Only the poor should drink, to forget their misery. Kings

not only on his incestuous brother, but on his father the king, who allowed this disaster to happen, and whose adultery set in motion these fatal dynamics, much as the adultery of Herod and Herodias forms the background for John the Baptist's relentless critique that leads to his subsequent arrest. Thus, in the Amnon-Absalom story we have elements that reappear in the story of Herod's banquet and its aftermath: the themes of sexual disorder or transgression (adultery, incest, rape) within a royal family, the resolve for revenge against a perceived enemy, and a banquet that offers the appearance of celebration, an occasion for drinking and entertainment, but that ends in an unexpected and unsanctioned execution.

Fatal Banquets Featuring Femmes Fatales

The story of Esther in both the Hebrew Bible and its Greek version, the Septuagint (LXX), provides another, closer parallel to the tale of Herod's banquet.[36] In the third year of his reign, according to the biblical book of Esther, the Persian king Ahasuerus (Artaxerxes) gives a sumptuous banquet lasting for several days, in which he literally orders unrestrained drinking (Esth 1:8). The result is what we might expect: heavy drinking brings a resultant loss of reason and control. "On the seventh day, when the king was merry with wine," he sends for his queen, Vashti, who herself has been giving a banquet for the women (Esth 1:9; LXX says that she gives a *poton*, a "drinking party"). He orders her to appear wearing her crown to "show her beauty" to his male guests. Vashti refuses, and the king is so enraged at her disobedience that he dismisses her as queen, demonstrating the undermined judgment and emotional volatility that appear to be the hallmark of unworthy rulers, who in diaspora Jewish texts like this are mainly Gentiles.

We could speculate, as much of the rabbinic commentary does, about the reasons for which Ahasuerus sent Vashti away, other than the reason given in the biblical text—as a bad example for wives to disobey their husbands. The *Esther Rabbah* 1.9 says that Ahasuerus ordered Vashti to appear nude, wearing only her crown.[37] Some of the rabbis, along with Josephus (*Ant.* 11.6.1) and some of the later Christian church fathers, approve of Vashti's refusal, of her cherishing modesty more than her crown, thus

---

have too much responsibility.

36. Anderson, "The Dancing Daughter," 137; Bach, "Calling the Shots," 103; Collins, *Mark*, 310; Kraemer, "Implicating Herodias," 337.

37. See b. Megillah 12b. See also Kadari, "Vashti," para. 6.

The Daughter of Herodias

refusing her husband's unreasonable drunken request. Their disapproval of this Gentile king's out-of-control banquet is apparent in their description of the guests' "indulgence" in the "pleasures of the dance," for which "dancers were provided, and charmed the company with their artistic figures displayed, and the purple-colored floor": purple was symbolic, not merely of royalty, but of Persian luxury; and *Persian* was for a long time a synonym in classical literature and the literature of late antiquity for *decadent*.[38] In this indulgence, "Ahasuerus followed the custom of the kings of Media, who had dancers before them at their carousals to entertain them."[39] Even though some of the rabbinic commentators disapprove of the disobedient wife Vashti, they placed the blame on the foolish Ahasuerus and his "lewd party," one of the hallmarks of which was entertainment by lascivious female dancing. In one version of the story, it is Vashti's head that is requested on a plate,[40] perhaps giving Mark and Matthew the kernel of an idea for the death of John. Flout an out-of-control ruler, and the consequences may be outrageous as well as dire.

In the Esther story, a new queen after Vashti must be chosen, and the young girl (*korasion*) Esther "pleased"[41] the royal eunuch in charge of selecting candidates (Esth 2:9), who in turn recommends her to the king. Ahasuerus proclaims Esther queen instead of Vashti, and announces another banquet to celebrate (2:18). Meanwhile, Esther's uncle Mordecai, who had counseled her not to reveal her Jewish upbringing, reveals to her a plot against the king, and thanks to Esther's information, the conspirators in the plot are put to death by hanging (2:19–23). Already her closeness to the king makes her responsible, albeit indirectly, for the deaths of two men.

Mordecai, like John the Baptist, does not care for Gentile celebrations of customs that would make him depart from his observant Judaism, and therefore he does not bow down before the king's odious official Haman, who consequently persuades Ahasuerus to give him the power to kill not only the offensive Mordecai but all the Jews in the kingdom. When Esther is informed of it, she risks her life to appear before the king and "wins his favor," so that he like Jephthah before him and Herod after him, vows that he will grant her anything she asks, "Even to the half of my kingdom," a phrase ominously and probably deliberately echoed in Herod's vow (Mark

38. Ginzberg, *The Legends*, 4:372
39. Ibid, 6:455–56.
40. *Esth Rabbah* 4:9, 12; Kadari, "Vashti," para. 14.
41. The Greek word used here is the same one used for the way in which Herodias's daughter's dance "pleased" Herod.

6:23; Matt 14:7). Unlike Herodias and her daughter, however, Esther simply asks the king and his henchman Haman to come to a banquet she herself will prepare (Esth 5:5), and when they are drinking, the king repeats his vow to grant her request, "Even to the half of my kingdom." Once again, Esther requests a banquet. But Haman, while flattered to be asked, cannot be content to dine with the king and queen while "the Jew Mordecai" is alive; his wife plots with him to persuade the king to have the troublesome Jew hanged, so that he may truly enjoy Esther's banquet. Unfortunately, Haman's own plot is foiled when Ahasuerus is reminded of the plot against him discovered by Mordecai, and honors the latter even more. Haman is still chafing about this turn of events when he is "hurried off" to the banquet prepared for him.

Apparently, these banquets are leisurely affairs, because it is not until the "second day,"[42] as "they were drinking wine," that the king repeats his vow to Esther for the third time, saying that she can have anything, "Even to the half of my kingdom." It is then that Esther tells him that she requests her own life and "the lives of my people," who are to be destroyed, with collateral damage to the king himself (7:4). When he asks who would do this, Esther names Haman, causing the king to be so uncontrollably angry that he absents himself, whereupon Haman throws himself (literally) on the queen's mercy, only to be discovered in this compromising position by the return of Ahasuerus, who resents the insult to his queen's person enough to order Haman's own hanging. In the end, Mordecai and Esther are given the king's authority to tell the Jews to retaliate by killing their enemies. Esther's ability to persuade Ahasuerus by softening him up at dinner has lethal consequences for her foes.

This story, most likely a novella written to encourage Jews in the diaspora, has several echoes in the story of Herodias's daughter's dinner dance, itself a probable fiction. First and most prominent is the manipulation of a powerful man, who is nevertheless blind to his own limits and prone to acting rashly, to achieve vengeance: the death of an enemy. Several feminist commentators on this story point out that a lack of "direct access to political influence" creates a need for such manipulation. As an apparently powerless person, Esther similarly provides a model for diaspora Jews in Persian society, who must use their wits to survive.[43]

---

42. According to Philip J. King, the ancient banquet known as the *marzēah* was open to both men and women of the upper classes, and might last for several days. See King, "The *Marzēah*," 98.

43. Dewey, "Mark," 470; Crawford, "Esther," 133.

The Daughter of Herodias

What is perhaps more interesting about this story's relationship to Herod's banquet and Herodias's daughter's part in it is that the theme of the high-stakes banquet persists throughout the Esther narrative; there are no fewer than four banquets, and only the culminating banquet Esther gives for Haman finally achieves her desired end: contriving his death. The many banquets also emphasize a setting in which a ruler's judgment is consistently diminished by drinking to excess, leading him to make rash and irrevocable vows, according to the formula "Even to half of my kingdom," as Herod vows to Herodias' daughter at his own banquet. Further, in both cases, the vow is elicited by the persuasiveness (verging on seduction) by a young woman (*korasion*). Granted that in the Esther story we have a new queen and not a queen's daughter, nevertheless Esther's uncle and guardian, Mordecai, raised her like a daughter; and Mordecai used his charge to achieve his own ends from a gullible king, just as Herodias did. While Esther provides one of the closer antecedents for the Salome narrative, other biblical stories, most likely known to the audiences of Mark and Matthew, contribute to a general framework of male fallibility and female seduction.

More Death While Dining: Jael and Judith

Although we have been searching for precedents to Herodias's daughter's dance and for precedents and parallels in texts, we have not mentioned her closest parallel in art: Judith. Judith has been another interesting puzzle for me. As a Protestant, I did not know about Judith because she appears in the Old Testament Apocrypha, a part of the Bible that has been rejected as Scripture by Protestants as well as Jews, and given secondary status by Catholics as part of the Christian Old Testament. When I began studying medieval religious history, however, I kept seeing depictions of a heroic female figure carrying a sword in one hand and a severed head in the other. Of course I wanted to know who she was, and why she was so often depicted in a positive light, as a heroine. She was not Salome; she was Judith, and had an entire book of the Apocrypha named after her.

Two women, each carrying a severed head. Beyond the fact that one had a sword and the other carried the head on a platter, how could the two women be differentiated? "Images of [Salome] are sometimes confused with those of the Jewish heroine Judith."[44] Judith may have supplied the model

---

44. *Art, the Bible & the Big Apple*, "Spotlight: Salome," 2. My thanks to Scott Newstok of the Rhodes College Department of English for this reference.

for an intimate relationship with the severed head of her enemy, which is later taken over in portrayals of Salome, who at times is depicted carrying John's plated head balanced on her own.[45] Salome, however, has usually been seen in art and literature as a seductive murderess, while Judith is almost always depicted as a heroine, as I had observed. Why the difference? The answer to the question lies in a closer look at Judith and her context. Like Esther, Judith is a heroine for a vulnerable Jewish population that must use cunning to prevent oppression or annihilation by foreign enemies.

Judith herself has a heroic albeit ambiguous forerunner associated with the foundational days of the Judges and with Israel's only female judge, Deborah: Jael. According to Judges 4, and its poetic version in Judges 5, the Canaanite king Jabin possesses the iron-age technology ("nine hundred chariots of iron") that allows his general, Sisera, to gain military superiority over the hapless Israelites (Judges 4:1–3). Despite this advantage, Sisera's army is routed by the Israelites, possibly because his iron chariots get weighed down in the Wadi Kishon, forcing him to flee on foot, seeking refuge with his allies the Kenites. Jael, the wife of Heber the Kenite, invites Sisera into her tent and gives him a drink (milk in 4:19, the more substantial "curds in a lordly bowl" in 5:25), and covers him up when he sleeps. He orders her to keep watch and to lie about his whereabouts (4:20). Without any motive being stated, she steals up on him and kills him by driving a tent peg into his temple with a hammer (or "workman's mallet," 5:21), "crushing," "shattering," and "piercing" his head (4:21; 5:26). In the poetic version of the story, in Judges 5, Sisera dies in slow motion, sinking to her feet, a warrior shamefully defeated "by the hand of a woman."

This story is pertinent to the Salome narrative for two reasons: first, it provides a model for the later story of Judith, who also slays with her own hand a sleeping foreign general in a tent; second, because even though there is no overt seduction in the Judges narrative, it is, like the story of Judith, a lesson in "sexual politics par excellence."[46] Jael lures Sisera to "come aside" to her (4:18); he is lulled by her hospitality (and perhaps by a veiled insinuation) into expecting that his needs will be met, only to have them radically disappointed, as she "emasculates" him.[47] Depending on the

---

45. These resemblances will be more fully discussed in chapter 2.
46. Niditch, "Eroticism and Death," 52.
47. Streete, *Strange Woman*, 58–59; Fewell and Gunn, "Controlling Perspectives," 405–6; Niditch, "Eroticism and Death," 52.

translation, she may even have driven the "phallic tent peg" between his "parted lips," rather than into his temple: this is a more violently erotic gesture, symbolizing rape, while Sisera's slow fall can be likened to the loss of an erection.[48] Whether we interpret Jael's actions as sexual or not, we could certainly say that the powerful warrior Sisera expects to be cared for and fed by a woman, and perhaps something more—he is, after all, in bed when she kills him. But his expectations lead him to trust a woman who beguiles him and is responsible for his death—a true femme fatale.

The connection between seduction and murder is even clearer in the story of Judith. Judith is a chaste widow who emerges from her pious isolation to rescue her town, the fictional Bethulia, from the Assyrian army under general Holofernes. The date of the work, another Jewish novella like the book of Esther, is hard to determine because of its many historical inaccuracies: the enemies of the Israelites are depicted not only as Assyrians but also as their successors the Babylonians, Persians, and Greeks, none of whom were enemies of the Jews simultaneously with the Assyrians, but all of whom conquered, dominated, or oppressed the Jews later in their history. The presence of the last group indicates a period in which the Jews encountered the Greeks, most probably during the period when the Greek Antiochene dynasty ruled Judea, ending with the Maccabean uprising and the founding of the independent Jewish Hasmonean dynasty in the late second century BCE. In terms of the story, however, it does not really matter what the name or nationality of the enemy is: "the enemy" in this book is an amalgam of all those hostile Gentile nations who want to subdue or obliterate the Jews. The name Judith, moreover, literally means "Jewish woman," and in its patriarchal context may be symbolic of a smaller, politically weaker nation fallen prey to these larger, more powerful kingdoms, a nation that like Judith can survive only through wiles and manipulation.

Judith will not allow her people to be conquered by the enemy or to face an even greater catastrophe, to make peace with them. Drawing lessons from Jewish history, she persuades the elders of her town to wait until "the-Lord will deliver Israel by my hand" (Jdt 8:33). In an astonishing prayer, which some readers find ethically compromised, Judith asks God to collude in her deception: "By the deceit of my lips strike down the slave with the prince and the prince with his servants; crush their arrogance by the hand of a woman" (9:10). To prepare for this deed, "that will go down through all generations of our descendants," she takes off her widow's clothing and

---

48. Fewell and Gunn, "Controlling Perspectives," 407; Fewell, "Judges," 75.

adorns herself with fine clothing, jewelry, eye makeup, and perfume—the weapons of seduction. Thus equipped, she goes with only her maid to the enemy camp, carrying a bag filled with kosher food, drink, and dishes. The Assyrian soldiers are amazed by her beauty, thinking that there are "women like this" throughout Israel who "will be able to beguile the whole world" if they are allowed. Little do they know.

Judith certainly beguiles the enemy commander, Holofernes. She flatters him into thinking that he is divinely appointed to be victorious. Charmed by her speech as well as her beauty, he invites her to stay in the special tent where he keeps his silver dinnerware, as potentially another precious possession. On the fourth day of her stay, Holofernes, apparently unable to wait any longer, invites Judith to a private dinner with only his personal servants in attendance, letting his chief eunuch know that he intends to have sex with her: "For it would be a disgrace if we let such a woman go without having intercourse with her. If we do not seduce her, she will laugh at us" (12:12). Judith does indeed have the last laugh: she gets the infatuated Holofernes to drink "a great quantity of wine, much more than he had ever drunk in any one day since he was born" (12:20). When his exhausted servants retire, leaving him alone with her, Holofernes lies "stretched out on his bed, for he was dead drunk" (13:2). Taking his own sword, Judith cuts off his head, giving it to her maid, who puts it in the food bag. Holofernes's head thus becomes simply more "dead meat," like the head of John, served up on a platter at a banquet. Triumphantly exhibiting the head to the elders of her town, Judith reassures them that it was only her face "that seduced him," that he has not had sex with her (13:16). Although one might jib at the technicality of the act of seduction, the narrative passes it by without negative comment. The discovery of the headless body demoralizes the Assyrians and emboldens the Israelites. The latter are consequently victorious. Now is the time for dancing: not only do the women do a victory dance in her honor, but Judith helps choreograph it. She and "all the people" also sing and dance a victory hymn: "Her sandal ravished his eyes, / her beauty captivated his mind, / and the sword severed his neck!" (16:9). Modestly, however, Judith returns home to her widow's life and to appropriate charitable deeds, never again threatening any man with her dangerous and deceptive sexual potency.

Except for the last part of her story—her retirement—we might truthfully call Judith (at least temporarily) a femme fatale. Margaret Stocker points out that Judith's story has analogues with sanctioned heroines like

Esther, but also with the less reputable Salome.⁴⁹ Although Judith has certainly fared better than Salome as an iconic heroine, like Herodias's dancing daughter, she has gone through many cultural permutations. In Stocker's opinion, "Judith's images, multiple and diverse, became a catalogue of prejudices, anxieties, inhibitions, and protests about the relations between women and men."⁵⁰ It has been even more the case with Salome. The story of Judith, as echoed in Herod's banquet, contributes a seductive female character who appears suddenly and unexpectedly (Judith does not appear until chapter 8!), a feast that leaves a powerful male impotent through excessive drinking, and a beheading that results in the head of the enemy being presented as a parody of food: Judith's food bag as parallel to Salome's platter. Yet another biblical precedent, however, contributes still more to the overall negative impression of Herod, Herodias, and by extension her daughter, with their contriving the death of a righteous prophet—the story of Jezebel and Ahab.⁵¹

SCHEMING QUEEN, MANIPULATED KING, PERSECUTED PROPHET

The name Jezebel, like that of Salome, has long been associated with immorality of a sexual nature, although if anything, she was overly loyal to her husband Ahab, king of Israel, procuring his heart's desire. The "whoredoms" of which she is accused by the usurper Jehu (2 Kgs 9:32) refer to her metaphorical "whoring" after foreign deities such as Baal and Asherah and being unfaithful to the true God of Israel, YHWH.⁵² Jezebel is a forerunner of the later Herodias, however, not least because she runs afoul of a powerful prophet, Elijah, and later his successor, Elisha, but because she "serves as an initiator and instigator of evil," plotting the death of an innocent man—two innocent men, in fact, the prophet Elijah and the citizen Naboth—for

---

49. Stocker, *Judith, Sexual Warrior*, 12–13.

50. Ibid., 135. See also Dijkstra, *Idols of Perversity*, 376–401.

51. Anderson, "The Dancing Daughter," 136–37, points to the intertextual associations with Esther, Salome's "shadow sister," with Judith, who is "Salome's obverse," and with Jezebel as the parallel to Herodias/Salome as John the Baptist is to Elijah.

52. See my discussion in Streete, *Strange Woman*, 62–65. The idea is that Jezebel's "painting her eyes, adorning her head, and looking out of the window (2 Kgs 9:30), which several commentators have claimed is acting like a prostitute, comes after the accusation of whoredom, and may very well be a gesture of defiance, especially if "adorning her head" means putting on her crown.

political purposes.⁵³ The fact that Mark the gospel writer seems to go out of his way to point out the resemblance of John the Baptist to Elijah (Mark 1:6; 2 Kgs 1:8), is also another link to the story of Jezebel, and invites a comparison between her and Herodias, another murderously vengeful queen.

In her story as we find it in 1 Kings 16–21 and 2 Kings 9:21–23, Jezebel is guilty prima facie because she is the daughter of the Gentile king of Sidon and imports her worship of the deities Baal and Asherah into Israel upon her marriage to Ahab, Israel's king (1 Kgs 16:31–34). A zealot for her religion, or simply a queen who will not tolerate challenges to the royal power, Jezebel threatens the prophets of YHWH, and when a victorious Elijah has the court-sponsored prophets of Baal slaughtered in retaliation for this royal persecution, she vows: "So may the gods do to me, and more also, if I do not make your life like the life of one of them by this time tomorrow" (19:3).

Jezebel, however, does not confine her machinations to threatening a resistant prophet. King Ahab wants to purchase the vineyard of one Naboth, which is beside his palace, but Naboth refuses because it is his inheritance. Like a disappointed child, Ahab takes to his bed and will not eat. Inquiring the reason for his depression, Jezebel chides him for his weakness as a king, and promises that she will give him "the vineyard of Naboth the Jezreelite" (21:1–7). She writes letters in Ahab's name to get Naboth falsely accused, tried, and condemned for "cursing God and the king," an accusation for which he is judged guilty and stoned to death (21: 8–14). Jezebel then tells Ahab that Naboth is dead, so he takes possession of the vineyard. When Elijah learns of it, he denounces Ahab and Jezebel and pronounces disaster upon them both, especially Jezebel, who will be eaten by dogs, a prophecy that eventually comes true (1 Kgs 21:20–24; 2 Kgs 9:30–37). In fact, Jezebel comes in for a greater condemnation than does her husband, because Ahab is weak, "urged on by his wife," and does in fact repent. Jezebel never does.

Nor does Herodias. The Gospels of Mark and Matthew draw a strong connection between the Ahab–Jezebel–Elijah narrative and that of Herod–Herodias–John.⁵⁴ Both narratives concern a prophet openly critical of a royal couple abusing power, abuse generated by the ruler's desire to do and have what he may not legally or morally, abetted by his ambitious and manipulative wife. Although Jezebel wields her power more openly than does Herodias, she nevertheless cannot achieve her aims without allies, like the

---

53. Hoffeditz and Yates, "Femme Fatale Redux," 207.
54. Kraemer, "Implicating Herodias," 337.

The Daughter of Herodias

elders who accuse Naboth falsely, to assist her in her schemes. Herodias uses her daughter to achieve her ends.

Another element besides the political links to both stories is religious conflict. Jezebel is a "whore," not because she contrives the death of Naboth and the near death of Elijah, both of whom oppose her. She is a "whore" because she fails to recognize the truth of God's prophet. In a similar way, Herodias is an adulteress who sends her adolescent daughter in to dance at a public meal so that she can silence the Baptist's criticism of her unlawful, adulterous conduct by contriving his death at the hands of her weaker husband. She does not even think of accepting John's call to repentance, a call that in Mark's narrative makes even Herod uneasy, just as Elijah's warning affected Ahab. Both queens bitterly resent prophetic criticism of their actions and aim at silencing it by any means necessary.

Religious difference in biblical narratives is frequently portrayed as sexual immorality, particularly when it is displayed by women, and especially by women who use their powers of sexual attraction and seduction to bring about the downfall or death of men that the biblical narrators deem righteous.[55] The power of outsider women—those outside the ethnicity, religion, or mores of the dominant voices of the texts—is usually depicted as sexual dominance of men and is always depicted as negative. The Hebrew Bible offers us numerous examples of the attractive yet destructive foreign or "strange" woman who is inevitably a seductress, adulteress, and femme fatale. Yet the real or apparent seductions and even murders practiced by the likes of Esther, Jael, and Judith are always explicitly or tacitly justified in the biblical narratives, because they aid in the survival of a nondominant minority and thus serve righteous and noble aims, the aims fostered and supported by the males of their community, whose values—primarily of survival—are promoted in the text.

Mark and Matthew portray neither Herodias nor Salome as achieving such aims. Indeed, as Jewish women, they are doubly to blame because they help to betray Jewish men: Herod, who fears he would appear shamed and possibly emasculated before his guests if he fails to keep the oath extracted from him by a mere girl, and John the Baptist, who insists on a return to Jewish fidelity to the law that Herod and Herodias have violated—and for that is unjustly executed. As Ross Kraemer argues, "Concerns about gender . . . play . . . [a] role in a narrative that implicates Herodias and her daughter in the death of John, through their exercise of indirect power and the

---

55. See Streete, *Strange Woman*, 1–19.

manipulation of a weak, emasculated ruler whose lack of sufficient masculine self-control enables Herodias to accomplish her destructive (female) desires."[56]

Textual echoes together with cultural assumptions have combined to create a narrative that not only constructs Salome as a sexually wanton and willful reflection of her mother, but also succeeds in dominating most if not all subsequent interpretations of both. Already in the gospels we have intertextual and intercultural connections that make it virtually impossible for Salome's dance to be understood as innocent: the setting of the formal banquet at court, with every possibility for drunkenness and bad decisions on the part of a despised or weak ruler; the type of entertainment usually expected and offered at such an occasion, and not by a princess of the court; Salome's adulterous and manipulative mother, Herodias; and the grim reward for her dance, the severed head of a righteous man offered like the pièce de resistance on a platter.

Scholars who try to rehabilitate Salome as the unwitting tool of her mother give up in frustration since the texts portray her as her mother's image as well as her instrument. For example, in trying to exculpate Salome childishly "imitating her mother's desire" for John the Baptist's head, René Girard only implicates her further—the daughter becomes symbolically imprinted with her mother's desires, the need for vengeance on the prophet, together with the sexual rapacity that he condemns in her mother.[57] The problem is complicated by the fact that the daughter also bears her mother's name, Herodias. The conflation of the two is an important step in the development of Salome as femme fatale. Whereas in the gospels it was Herodias who stage-managed Salome, later it is Salome who pushes her mother into the background and becomes the one responsible for seductively persuading Herod, which leads to the desired end of the Baptist. As his death grows more prominent in Christian theology, Salome's role in that death becomes correspondingly more important, as will be seen in chapter 2.

---

56. Kraemer, "Implicating Herodias," 347.
57. Girard, "Scandal and the Dance," 313, 318.

2

Salome and the Head of John the Baptist

THE BONES OF THE BAPTIST

John the Baptist, like Jesus after him, was executed in the chaotic days of the first half of the first century CE, during the Roman domination of the Mediterranean. Three hundred years later, Rome still dominated the Mediterranean, but the empire had changed. Instead of treating the members of the Christian sect as renegade Jews and practitioners of an illegal superstition and subject to punishment as criminals, traitors, and enemies to state order when they came to public notice, the officials of the later empire were, for the most part, Christians themselves. They believed that the unity of the empire depended on fidelity to the one God, and equally on allegiance to the divinely appointed emperor who ruled the world below. Thanks to a decree from Constantine and his coemperor Licinius (the Edict of Toleration), Christianity was recognized as a legal religion in 312, just seven years after Christians had undergone the most virulent persecution; acceptance of Christianity happened before Constantine became the sole ruler of the Roman world, he believed, through divine sanction.[1] Through a decree of one of Constantine's successors, Theodosius I (380), Christianity was subsequently made the official religion of the Roman Empire.

Yet although Christian writers developed a deft apologetic by which they attempted to shift the blame for the death of Jesus and the persecution of his followers away from the Romans, whose empire they had inherited, they did not forget, nor did they cease to celebrate, those who had borne

---

1. Eusebius, *Life of Constantine*, 28.

witness to their faith in their own bodies, suffering and dying for Christ and as Christ had: the martyrs, whose very title—*martys*, in Greek—meant "witness." Their blood, as the fiery church father from North Africa, Tertullian, proclaimed, was the "seed" of the church.[2] Bodily suffering, even more than spiritual experiences, showed that one belonged to Christ. The apostle Paul's "boast" was that he suffered bodily harm for the faith, and "bore on [his] body the marks of Christ" (Gal 6:17). The hallmark of emerging orthodox Christianity, as opposed to its more spiritual, gnostic form, was that Jesus himself had come in a human body, had truly suffered, had truly died, and had been raised in bodily form from the dead. And although Christian martyrdoms at the hands of the imperial powers had come to a halt after the Edict of Toleration, the power of God could still be inscribed on a body, by its refinement through controlling the passions and denying sensual and sexual indulgence in the physical and spiritual training regimen known as asceticism. The great century for the flowering of Christian monasticism was the fourth, not coincidentally the same century that saw the legalization and eventual domination of institutional, orthodox Christianity and the cessation of other forms of bodily *martyria* or witness. John the Baptist therefore became revered as doubly holy, in that he had lived an ascetic life, much like those of the fourth-century desert monastics, and had died because of his fidelity to God's law. He was, moreover, the ultimate witness (*martys*) to Christ, who testified to him as his forerunner and prophet.

The fourth century saw the development of a cult of venerating the martyrs; shrines were built at their tombs, which became sites of pilgrimage, where the faithful might be in touch with the powerful presence of the martyr. With this veneration came an increased concentration on and acquisition of the material remains (*reliquiae*) of the martyrs, their relics. Anything having had physical contact with a holy man or woman during his or her earthly life, especially body parts, was numinous. The *disjecta membra* of the martyrs were particularly poignant, as they bore witness themselves to the terrible ways that martyrs' bodies had been tortured and torn apart because martyrs would not renounce their faith. And just as the martyrs became known as "conquerors," these body parts were symbols of victory over persecution, evil, and death.[3] They were also a form of physical

---

2. Tertullian, *Apologeticus* (*Apology*) 50.13.

3. See L. Stephanie Cobb's detailed treatment of this subject in *Divine Deliverance*, especially 125.

connection between the living and the powerful dead, who could intercede for them in heaven.

A great impetus to the veneration of the relics of the saints was Constantine's mother Helena, herself a convert to Christianity and the first distinguished Christian pilgrim to the Holy Land in 327. Although accounts of her pilgrimage are piously embellished, most of them agree that she visited the tomb of Jesus, now the Church of the Holy Sepulcher, and "discovered," or had discovered for her, fragments of the True Cross and other materials related to Jesus's passion. This discovery, known in Latin as the *Inventio*, or "finding,"[4] most likely gave an impetus to the finding of other relics related to Jesus's life and death, and to the lives and deaths of the early saints. These included the remains of Jesus's supposed relative and prophetic predecessor, John the Baptist.

Both Mark (6:29) and Matthew (14:12) report that after his execution, John's disciples took his body away for burial, but neither says anything about the whereabouts of the head after it was presented by Salome to Herodias. According to early church historians, the saint's body was discovered in a tomb in Sebaste in Samaria, where a church was built above it and where, according to Saint Jerome (347–420), who verifies the location, which his friend Paula visited, miracles occurred.[5] Although two different churches—Saint Sylvester in Capite in Rome, and Amiens Cathedral in France—both lay claim to the head of John the Baptist, a long-standing church tradition holds that the actual head was found in the fourth century, during the heyday of "findings," on the Mount of Olives, where it had been hidden after it was rescued from Herodias's dishonorable clutches. Eventually, the head supposedly reached Emesa, and later Constantinople. According to the Byzantine historian Sozomen (400–450), in his *Church History*, the Emperor Theodosius I, who was also responsible for making Christianity the religion of the empire, thanked the relics of Saint John for an important victory in 394.[6] The remains of John at Sebaste were reportedly burned and scattered by the followers of Julian the Apostate,[7] but some of them were rescued by monks and reached various places around the world,

---

4. It is almost irresistible not to connect the Latin term to its English derivative, "invention."

5. Jerome, *Letters*, 46.13.

6. Kazan, "The Head of John the Baptist"; Sozomen, *Ecclesiastical History* 7.21.

7. An improbable version of this story appears in the thirteenth-century popular compendium of saints' stories, Jacobus da Voragine's *The Golden Legend*, which says that the bones of the Baptist were burned "on the very day" of his martyrdom.

including the Bulgarian monastery of Sveti Ivan (Saint John), where pieces of bone were recently identified as belonging to a man who lived in the first century, who may have been John the Baptist.[8] The recent public excitement generated by this discovery—a possible link to a biblical character related to Jesus—can give us some idea of how important it was to people in early and medieval Christianity to have material, tangible evidence of a revered holy man, the "Blessed Forerunner" of Christ.

HERODIAS, SALOME, AND THE HEAD

This brief recitation of the tangled posthumous history of John the Baptist shows how important his relics became, consequently bringing to the fore the terrible nature of his death and the culpability of those who caused it. Ross Kraemer claims that the narrative of John's death as we find it in Mark and Matthew is constructed so that it suits two propagandistic purposes: first, that "the body [of John] is desecrated" in a manner intended to prevent bodily resurrection, and that serves as an important distinction between Jesus and John, as Jesus's body remained whole; second, by associating the decapitation of John with Herodias and by extension with her daughter, Mark draws a sharp contrast between the scheming, seductive, and murderous women among the Herodians and the virtuous Galilean women who support Jesus, follow him loyally to the cross, and become the first witnesses to his resurrection.[9]

    I will add one other possible motive the gospel writers might have had to involve Herodias and her daughter in John's death, together with an important consequence. In Christian apologetic responses to the reality that Rome could no longer be thought of as the "Great Whore," drunk on the blood of the saints, but had fostered Augustine's "City of God" on earth, the church, Romans were exculpated as far as possible from involvement in the death of Jesus and the early martyrs; the blame correspondingly was placed on others. Who better to blame for the death of the very first "witness [*martys*] to the light" (John 1:6–8) than the Herodians, whom many Judeans regarded as illegitimate rulers?[10] Jesus had warned his followers to beware the "leaven of the Pharisees and Herod" (Mark 8:15; parallel Matt 16:6), and according to the Gospel of Luke, Jesus was warned against "that fox,

---

8. Than, "John the Baptist's Bones Found?"
9. Kraemer, "Implicating Herodias," 341–49.
10. Ibid.

Salome and the Head of John the Baptist

Herod," who wanted to kill him, believing that he was John risen from the dead (Luke 13:32). As we have seen, Josephus mentions the Jews' belief that Herod's forces lost to Aretas's army because he had killed John the Baptist; the loss was therefore a punishment "from God" (Josephus, *Ant.* 18.5.2). Herodias herself, according to Josephus, initiated her divorce against "the laws of our country," and was so loyal to Herod that when her own brother Agrippa, between whom and Antipas was no love lost, accused him of conspiracy and engineered his exile[11] to Lugdunum in Gaul, she went with him, presumably accompanied by her daughter (*Ant.* 18.246-52). All of Herodias's scheming thus came to naught, thanks to the Roman government, which is therefore the ultimate instrument of retributive justice against the Herodians, and not to blame for John's death.

An important consequence of charging the decapitation of John to Herodias, and collaterally to Salome, is that from that point they both continue to be associated with the severed head, an important symbol that generates Salome's first "afterlife." From the time of the Greek philosopher Aristotle, whose "natural philosophy" remained dominant in the Christian world well through the Renaissance, males were associated with the head (and therefore with thinking, reason, and self-control) and females with the body (and therefore with senses, physicality, and the passions).[12] The apostle Paul famously expresses a Christian version of this idea in 1 Cor 11:3: "But I want you to understand that Christ is the head of every man, and the husband is the head of his wife, and God is the head of Christ." The woman is therefore body. Paul, or more likely one of his male disciples, also speaks of a husband needing to care for his wife "as his own body" in Eph 5:25-33.

In this context, John's head is symbolic of both his manhood and his prophetic authority, and the instigation behind its removal represents a subversion of Herodias's role as subject to the "headship" of her husband, and to the authority of God and the law of Moses, represented by the Baptist. As a relic, John's head is a material reminder of the reason that it was taken from his body and buried in a separate place, thanks to the passions of Herodias. The fact that the head is "out of place" could also serve as a reminder of Herodias's "out of place" behavior in Herod's court, and

---

11. What happened in that exile, including the sad end of "Herod's daughter" is recounted in the apocryphal *Letter of Herod to Pilate*, which will be discussed later in this chapter.

12. Aristotle, *On the Generation of Animals* 737a25; Aristotle, *The Politics* 1.1-2; cited in Streete, *Redeemed Bodies*, 18-21.

even more as a reminder of the behavior of her daughter, who should not have been at Herod's banquet at all. As a minor, a female child, supposedly without developed reason and self-control, she could hardly have helped but listen to her mother, but should not have been used to manipulate her stepfather to achieve her mother's unlawful ends.

The discovery of the skull of the Baptist in the fourth century reinforced the association of the head with spirituality, manhood, self-control, and authority. In this same period, a legend about the shameful treatment of John's head after his death began to develop. In his *Apology against Rufinus*, Jerome says that Herodias "pierced the tongue that spoke the truth with the pin that parted [her] hair."[13] Later embellishments of this legend show Herodias using a knife or fork, taken from the banquet table, to stab John's tongue.[14] An early Christian legend has the head come to life. When Herodias's daughter is presented with the head, the result of her request, she begins weeping with remorse over what she has done, and a "wind from God" issues from the mouth of the Baptist, literally blowing her away. She is condemned to fly through the air forever, lamenting her crime.[15] Other accounts have Herodias herself being whirled into the air, where she reappears with or as the pagan goddess Diana in the "Wild Hunt," a cavalcade of witches tossing the head of the Baptist as if it is a ball. This legend is adapted by Heinrich Heine, in his 1843 poem, *Atta Troll*, which attributes John's decapitation to desire on the part of Herodias: "For why would a woman want the head of a man she did not love?" Herodias's desire (and obsession with the head) will later be transferred to her daughter by Oscar Wilde in his play *Salomé*.[16]

THE DEVIL IN THE DANCE

In the fourth- and fifth-century Christian church, most of the vilification for the death of John rests on Herodias, but there is one church father who

---

13. Jerome, *Against Rufinus*, 539–40.

14. As in paintings by Rogier van der Weyden and Peter Paul Rubens (Neginsky, *Salome*, 62).

15. Magliocco, "Who Was Aradia?" 2. *The Golden Legend* reports the tale that Herodias "taunted" the head "gleefully," but "by God's will the head breathed in her face and she expired." See https://sourcebooks.fordham.edu/basis/goldenlegend/.

16. Much more about Romantic, Symbolist, and Decadent interpretations and versions of the Herodias/Salome/Baptist story will be found in chapter 3.

will not let us forget the role of her daughter: John Chrysostom (347–407). The "golden-tongued" patriarch of Constantinople was bold enough to denounce even the Empress Eudoxia for her opposition to him, portraying himself in the role of John the Baptist and the empress as Herodias/Salome: "Again Herodias raves; again she is troubled; she dances again, and again desires to receive John's head in a charger."[17] In his *Homily on Matthew*, however, he assigns responsibility for "diabolical" behavior to the daughter herself. He also denounces Herod's banquet as demonic:

> O diabolical revel! O satanic spectacle! O lawless dancing! And more lawless reward for the dancing. For a murder more impious than all murders was perpetrated, and he that was worthy to be crowned and publicly honored, was slain in the midst, and the trophy of the devils was set on the table.

He goes on to accuse the dancer of two sins: "Her reproach is twofold: first, that she danced, then that she pleased him [i.e., Herod], and so pleased him, as to obtain even murder for her reward." While Chrysostom does not excuse Herod for his "savagery," he finds the dancer the guiltier party. Herod at least is "sorry" for his oath, but Salome's "madness" does not allow her to take Herod's sorrow seriously: "When she too ought to admire, yea, to bow down to him, for trying to redress her wrong, she on the contrary even helps to arrange the plot, and lays a snare, and asks a diabolical favor." Although he suggests that Herod may have been "the worst transgressor of all," because he was supposed to be in control, Salome is nonetheles complicit in the drunkenness, luxury, and depravity of the banquet because she incites the "irrational pleasure" that subverts the chief male virtue, self-control. The girl is thus the more to blame, since she, "because of whom the marriage was illegal, who ought even to have hid herself, as though her mother were dishonored by her, comes making a show, and throwing into the shade all harlots, virgin as she was." Chrysostom is also very clear on his belief that the dance was immoral and intended to arouse sexual passion, as in his view such dances, even at wedding banquets, are. The devil who "danced in her [i.e., Herodias's daughter's] person" is still looking to capture other souls.[18]

With Chrysostom, two important traits of later versions of Salome emerge: (1), that she was a virgin, an idea exploited quite thoroughly in

---

17. Socrates Scholasticus, *Church History* 6.16.
18. All the above from John Chrysostom, *Homilies on Matthew* 48.3–9.

nineteenth-century portrayals; (2) that despite her virginity, through her "leapings and boundings" in the dance, she elicited Herod's desire, just as Chrysostom warned that the female "dancers of our time" make men slaves to passion and steal their souls. Salome is thus a virgin who acts like a whore, and whose desire, perversely, is not satisfied even by illicit intercourse but only by the death of a righteous man. Chrysostom's Latin contemporary, Ambrose, bishop of Milan (337–397), mentor to Augustine and frequent writer and advisor on female virginity, writes the treatise *On Virginity* to his sister, Marcellina. In it, he lists virgins she ought to emulate, like the martyrs Thecla and Agnes, who faced their own deaths rather than sacrifice their virginity. He also gives her an example of a virgin gone wrong. At Herod's "banquet of death," he tells her, the daughter of the queen is "brought forth to dance in the sight of men." But her seeming passivity vanishes, as Ambrose continues in colorful vein:

> What could she have learned from an adulteress but loss of modesty? Is anything so conducive to lust as with unseemly movements thus to expose in nakedness those parts of the body, which either nature has hidden, or custom has veiled, to sport with the looks, to turn the neck, to loosen the hair? Fitly was the next step an offense against God. For what modesty can there be where there is dancing and noise and clapping of hands?[19]

Clearly, for the fathers of the church, it was the dance that was the evil instrument of John's death. Virgin though she may have been, Salome had three grave counts against her modesty: her mother was an adulteress, because she divorced her husband to marry his brother; as her mother's daughter, she appeared before drunken men whose judgment was already shaken by drink, at a dinner party; and she performed a dance that in and of itself was made up of bodily movements guaranteed to arouse lust.

Even before Chrysostom and Ambrose, Christian writers such as Tertullian (155–240), inclined to ascetic behavior, condemned theatrical shows as an unholy combination of the pagan deities Bacchus and Venus, "demons of drunkenness and lust."[20] From Ambrose's time, when Christianity was defining itself as respectful of Roman institutions like self-control, female virginity, and chastity within marriage, we have ample evidence of women dancing in the manner he describes as *lascivia saltatio* (lascivious leaping), seminude, and with the immodestly loosened hair he decries.

19. Ambrose, *On Virginity* 3.6.27; cited in Johnson, *Salome*, 157–58.
20. Tertullian, *De Spectaculis* 10.

Some of these women may have performed not only in public but at private parties. They were undoubtedly prostitutes and slave girls who were the sexual property of their owners. Female dancers called *saltatrices* (leaping dancers) and even young girls called *saltatriculae* (little leaping dancers) performed dances of an acrobatic or gymnastic kind on the stage, possibly like those depicted in a fresco from the fourth-century Villa Romana del Casale, where the women are dressed in something like ancient bikinis. The scene may actually represent a staged female athletic contest, but clearly it was meant to be a spectacle for entertainment.[21] Epitaphs of some of these professional dancers show that they could be as young as nine years old, like a girl called Julia Nemesis, possibly known by her stage name.[22] For a princess to appear in public like this, pace F. F. Bruce, was entirely disreputable, never mind that her mother put it up to it.[23] We might get a sense of how shocking this was by reading the sixth-century Christian historian Procopius's gossipy tale of the former life of Justinian's empress, Theodora, a mime (and probable prostitute) whose signature dance in the theater was performed with only a G-string, and whose "impudent" and "provocative" behavior in private, when she danced completely nude, was intended to make others equally audacious.[24] One would never guess her past from looking at the stately and saintly (and richly clothed) figure presenting the Eucharistic wine in the mosaics of San Vitale in Ravenna.

THE DANCER IN THE DANCE

One would probably never see lewd behavior in the first extant visual representation we have of Salome. In a sixth-century fragment from the gospel of Matthew in Greek, from Sinope on the Black Sea, dating from approximately the same era as the mosaics of San Vitale, we do not even see her dancing. A valuable object of Byzantine art and piety, the manuscript is written in gold letters on purple-dyed vellum, both royal colors.[25] The illuminated miniature accompanies the passage in Matthew 14:1–12 that describes the feast of Herod. Herod and his guests are reclining in Roman

21. *Carnaval*, "Roman Dance," illustration 4.
22. Corpus Inscriptionum Latinarum 6.10143, cited in Hall and Wylos, *New Directions in Ancient Pantomime*, 117.
23. Bruce, "Herod Antipas," 6–23.
24. Procopius of Caesarea, *The Secret History* 9.
25. Rodney, "Salome," 193.

fashion, while Salome stands. Both Herod and Salome wear diadems of what appear to be pearls, indicating their royal status and wealth, while a servant presents a large platter containing John the Baptist's head to the girl, to whom Herod points. On the right is depicted a prison, with two men who are probably John's disciples, their arms raised, exclaiming over the body. Salome's pose is static: she is a little smaller than the other diners, her size indicating her lesser status (and her age), and is fully clothed. There is no indication that she has been rushing around dancing and consulting with her mother. Her face as she receives the head is expressionless, perhaps in contrast to the expressions of John's disciples.

In another early representation of the banquet scene in a late ninth-century book of gospels from Chartres,[26] Salome is shown dancing in an animated scene that combines the feast, the dance, and the decapitation all in one. The dancer is fully and richly dressed, her movements indicated mainly by her raised arms and the swirling of her skirt, movements that are ironically replicated by the clothing of John the Baptist as he sinks to his knees when the swordsman strikes.[27] Salome, however, is fully absorbed in her dance, turned away from its result. Without words, this full-page illustration encapsulates the whole story: the dancing Salome is the link between Herod's luxurious feast and the decapitation of John.

The Romanesque period in art (1000–1200) corresponds with the beginning of the Crusades (1095) and the consequent rise in traffic in relics from the Holy Land, including the head of John the Baptist at Amiens Cathedral, brought back by Canon Wallon der Sarton from the sack of Constantinople during the Fourth Crusade (1204).[28] Veneration for the Baptist increased during this period, while the role of the "dancing girl" who caused his death was heightened and made both more sensuous and more immoral. It is also in this period that Salome begins "to emerge ... as an important subject in painting and sculpture," always dancing. But since the dance was never described in Scripture, it was left to the imagination of the artists, even more than the theologians, to depict it.[29] In fact, one could say that in the medieval period, artistic representations of the Salome

---

26. Paris, BnF, ms. Latin 9386, fol. 146v. Also cited by Baert, "The Dancing Daughter," 16.

27. Commenting on the Chartres illumination, Voyer "Le corps du péché," 71, claims that Salome dances "like a maenad." If so, she is a very restrained one.

28. *Atlas Obscura*, "The Head of John the Baptist at Amiens Cathedral," par. 2

29. Zagona, *The Legend of Salome*, 20–21.

narrative served not only as a complement to theology, but as a distinct expression of it.

We can almost pinpoint the change in the role of Salome and her dance by looking at two early twelfth-century series of sculptures on the capitals of columns in two monastic institutions in the same city, Toulouse: the cloister of the Benedictine monastery of Notre-Dame la Daurade and the chapter-room attached to the Cathedral of Saint Étienne, where the Augustinian canons attached to that cathedral gathered.[30] The sculptures for the Benedictines are rather austere, and appear to be a strict interpretation of the Salome episode as depicted in Mark's gospel: an orderly narrative depicting feast, dance, beheading, and presentation of the head. Salome dances alone in a rather confined space; the emphasis here is on Herod and his feast. He is resolutely not looking at Salome. She is depicted again, presenting the head to her enthroned mother (Mark 6:28). End of story.

The sculptures at Saint Étienne, however, executed presumably by one Gilabertus about 1120–1190, at a slightly later date than those in the Benedictine monastery (1100–1110), have figures that are much more active and sensuous. The sculptor also depicts a definite relationship between Herod and Salome. While Salome is never actually shown in the act of dancing, we see the dance's aftermath. On one face of the double capital from the chapter-room, Salome is depicted with a lithe, sensuous body, her long hair flowing loose—a sign of sexual abandon as well as of the unmarried state—leaning in towards Herod, who leans down to cup her chin in his hand. There is a clear intimate, erotic stamp on the scene, seemingly more than a chuck on the chin to a favored stepdaughter. This is the point at which the dancer and the dance have "pleased" Herod very much: it "reads as a seduction."[31] Salome's seductive complicity in the death of the Baptist is indicated by the other sculptures on the face of the capital. She appears in duplicate, swaying towards the executioner of John, from whom she receives the head, and then swaying towards Herodias, to whom she presents the head. Salome is in complete control of the other characters in this drama as she "wins" the head, possibly the object of her desire.

Apart from the possible differences in the gospels used by the programs at La Daurade and Saint Étienne (the former preferring Mark, the latter Matthew), a difference also appears in how the story is interpreted

---

30. For a complete art-historical description and analysis of these two sculptural programs, see Seidel, "Salome and the Canons," 29–66.

31. Ibid., 29.

in a scant twenty-five years, a difference that may reflect more than the difference between two orders of religious—the cloistered Benedictines and the secular Augustinians. The Benedictine sculptures seem to "invite neither meditation nor moralization," depicting a scriptural event rather straightforwardly.[32] In the Augustinian chapter-house, however, Salome is doing some fairly blatant sexual temptation, to which Herod clearly succumbs, in the first artistic representation of a relationship between the lecherous king and his nubile stepdaughter. The Saint Étienne capital veers dangerously in the direction criticized by the reforming Cistercian and major medieval theologian Bernard of Clairvaux, who thundered against such sculptural programs in his *Apology* (1124), by claiming that elaborate decorative schemes make the brothers forget the Scriptures to which they allude and evoke sensual pleasure rather than act as a stimulus to piety or meditation.[33] The canons might have justified their decoration by seeing it as scriptural and instructional. Perhaps, as Linda Seidel suggests, the Augustinian capitals serve as a warning against the temptations of too much involvement with the world, always a risk for secular (noncloistered) clergy, as evidenced by two church councils warning clerics against relations with women.[34] In that case, Salome serves (not for the last time!) as the representation of feminine seductiveness, the dire result of which is the death of an ascetic holy man. The message is clear: Clergy, beware!

DEVELOPING THE DANCE

The "dance of Salome" continues to be developed throughout the Middle Ages, using as its model the performances of itinerant female street performers called *jongleuresses* or *jongleresses*, who were known for their acrobatic and gymnastic abilities that were perhaps descended from the fourth-century *saltatrices*.[35] According to William E. Jackson, "The figure of Salome was one of the most popular figures for portrayal by the medieval jongleuress."[36] The German medieval author Ava of Melk (or Göttweig), who wrote a number of poems about church history and incorporated in them popular medieval ideas about the Bible, also wrote a poem about John

32. Ibid., 58–60.
33. Bernard of Clairvaux, *Apology*, par. 1–6.
34. Seidel, "Salome and the Canons," 58–60.
35. Walker Vadillo, "Salomé," 97–98.
36. Jackson, *Reinmar's Women*, 233–34.

the Baptist, "Johannes," in which she describes the dance of "the daughter of Herodias," who "danced like an acrobat."[37]

Several medieval artists also depict Salome's very acrobatic dance in such a way that makes one think they had seen such performances. A decree by William, Bishop of Orléans, issued in 867, sternly instructs priests who attend banquets not to allow these "*saltatrices*," who dance in the shameful "manner of the daughter of Herodias," to come near them.[38] Several medieval depictions show Salome as having the back-arching and "trained suppleness" so decried in Theodora's case by Procopius. On the eleventh-century door of the church of Saint Zeno in Verona, Salome is bent over backwards in a near-perfect circle; in a festal missal from the Abbey of St-Jean-sur-la-Celle, Amiens (1323), she is bent over backwards in an exactly perfect circle; in the tympanum of the twelfth-century north portal of the west front of the Cathedral of Rouen, she dances on her hands, a dance known in the Middle Ages as the Dance of Salome, just as post-Wilde dancers would call their vaudeville performances the Salome Dance.[39] Something called the Dance of Salome was also performed in the medieval Mystery plays. Based on the Bible and embellished with folk tradition, these performances were intended, like the column capitals of Saint Étienne, to instruct as they entertained. At least one of these plays depicted Herod's feast, together with Salome's dance and John's beheading.[40] Through the frequent association with dancing, as performed by female street musicians and dancers of low repute, Salome became the "personification of ... the flesh," unlike the ascetic John, who "symbolized the life of the spirit."[41]

A remarkable instance of the association of Salome and her exotic dance with John the Baptist and his beheading is found in a double illumination that appears in a manuscript of Anselm's *Prayers and Meditations* from about 1150, once owned by a convent in Littlemore, England.[42] On the

---

37. Ava of Melk, "Johannes," lines 284–91, in Rushing, trans., *Ava's New Testament Narratives*, 30, cited in Walker Vadillo, "Salomé," n15.

38. William of Orléans, PL 119, 79, cited in Dronke, trans. and ed., *Nine Medieval Latin Plays*, xxv.

39. Walker Vadillo, "Salomé," 97–98.

40. Dronke, trans. and ed., *Nine Medieval Latin Plays*, xxv–xxvi n21, claims that a play like this existed as early as the ninth century.

41. Ibid., citing Bornay, *Mujeres de la Biblia*, 192–94. See also Voyer, "Le corps du péché," 73–74."

42. Bodleian Library, MS. Auct.D.2.6., fol. 166v, roll 333.1, frame 14. My thanks to Dr. Sally Dormer, medieval art historian at the Victoria and Albert Museum, for pointing

left-hand side of the manuscript, a crowned Herod and Herodias sit, food in hand, at a sumptuous table under three columned arches. Under one of the arches is a female figure with long hair, presumably Salome, poised upside down, her head balanced precariously in a vee made by two swords that she holds in her hands. Her knees are draped over another sword, while a fourth appears to be aimed at her side. In the historiated initial S that appears beside this remarkable scene are contained two smaller scenes. In the lower one, an executioner raises a large sword to behead John the Baptist; in the upper register, a kneeling Salome presents his head to Herodias, who raises her arms in exclamation. The fantastic dance depicted here may have its origins in the "daggers dance" from Muslim Spain, and may have been adapted for street performance by *jongleuresses*.[43] If the dance is "Moorish," it makes Salome more of an exotic outsider and even a dangerous figure to medieval Christian audiences, a forerunner of the seductive "Orientalizing" portrayals of Salome that emerge in the nineteenth and early twentieth centuries.

The possible textual context for this illustration is that it forms a transition in the manuscript from Anselm's prayer to Christ and the Virgin Mary to the one that follows: a prayer to John the Baptist. Scripturally, the two most salient features of the Baptist's brief but important appearance in the New Testament gospels are his baptism of Jesus and his execution by Herod (hence his association with Salome and her dance). It could be that the sinuous initial S that forms the first letter of the first word of Anselm's Latin prayer to John, "*Sancte*," could be a subtle reference by the illuminator to the story of the sensuous dance and John's beheading. Given the medieval love for allegory, it is not entirely impossible. Although nothing in the prayer itself mentions the specific manner of John's death, he is called a martyr. The illustration of Salome's sword dance may therefore by an allusive foreshadowing of John's beheading by the sword. For Cécile Voyer, the swords also represent Salome's seductive ability and her cruelty: she can juggle the phallic swords without difficulty.[44] For Anselm, John was the forerunner of Christ, and in his prayer to the saint, he links John and Jesus: the former was chosen by God in his mother's womb; the latter was born of the pure womb of Mary. According to medieval typological think-

---

me to this illustration.

43. Walker Vadillo, "Salomé," 97–98. See also Réau, *Iconografía del arte Cristiano*, 512.

44. Voyer, "Le corps du péchê," 85.

ing, John the Baptist was a type of Christ, so his execution by the sinful Herodians foreshadows Christ's death for sin. Anselm's prayer to John also contrasts the "blessed" saint with himself, who "busied myself with sordid sins."[45] It may not be too far of a stretch, given the medieval propensity for allegory, typology, and allusion, to view Salome also as a representative of the wicked, contrasting with the blessed John. Although Anselm does not specifically state this in his prayer to Jesus and Mary, the monastic copyist and illustrator of this text would not have been unaware of Simeon's famous prophecy to Mary as he blesses the infant Jesus: "And a sword will pierce your own soul [heart] too" (Luke 2:35). Swords do appear to pierce the heart and side of Salome as she dances: just as Jesus and John are linked as righteous martyrs, so Mary and Salome are linked by the sword as bringers of birth and death respectively. Taking Seidel's suggestions about the import of the story of Salome's dance at Herod's banquet to the canons of Saint Étienne, it may be that this illustration, in the possession of the nuns of the Littlemore convent, may have served as a warning to these Christian virgins not to become like the notorious dancing virgin, but more like the Blessed Virgin herself.

Another stunning and "iconographically unique" drawing of John the Baptist was also in the possession of a community of monastics and may have been made for the devotions of a fourteenth-century Oxford scholar-monk John of Lingfield.[46] An illustration for John of Dumbleton's *Summa logiae et philosophiae naturalis*, it is a full-page representation of John the Baptist, who is clothed, not simply in his traditional camel's hair garment (Mark 1:6; Matt 3:4), but in an entire camel's skin, complete with head. The illustration is perhaps also unique for its representation of Salome as a tiny, crushed figure being trampled by the giant figure of the victorious Baptist, who, typically in art of this period, points to a round, "paten-like disc"[47] containing a representation of the Lamb of God, Christ, as proclaimed by his forerunner John in the Gospel of John (1:29). Since the Lamb of God as the sacrificial victim who "takes away the sins of the world," this disc may also represent the paten or plate for the Eucharistic host. Inscribed with the image of the "lamb that was slain" (i.e., Christ), from the book of Revelation,

---

45. Anselm, "Prayer to St. John the Baptist," in Anselm, *The Prayers and Meditations*,

46. Luxford, "Out of the Wilderness," 137. Once again, I am indebted to Sally Dormer for alerting me to this illustration. See also the catalog of the V & A exhibition, Browne et al., eds., *English Medieval Embroidery*.

47. Luxford, "Out of the Wilderness," 140.

The Salome Project

it may also be prefigured by the head of John the Baptist offered on a platter by Salome to her mother, Herodias. If that allusion is being made here, it is played down, as Salome, not John, is the victim, whom he "subjugates and neutralizes."[48] Here, Salome is bent backwards in an awkward pose,[49] while John places his left foot firmly on her genitals. A better illustration of the conquest of lust could not be found, and is reinforced by the downward-pointing head and tongue of the dead camel, which appears exactly in the center of John's own genital area. Since the camel was a symbol of the virtue of temperance in the Middle Ages,[50] the conquest of lust by temperance is doubly illustrated: for John, lust is indeed conquered. Julian Luxford, who describes this remarkable image in copious detail, regards this illustration, like the sculptures of Saint Étienne and the Anselm illumination, as an admonishment to "a university-based monk with readier access to secular temptations than existed in the cloister,"[51] but in this case, the illustration reminds the monk of the triumph of asceticism, illustrated by the figure of John, rather than of the possible fatal consequences of yielding to temptation. As an illustration of a work of philosophy, it also reminds the scholar of the necessity of letting reason (the ascetic John) control the passions (the lascivious Salome).

"THE DANCE OF DEATH"

Fourteenth-century illustrations of Salome show her dancing, not for, but with, the Baptist's head. A fresco from the Church of the Holy Apostles in Thessaloniki from the early fourteenth century shows an athletic Salome who dances with the head of the Baptist in what looks like a basket or shallow bowl, a fit receptacle for an offering at a feast, which she balances precariously on her own head. She dances with the head again in a fresco from the fourteenth-century Church of the Hodogetria in Peč, Kosovo, holding it in a receptacle on her head with one hand, looking dreamily off to the side. A spectacular fourteenth-century mosaic from the Basilica of San Marco in

---

48. Ibid., 147.

49. Ibid.,140. I cannot agree with Luxford's assertion that Salome's posture echoes that of the numerous "acrobatic" depictions of her dance in this period. While she is bent backward, she appears to be totally flattened by John's giant, conquering, and subduing foot.

50. Ross, *Medieval Art*, 14.

51. Luxford, "Out of the Wilderness," 141.

Salome and the Head of John the Baptist

Venice shows a Salome richly dressed in an elaborate ermine-trimmed garment with long sleeves, dancing as if in a trance while she balances the head of John in its plate on her own head with one hand.[52] The motif seems like an after-dance—Salome rejoicing in a victory lap with her prize—reminiscent of the biblical heroines Jael and Judith. It may also relate to a Bulgarian legend that Salome refused to dance before she received the Baptist's head.[53] Yet this tale may also be, like the association of the head with Herodias, the first suggestions of a quasi-erotic relationship, "a masturbatory pleasure [that] manipulates the horrible relic into a fetish."[54]

Salome's own head is associated with the head of John through her dance in another development of her afterlife, as contained in the apocryphal *Letter of Herod to Pilate*, dating from the sixth or possibly early seventh century, which has an interesting afterlife in some later literary and artistic representations.[55] New Testament apocryphal materials often attempt to fill in details left out by what became the canonical New Testament, the "official" story of the church, by using legendary material. They also frequently attempt to rehabilitate even the more monstrous characters of the New Testament, especially if they were associated with the Roman government, now Christian. We find this tendency over and over in apocryphal stories of the end of Pontius Pilate, who is somewhat exculpated from ordering the execution of Jesus even in the canonical gospels. We find it also in the instances of Longinus, the centurion who supposedly crucified Jesus (unnamed in the gospels), and even in Herod Antipas.

In this apocryphal letter, Herod writes to Pilate, to tell him of the sad end of his "daughter," which has served as punishment for his whole family:

> It is in no small sorrow ... that I write to you. My dear daughter Herodias [*sic*] was playing upon the water (i.e., the ice), and fell in up to her neck. And her mother caught at her head to save her, and it was cut off, and the water swept her body away. My wife is sitting with the head on her knees, weeping, and all the house is full of sorrow ... My wife's left eye is blinded through weeping ... because we mocked at the eye of the righteous.[56]

52. Again, I am indebted to Sally Dormer for both these images.
53. Voyer, "Le corps du péchê, 77–78.
54. Kristeva, *The Severed Head*, 83. Anderson, "The Dancing Daughter," 127, refers to the medieval veneration of John's head on a platter, cited in Collins, *Mark*, 313n143.
55. One of the most compelling is "A Dance of Death," written in the early twentieth century by the pseudonymous Michael Field. This poem will be discussed in chapter 3.
56. *The Letter of Herod to Pilate* 1–3.

This account evokes a sense of righteous satisfaction for the death of John: a head for a head, a figurative eye for an eye; the head of her beloved daughter in Herodias's lap, rather than the head of her enemy, John. Yet it also seems to excuse what appears to be a childish Salome from full complicity in John's death: she is "playing" on the ice. This apocryphal story is repeated by the Byzantine historian Nicephorus Callistus Xanthopoulos (1256–1335), who treats it as a retribution for the "lethal leaping" of the "viper . . . taught by her mother."[57] Jacobus da Voragine's popular late thirteenth-century *Golden Legend* has two versions of Herodias's daughter's death. In one, she is merely "walking" on an icy pond when the ice gives way and she is drowned; in the other, "the earth swallowed her alive." There is no decapitation in either version.[58]

A more benign version of this tradition has Salome take the well-worn path to repentance followed by the "harlot saints," former wealthy courtesans who retreat to the desert to live out rigorous lives of solitary expiation for their sins. In one version of this tradition, Salome herself escapes beheading by Herod and lives in the desert, clothed in animal skins and eating locusts and wild honey, like John the Baptist in Mark 1:6. She comes to believe in Jesus as the messiah, and wanders about as an itinerant preacher of the gospel. On one of her many wanderings, she is crossing a frozen lake, when the ice breaks. As in the previous accounts, she is decapitated by the shards, but not before calling on the names of John the Baptist and Jesus before she dies. Her severed head is later seen on the "plate" of silver ice, surrounded by a golden nimbus, like that of a saint.[59] Oscar Wilde knew of this tradition but apparently rejected the idea of a Saint Salome. Salome's career as a repentant sinner and convert who expiates her complicity in John's death is resurrected by the American poet J. C. Heywood's "dramatic poems" about Salome—which may have been the reason Wilde rejected his version—and Michael Field's poem, "A Dance of Death."[60] Very little of the repentant Salome seems to have appealed to subsequent generations. It was all well and good to have her own decapitation expiate John's, although Wilde, as I noted, rejected it, opting instead to have her crushed

---

57. Nicephorus Callistus Xanthopoulos, *Ecclesiastical History*, 1.19. The English translation is mine. This story inspired a poem by the Welsh metaphysical poet Henry Vaughan, "The Daughter of Herodias." See Janes, *Losing Our Heads*, 3.

58. Jacobus de Voragine, *The Golden Legend*, chapter 125.

59. Richardson, "Michael Field's 'A Dance of Death,'" 1n3.

60. Both will be explored in chapter 3.

under Herod's soldier's shields, but later writers wanted more. The pairing and contrast of Salome, representing tantalizing yet deadly sexuality, and John the Baptist, representing denial of the flesh and its sexual temptations, proved irresistible.

In Muslim traditions, which revere John the Baptist as the prophet Nabi Yahya,[61] Salome is portrayed as even more of a temptress than in Christian legend, even guiltier for John's head than is her mother, Herodias. In one Muslim legend, Herodias does not appear at all, or at least not by that name. According to the fourteenth-century Sunni scholar and historian Ismail Ibn Kathir, John the Baptist, "Allah's beloved prophet," denounces a prospective marriage between Herod Antipas and his niece, Salome, as incestuous and "against the Law of the Torah." Salome, who is angry at this challenge to her plans "to rule the kingdom with her uncle," engineers a solo plot to kill John. She dresses "attractively," and sings and dances to "arouse Herod's lust." The plot is effective. Salome requests John's head, telling Herod that "he has defiled your honor and mine throughout the land." She offers herself to him in recompense for the head. "Bewitched by her charm," Herod fulfills her "monstrous request," and the "cruel woman gloat[s] with delight." In the end, however, John's death is avenged with "severe punishment," not only of Salome but also by the destruction of "all the children of Israel" by invading armies, presumably the armies of Aretas, but perhaps an allusion to the destruction of the Jewish nation by the Romans.[62]

SALOME'S ALLEGORICAL AFTERLIFE

At the end of the Middle Ages, as with so many other aspects of European culture, a new interpretation of Salome and John the Baptist emerged: one in which Salome is neither the childish pawn of an ambitious mother nor a disreputable, seductive dancer—although the latter image survived and thrived—but an allegorical emblem. Like the writers, artists, and theologians of the Middle Ages, their counterparts in the Renaissance loved typology, the idea of the "prefiguration" of characters and objects in the New Testament and church history by those in the Old Testament and even

---

61. The Great Mosque of Damascus (Umayyad Mosque) has a shrine containing the supposed head of John the Baptist. See Sacred Destinations, "Great Mosque of Damascus," para. 2.

62. Ibn Kathir, "Prophet Yahya."

in classical culture. Like their predecessors, they also loved allegory—the reading of the Scriptures, whose literal sense was crude and repellent to readers and interpreters steeped in classical philosophy and literature—as symbolizing something higher, more intellectual, and more spiritual than the literal sense indicated.

In the writings of the church fathers of the early Christian period, and in the Middle Ages in general, Salome symbolized sexual abandon, women's carnal nature, and the temptation of the flesh—identified with the female—that might cause a man to lose his head, the seat of reason and authority, as in the cases of Herod (figuratively) and John (literally). While these ideas are not entirely abandoned in the Renaissance, the divide between spirit and flesh becomes less sharp, and physical beauty can be admired without the admirer inevitably succumbing to the temptations of the flesh and of lust.[63] Beginning in the fifteenth century with the Flemish artist Rogier van der Weyden, artists returned to representing a fully clad, young but not childish Salome, who is not now engaged in her dance. Instead, she is often shown being presented with, holding, or presenting the head of John the Baptist on a platter, but she is not looking at it. Rather, she turns her head away. It would not be too far a stretch to think that in the Renaissance, with its often-expressed reverence for reason over passion, Salome is shown to have come to her senses, fully conscious of her role in John's death and repelled or ashamed by the result of her actions.[64] The viewer is thus also allowed to gaze at a beautiful young woman who is not overtly eroticized.[65] Image after image painted in the Renaissance preserves this glance away from the head. Nevertheless, an alternative interpretation of Titian's two paintings of Salome with the head of John the Baptist suggests that the erotic element is still present, even with the sideways glance. In his earlier 1515 painting, Salome exhibits the typical Renaissance turn from the head, possibly in regret. In his 1550 painting, Salome lifts the head high, while she turns toward the viewer, away from her trophy. In both, however, it has been suggested that the bare arm of Salome is suggestively, even erotically, touched by the long hair of the dead John.[66] The eroticism, if it is indeed there, is implicit rather than explicit.

---

63. Zagona, *The Legend of Salome*, 21–22.
64. Neginsky, *Salome*, 26.
65. "Amy," "Dancing Seductress: Salome," par. 3
66. Museo Nacional del Prado, Madrid, "Titian, Salome."

Salome and the Head of John the Baptist

It is not by accident that these images parallel those of the other young woman whose actions result in a man's death by beheading, although she is herself the executioner: Judith. When Renaissance artists depict Judith with the head of Holofernes, they usually show her not looking at her gruesome prize, as either turning directly towards the viewers, implicating them in her deed, or turning pensively away from the head. For example, Artemisia Gentileschi, who earlier depicted Judith in the bloody act of sawing off the head (1614–1618), later (1625) depicted her after the deed was done, turning aside from the viewer and from the head, holding up her hand as if to shield herself and the result of her actions from the light of the candle on the table.[67] Like Salome, Judith uses her physical attractions to bring about the death of her enemy, the achievement of her desire. The interpreters of Judith's story can veer between seeing her as a virtuous defender of her people against annihilation and viewing her as a woman who craftily uses her physical and sexual attraction to lure a man to a horrible death. What seems dominant, however, in many Renaissance paintings, both of Judith and Salome, is the image of regret over causing a man's death, not willful ignorance of the implications of their actions.

In keeping with the medieval love for allegory and symbolism, Renaissance artists retrieved from earlier theologians an idea of Salome that also helped them redeem her from her shameful participation in the death of the prophet, martyr, and forerunner of Christ. The offering of John's head on a platter at a feast came to prefigure the offering of the body of Christ in the Eucharist to believers.[68] Correspondingly, Herodias and Salome also have symbolic roles to play in this understanding of the church—roles that, like Judas the betrayer of Christ, they were divinely destined to play. A Frankish theologian of the late eighth century to early ninth century, long taken to have been the much earlier church father Jerome, is responsible for expressing this symbolism by interpreting figuratively Jesus's saying in Luke 16:16: "The law and the prophets were in effect until John came; since then the good news of the kingdom of God is proclaimed, and everyone tries to enter it by force [i.e., violently]." For this author, later called Pseudo-Jerome, the imprisonment of John means "the end of the old Law." Herodias signifies the synagogue; "the girl dancing at the banquet [i.e., Herodias's daughter] symbolizes the pagans dancing before their idols," and the "head of John on the plate symbolizes the body of Christ on the altar." The "girl," presum-

---

67. Wikipedia, "Judith Slaying Holofernes."
68. Voyer, "Le corps du péché," 79; See also Reed, "Rogier van der Weyden," 7–8.

ably Salome, symbolizes also "the Church that comes from the Gentiles," a reference to Paul's discussion of the reason for the acceptance of Jesus more readily by non-Jews than by Jews in Romans 9–11; "and she brings it to her mother, meaning the conversion of the Jews."[69] In this commentary on the Gospel of Mark, Pseudo-Jerome explains that John's head signifies that "the head of the Law, which is Christ, is severed from his body: that is, the Jewish people, and given to the Gentile girl: that is, to the Roman church." When Salome gives the head to her mother, "the adulteress," the gesture demonstrates that "the Synagogue, now astray, will believe in the end."[70] Both Herodias and her daughter will finally be redeemed, but the moment is yet to come. Salome's glance away from the head, her reluctance to look at it, could symbolize the pagan (Gentile) reluctance to believe, or it may indicate that the church does not allow the unbaptized to receive the sacrament.[71] The afterlife of a chastened and repentant Salome, however, is not pursued to any degree until its flowering in the nineteenth century with the epic trilogy of the American writer J. C. Heywood, and even then it continues to be a fairly minor strain in the master narrative of the seductive and fatal virgin.

At least one Protestant artist of the Reformation, Lucas Cranach the Elder, preserved the tradition of Salome's full frontal gaze away from the head of John the Baptist. Cranach, who seems to have had an "obsession with severed heads," painted five pictures of Salome with the head of John the Baptist, and four of Judith with the head of Holofernes.[72] A staunch friend and supporter of Martin Luther, Cranach developed "a new Lutheran iconography, holding, with Luther, that "art . . . is useful for the purposes of promoting memory and serving as a witness (a record of beliefs)." Thus, art for the Reformers remains a means of expressing theology, and has a "distinctly didactic character."[73] Cranach's Salome is never depicted dancing, although Luther himself had nothing against dance, holding it "a remarkably pleasant pastime," provided it was not lascivious.[74] In all of Cranach's

---

69. References, as well as discussion from Reed, "Rogier van der Weyden," 14n38. This passage is taken from Pseudo-Jerome's *Exposition of the Four Gospels*, on Matt 14:1-12 (PL 30, col. 570–71). The English translation from Latin is mine.

70. Reed, "Rogier van der Weyden," 14n39.

71. Ibid., 8, 14n45.

72. Ferrebee, "Cranach's Obsession with Severed Heads."

73. Smith, *The Northern Renaissance*, 373–74.

74. Luther, "Table Talk," no. 3477.

paintings of Salome, moreover, she is always fully and elegantly dressed, perhaps as an indication of her royal status.

Albrecht Dürer, another artist and adherent to the Lutheran cause, depicts Salome and the head of John the Baptist in two prints, the new technological medium of the Protestant "revolution." In *The Beheading of Saint John the Baptist* (1510), Salome, again elegantly dressed, receives the severed head directly from the executioner. In *The Head of John the Baptist Brought to Herodias* (1511), a willowy Salome proudly presents her trophy to a matronly Herodias and to Herod. This time, it is the queen and king who turn away from this gruesome addition to their dinner table—Herodias in disgust, Herod in sadness. These two prints suggest that Dürer saw Salome, rather than Herodias or Herod, as the active agent in John's decapitation.[75]

Catholic artists during the Counter-Reformation (1545–1648) have little to add to these rote depictions, and do not respond directly to them. The most famous of these artists, Peter Paul Rubens, depicted Salome in three paintings—of the beheading, of receiving the head, and of presenting the head of John the Baptist at Herod's feast.[76] Each time, Salome appears as a voluptuous young woman sumptuously dressed in scarlet—perhaps an indication of her wealthy status and her dubious reputation as a "scarlet woman"—but undoubtedly as a royal personage, permitted to wear such bright colors. It is hard to imagine this stately figure dancing anything other than a courtly dance, although in the version of *The Feast of Herod* in the National Gallery of Scotland, the dance is implied by the rollicking boy in the left foreground, rolling what appears to be a tambourine. This figure may also be an echo of the innocence of Salome's childish dance. It is Herodias rather than Salome who is the active party in the presentation, using her fork to stab at John's tongue, as if she were prodding a particularly luscious cut of meat.

The magisterial Reformers nevertheless have little to say about Salome, perhaps because they have a greater image of feminine evil to hand in the Great Whore of Revelation, the woman seated on seven hills who in their theology is indubitably Catholic Rome in the guise of Babylon, "mother of whores and of the earth's abominations" (Rev 17:5), symbolizing the

---

75. Both woodcuts are in the collections of the Metropolitan Museum of Art, New York.

76. It is possible that Rubens himself only painted the last one; the first two may be by his studio. But all three have the young woman in the red dress.

papacy. A woodcut in the Luther Bible of 1523, by Hans Burgkemair the Elder, depicts the Great Whore wearing the papal tiara.[77] John Calvin's stated opposition to images and representations did not allow for an actual Calvinist religious art, even of a didactic nature.[78] For both Luther and Calvin, moreover, the important personage in the story of Herod's feast and its aftermath was John the Baptist, but only as the forerunner and predictor of Christ.[79] Calvin, however, did not miss an opportunity to castigate Herodias, Salome, and the laxity of the Herodian court in general:

> Hence, too, it appears what sort of discipline existed in his [Herod's] court; for though most people at that time thought themselves at liberty to dance, yet for a marriageable young woman to dance was a shameful display of the influence of the strumpet. But the unchaste Herodias had moulded [sic] her daughter Salome to her own manners in such a manner that she might not bring disgrace on her.[80]

Artistic representation was not the only means by which Protestants depicted their own version of the story of Salome, Herodias, and John the Baptist. According to Detlef Melz, Protestant authors from the early sixteenth century into the seventeenth, during a revival of tragedy on the stage, produced an increasing number of tragedies that treated the theme of martyrdom—especially as depicted in the Bible, since Protestants at that time were likely avoiding anything that lacked biblical authority, not to mention the cult of the martyrs, saints, or relics. John the Baptist was thus a character ready to hand for several playwrights, including the celebrated Hans Sachs.[81] Sachs's play, *The Beheading of John* (1580), like the art of Cranach and Dürer, supports Protestant theological and political aims, and "expresses his bitter disappointment at the developments unfavorable to German Lutheranism, specifically the punishment of the preacher Veit Dietrich and the exile of Andreas Osiander. The latter event explains Sachs's introduction of the motif of exile into the dialogue between Herod, Herodias, and Salome, for which neither the Bible nor Josephus's *Jewish Antiquities*

---

77. Wikipedia, "The Whore of Babylon."
78. Calvin, *Institutes* 1.11.2 and 1.9.8.
79. Luther, "4th Sunday in Advent."
80. Calvin, *Commentary*, Matthew 14:3–12 (Mark 6:17–29). See https://www.ccel.org/ccel/calvin/calcom31.html/.
81. Melz, *Das protestantische Drama*, 527–28.

offers a precedent," although there is ample precedent of the Herodians' exile to Gaul in the apocryphal and legendary materials.[82]

As the narrative of Salome in art progresses through the Renaissance and the Reformation, the dance is downplayed and the connection with the severed head of the Baptist enhanced. Overall, in the postbiblical development of Salome representations and Salome's connection to John the Baptist's decapitated head, whatever she is given to symbolize, positive or negative, is the result of mythological and theological reflections on aspects of "the feminine," rather than any attempt to portray or to understand a historical woman. Salome's body, even as abundantly and sumptuously clothed by Renaissance and Reformation artists, is still a body. Perhaps the richness and detail of the clothing itself contributes even more to a sense of materiality and physicality, signifying a woman who can only possess a man's head, the seat of reason, through contriving its removal, and one who has the power to do so.

82. Wailes, "Hans Sachs," 399.

3

Salome Counter Salome

SALOME ON THE VERGE

As the Salome story in art, literature, and theology progresses through the Renaissance and Reformation, her dance is downplayed, while the close connection between Salome and the head of John the Baptist strengthens. In contrast, the portrayal of Salome as a seductress declined from the sixteenth to the early nineteenth century, when her importance waned, as did the retelling of her story in its variants. Many of the artistic representations from this period concentrate on the act of beheading rather than the dance, and on John rather than Salome. Toni Bentley refers to the period between the seventeenth century and nineteenth century as Salome's "artistic hibernation."[1] Helen Grace Zagona notes three "peaks of interest" in Salome: early Christianity, the Middle Ages, and the post-Romantic era, characterized as the era of Decadence.[2] Over 388 versions of the Salome legend in art, drama, history, literature and opera appeared in the nineteenth century and blossomed internationally from their beginnings in Paris. While the preponderance of these covered the years from 1860 to 1920, versions of a Herodias/Salome narrative appeared as early as 1832, with a play by Silvio Pellico called *Erodiade* (*Herodias*).[3] In this five-act play, Herodias is the chief instigator of the Baptist's death, while Salome is

---

1. Bentley, *Sisters of Salome*, 20.
2. Zagona, *The Legend of Salome*, 22.
3. Pym, "The Importance of Salome," 311–12. During this period, there was a significant absence of theological reflection on the subject.

a "marginal" character, described as a girl who is "ten or twelve years old."[4] These characterizations are closer to their biblical origins than the much-embroidered ones they will later become. Salome is not yet the femme fatale that she will be. She is generally confused with Herodias until 1866, after which she emerges, not exclusively but predominantly, as the sultry dancing Salome.[5] The femme fatale characterization appears to be the result of the influence of Romanticism, coupled with the Gothic imagination and the emergence, in Western imperial Europe, of the concept of Orientalism, out of which evolves the figure of *la belle juive* (the "beautiful Jewess") as both victim and predator. Because so many versions of the Herodias/Salome narrative arise in the nineteenth century and later, many of them interacting with each other, it will be necessary to focus on only the more influential and pivotal, although I will include some of the more marginal and outré, as they illustrate the wide attraction of the dancer and her dance. The most famous modern representation of Salome, Oscar Wilde's 1891 play of that title, is itself influenced by the literary works of Heinrich Heine, Gustave Flaubert, Stéphane Mallarmé, Joris-Karl Huysmans, and marginally by the American J. C. Heywood's florid dramatic trilogy on Herodias and Salome; and by the paintings and drawings of Gustave Moreau. More than any other, however, Wilde's *Salomé* had a major influence on how the character was interpreted, from its first appearance to the present day.

THE ROMANTIC IMAGINATION AND HEINE'S *ATTA TROLL*

The Romantic era "came into full flower towards the end of the eighteenth century," signaling a reaction against the Age of Reason and the Enlightenment. Originally intended as a pejorative label (like *Gothic* in architecture), the Romantic and Romanticism played upon the imagination, even incorporating the fantastic,[6] and prepared for the later Decadent image of the fatally attractive Salome. The Romantics were also interested in folkloric legends, often of a macabre nature, including one about a character called Aradia, who was probably an early form of Herodias.[7] Herodias and the Roman goddess Diana "are linked in folk legend from the ninth century

---

4. Boccaccini, "Erodiade (Herodias/1832 Pellico), play."
5. Pym, "The Importance of Salome," 316.
6. Praz, *The Romantic Agony*, 11–13.
7. Magliocco, "Who Was Aradia?" para. 5.

CE onward." This is especially true of Diana in her manifestation as Hecate. Unlike Diana's manifestation as a virgin huntress, the goddess Hecate is associated with secret rituals (sometimes of a sexual nature), with the spirits of the unquiet dead who haunt crossroads at night, and with the supernatural beings called faeries, who cross the borders between the living and the dead, to lure the living into the underworld or faerie realm. One of these, Fey Aboundia, or Domina Abundia, is a kind of goddess of plenty, as her name implies, who helps houses in which she and her followers receive hospitality, but curses others who reject them.[8] This folklore complex absorbed other elements, such as naked dancing and flying through the night on a "wild hunt" or cavalcade.[9] The German poet Heinrich Heine, whom Jeffrey Sammons credits in his biography with a fairly typical Romantic love of the folklore of the Rhineland, incorporates Diana, Fey Aboundia (as "Habondia," the "Celtic sprite"), and Herodias (Aradia) as members of a haunted hunt, appearing appropriately on the Eve of Saint John the Baptist, in his epic poem, *Atta Troll*.[10]

Contributing to the picture of a predatory female, and assisting in the development of the classic fatal female character indelibly associated with Salome in the latter part of the nineteenth century and in the early twentieth was the emergence of the Romantic tradition of *la belle dame sans merci*. The figure of the unattainable but desirable beloved, reflecting the Romantics' medieval interests, is originally derived from courtly love poetry and the *romans* (romances) it produced. The term itself—*la belle dame sans merci*—comes from a fifteenth-century poem of that title by Alain Chartier.[11] In Romanticism, *la belle dame* is the attractive but pitiless beauty who seduces and "kills the man she loves,"[12] best known from John Keats's 1819 ballad of the same title. In it, the male victim/speaker, encountered "alone and palely loitering,"[13] has been made sexual captive to the point of possession and near death by the erotic and exotic "faery's child," who enslaves the knight by her "sweet moan" and the deceptive appearance of love for him. Warned in a dream by her other dead or near-dead victims, he escapes her, but cannot escape her "thrall."

8. Ibid., para. 11.
9. Ibid., para. 27.
10. Sammons, *Heinrich Heine*, 35–42.
11. "La Belle Dame sans Merci: More Notes," in *Keats' Kingdom*.
12. Praz, *The Romantic Agony*, 215.
13. "La Belle Dame sans Merci: A Ballad," in *Poems by John Keats (1795–1821)*.

Salome Counter Salome

As Mario Praz notes, "Pleasure and death are intertwined" in several of Keats's poems.[14] In "Lamia," a snake-woman possesses and is possessed by a young philosopher until he learns her true identity, and dies. In "The Eve of St. Agnes," the lovers Madeline and Porphyro are able to achieve their desires—she, to enjoy him in a vision; he, to enjoy her physically—but they create evil dreams, havoc, and death for others. In "Isabella," the heroine cuts off the head of the lover whom her brothers have murdered and buries it in a pot of basil. When the pot is stolen from her, she goes mad and dies. Thus, the poet portrays the Romantic subjection of virtue ("La Belle Dame"), reason ("Lamia" and "Isabella"), and even purity and holiness ("The Eve of St. Agnes") to desire. Keats wrote of his own personal attraction to a "young Anglo-Indian girl" who had "the Beauty of a Leopardess [*sic*] . . . I should like her to ruin me."[15] The Romantic nexus of irresistible, savage, and fatal love, together with a strong Orientalizing flavor, could not be any clearer. As will be seen in later portrayals of Herodias or Salome as the femme fatale, these Romantic themes foreshadow the Gothic and still later the Decadent: "Love and death, temptation and duty, dream and waking, and the murky suffering of the consequences of ungoverned emotion; ecstasy and its aftermath of despair; the otherworldly seductress . . . the fraught duality of Eros and death."[16]

The link between eroticism and death is also applied to Herodias/Salome in Heine's epic poem, *Atta Troll* (1842–1846). Its hero is a dancing bear who escapes from his captivity, has a series of picaresque adventures, and ends up being recaptured and turned into a bearskin rug that warms the narrator's toes. Heine wrote that he intended the poem "for my own pleasure and enjoyment," in the manner of the Romantic school that he thought he was now—playfully or otherwise—repudiating.[17] Heine's "Sommernachstraum" ("Midsummer Night's Dream") is a complex political allegory and parody, but it is also a phantasmagorical poem in which Herodias, like Aradia, appears as a member of a cursed or haunted hunt, to which she has been condemned for instigating the murder of John the Baptist. As she rides by with the ghostly band that includes two other (nonhuman) women, the goddess Diana and the Celtic sprite Habondia, the poet (as narrator) relates his attraction to her, wondering,

14. Praz, *The Romantic Agony*, 285n17.
15. Ibid.
16. Earl, "John Keats: 'La Belle Dame sans Merci.'"
17. Phelan, *Reading Heinrich Heine*, 114.

> Was she too a lady-devil,
> Like the other female figures?
> Be she devil, or an angel,
> I don't know. Just so with women,
> One's not certain where the angel
> Stops, and where begins the devil.[18]

In this respect, Herodias is not unlike Keats's Lamia, "who seem'd, at once, some penanced lady elf, / Some demon's mistress, or the demon's self."[19]

Heine describes his Herodias in exotic Eastern terms, noting her "fevered visage," on which lay the "oriental magic"; her "precious clothes" that reminded him of "Scheherezade's old stories"; her "soft red lips, red like pomegranates"; her "little curved nose, like lilies," and her limbs, "like the palms of an oasis" (20.18–19). Some of this Orientalizing language, reminiscent of the Song of Songs, will reappear in Wilde's *Salomé*. As if anyone had questioned her lineage, Heine asserts, "Yes, she really was a princess, / Was the queen of all Judea, / And the lovely wife of Herod, / Who the Baptist's head did covet" (20.21). In Heine's telling of her story, Herodias has not instigated the death of John because of his incessant criticism of her adulterous marriage to Herod: she has him killed because she desires him. For her "blood-guilt," Herodias is forced to keep carrying—and kissing—the head of John the Baptist. The themes of thwarted desire and the kissing of the dead Baptist's head are later employed by Oscar Wilde in his *Salomé* as proof that Salomé is sexually "monstrous." Heine claims that at one time Herodias loved John, even though this idea is far from supported in the biblical texts. The proof of her "blood loving" is, counterintuitively (except in Romantic poetry) the head: a woman would not crave the head of a man she does not love (20.25). In turn, Herodias dies of "love's dementia," and is buried in "Old Yerushalayim," but is brought back to life, to toss the head like a spectral ball, "with childish laughter," as she rides in the wild hunt. The poet/narrator himself longs for Herodias, believing that she is flirting with him: "Why has thou regarded me so tenderly, Herodias?" (19.34). He confesses, "I love thee above all others! . . . I love thee, departed Jewess!" He urges her, "Love me and be my beloved!" and asks her, somewhat grotesquely, to "catapult the bloody *dummkopf* / With his platter!" (20.22–24).

---

18. Heine, *Atta Troll*, 19.16–17.
19. Keats, "Lamia," in *Poems by John Keats (1795–1821)*, stanza 36, line 55.

Heine's poem lays the foundation for the "fatal attraction" that Herodias/Salome has for John the Baptist, and the fascination that the poet or playwright has for the bloodthirsty object of his own desires.

An intriguing part of the characterization of Herodias in Heine's poem is the "oriental magic" that "lay upon her fevered visage" (20.18). Contributing to this magic is the fact that she is a "princess of Judea," a "Jewess," with whom the author is fascinated. As she "reclines" on her white palfrey, Herodias is accompanied by equally exotic dark-skinned Muslim "Moors." Heine himself had a complicated relationship to Judaism. Born Jewish, he later was baptized a Lutheran in 1825 to assimilate to European culture. Because of his political activities and inclinations, he lived in Paris as an expatriate for twenty-seven years.[20] In his *Confessions* (1854) Heine later identifies himself with Judaism as well as with Christian traditions and rejects "communist atheism."[21] An unfinished novel, *The Rabbi of Bacharach*, centered on the medieval persecution of the Jews.[22] He was also fascinated by the Muslims of medieval Spain, who were called Moors in his time, and their relationship to the Christians in three works focusing on the tragic young "Moorish" character Almansor.[23] In "Donna Clara," a poem in his *Book of Songs* (1827), Heine parodies European anti-Semitism by having "the daughter of the Alcalde" fall in love with a man she thinks is a Christian knight, and not one of those "nasty Jews." He lies to her, telling her that he has "Not a drop of blood that's Moorish, / Nor a taint of Jewish foulness," and becomes her lover. When she asks his identity, he says he is the son of Rabbi Israel of Saragossa.[24] This ambivalence towards Judaism appears also in his poetic portrayal of Herodias/Salome in *Atta Troll*. Heine sees her literally and figuratively from a distance as an exotic Middle Eastern "Other," as if her femaleness makes her either more Jewish—or at least Jewish in a different way—than he is, perhaps in the way that Judith Plaskow speaks of the Jewish woman in a Gentile society as the "Other's Other."[25] It does not seem, however, that Heine as narrator in *Atta Troll* is thinking of himself as a Jew, but as a European non-Jew attracted to an "Oriental" Jewish woman.

20. Wikipedia, "Heinrich Heine."
21. Phelan, *Reading Heinrich Heine*, x.
22. Sammons, *Heinrich Heine*, 95.
23. Ibid., 69.
24. Heine, "Donna Clara"; see also Marshall, "Donna Clara."
25. Plaskow, "The Wife/Sister Stories."

Through the lens of this Orientalism, Heine can see himself as culturally European and not Jewish. This is a theme to which we shall later return.

ORIENTALIZING HERODIAS AND SALOME

The term *Oriental* carries with it a host of cultural and political associations, expressed in the concept of Orientalism, as defined in the landmark book with that title by Edward Said. According to Said, the concept arises in "late eighteenth-century" Europe, in part as a result of Napoleon's campaigns in Egypt and Syria, as "a Western style for dominating, restructuring, and having authority over the Orient,"[26] a realm that is manifestly different from and "Other" than the West, and therefore signifying both allure—often expressed as sexual—and also "danger and threat."[27] Said observes that literary travelers to the "Orient"—usually meaning Egypt, Palestine, and the Levant—like Gustave Flaubert, whose *Salammbô* and "Hérodiade" heavily influenced Oscar Wilde, formed a European "community of thought and feeling" like that of the Romantics described by Praz in *The Romantic Agony*. Their work was informed by "the imagery of exotic places, the cultivation of sadomasochistic tastes . . . a fascination with the macabre, with the notion of a Fatal Woman, with secrecy and occultism."[28]

A better term for this phenomenon might be the more active and deliberate "Orientalizing," the construction of a set of stereotypes, positive and negative, that distinguished European culture from that of the "East."[29] *Oriental* also came to symbolize the feminized or effeminate male and the mysterious female who renders men weak or effeminate, under the control of desire, expressing the Western fear of effeminacy. One could also add to this Oriental sensibility a heightened awareness of the sensual, and an engagement with the sense of sight in particular, giving rise to the multilayered and literally color-full descriptions and depictions from artists and writers such as Heine, Flaubert, Moreau, Mallarmé, Huysmans, and Wilde.

It is probably no accident that Salome's dance came back both into art and literature in the mid- to late nineteenth century as an Orientalized, highly visual experience that attracted the gaze of artists, writers, and their audiences. It usually involved veiling—symbolizing the mystery

26. Said, *Orientalism*, 3.
27. Ibid., 26.
28. Ibid., 180.
29. Ibid., 181.

stereotypically attributed to the Orient—together with its equally stereotypical seductivity, symbolized as those veils are removed one by one. As Tatiana Petzer observes, the veil becomes stylized as "an attribute of the *belle femme orientale*, or that of the dancing *femme fatale orientale*, but more generally into an ambiguous and mutable object representing 'the Other.'"[30] The symbolism of veiling is carried forward into Oscar Wilde's *Salomé* and its consequent imitators as a form of seduction.

Flaubert and His Oriental Heroines

One of those most fascinated by the constructed, alluring Orient that was based on his travels and antiquarian studies was Gustave Flaubert. "Flaubert's writing both before and after his visit [to the Middle East, in 1849–1850] is soaked in the Orient," and in particular its "sensual and sexual aspects."[31] From his visit Flaubert saw veiling as concealing "a deep, rich fund of female sexuality."[32] His travel to Carthage in 1858, together with his extensive historical research, produced one of his Oriental novels, *Salammbô*, published in 1862. Its protagonist is a Carthaginian priestess of the goddess Tanith, and daughter of Hamilcar Barca, the Carthaginian general and father of Hannibal, who is surprisingly not prominent in the novel. Salammbô is beloved of Hamilcar's enemy, the rebel Libyan Mâtho. The plot revolves around a revolt of barbarian mercenaries against Hamilcar and the Carthaginians. The rebels are temporarily successful because of their theft of the sacred veil belonging to the goddess Tanith, the *zaïmph*, which has mystical power. Salammbô, in a Judith-like move, spends the night with Mâtho in his tent, and out of love for her he gives her back the veil. After various intrigues and battles on both sides, Mâtho leads a futile attempt against Carthage, is captured, tortured, and dies before Salammbô, who has been promised to Hamilcar's ally, formerly a rebel, Narr' Havas. He drinks to the victory of Carthage, but Salammbô dies of the shock of Mâtho's death.

According to Lisa Lowe, Flaubert's novel, much like Heine's epic poem, creates an Orientalized woman as an object of desire: "In the novel *Salammbô*, the representations of the Orient as cultural opposite of the Occident are eroticized and feminized; the object of the Orient is praised

30. Petzer, "Veils in Action," 249.
31. Said, *Orientalism*, 181.
32. Ibid., 182.

as a female object."³³ Salammbô is described by Flaubert as an object of restrained sexuality: as a virgin priestess of Tanith, "she had grown up with abstinences, fastings, and purifications, always surrounded by grave and exquisite things."³⁴ Nevertheless, her virginity is tormented through her being possessed by the goddess Rabetna, another aspect of Tanith, although she loves Tanith in her more chaste personification as the moon, who dwells beneath the sacred veil, the *zaïmph*, and who "inspires and governs the lives of men."³⁵

Salammbô's first appearance, to rebuke the mercenaries at their unruly feast, where they are celebrating their victory at the battle of Eryx, Flaubert describes in a richly layered, intensely visual, and nearly inhuman fashion:

> Her hair, which was powdered with violet sand, and combined into the form of a tower, after the fashion of the Chanaanite maidens, added to her height. Tresses of pearls were fastened to her temples, and fell to the corners of her mouth, which was as rosy as a half-open pomegranate. On her breast was a collection of luminous stones, their variegation imitating the scales of the murena. Her arms were adorned with diamonds, and issued naked from her sleeveless tunic, which was starred with red flowers on a perfectly black ground. Between her ankles she wore a golden chainlet to regulate her steps, and her large dark purple mantle, cut of an unknown material, trailed behind her, making, as it were, at each step, a broad wave which followed her.³⁶

Perhaps the most exotic part of this entire description is the "chainlet" that confines her steps. According to Lowe, this *chaînette*, which is ultimately broken when she seduces (or is seduced by) Mâtho in his tent, "defines and confines Salammbô's sexuality," and is a sign of desire whose breaking defines Mâtho as well, as the Occident asserting itself over the desired feminine Orient.³⁷

But what has Salammbô to do with Herodias or Salome, other than to provide the model of an Orientalized woman as an object of desire? Not only did Flaubert develop this figure in another Oriental tale, "Hérodiade," but his *Salammbô* influenced the depiction of Salome and her dance in Gustave

---

33. Lowe, "The Orient as Woman," 45.
34. Flaubert, *Salammbô*, in *Greatest Works*, 316.
35. Ibid., 317.
36. Ibid., 290.
37. Lowe, "The Orient as Woman," 50–51.

Moreau's series of paintings on the subject. According to Françoise Meltar, "Flaubert's description of Salammbô is almost identical to Moreau's vision of Salome," including the chainlet.[38] Not only that, but Moreau's paintings also "help to motivate Flaubert's story of Salome." Moreau's painting *Salome Dancing before Herod* appears in a fevered meditation by the aesthete Des Esseintes in Huysmans's *À Rebours* (*Against the Grain*), and in turn, along with Flaubert's "Hérodiade," contributed to Wilde's *Salomé*.[39] Wilde even writes, "My Salomé is a mystic, the sister of Salammbô, a Saint Thérèse who worships the moon."[40]

Moreau and His Salomes

Henri Regnault had already exhibited a sensual, robust, and peasant-like Salome in the Paris Salon of 1870. Gustave Moreau exhibited two influential and carefully worked out paintings of Salome in the Salon of 1876: *Salome Dancing before Herod* and *The Apparition*. The first, arrived at after one hundred twenty drawings, was heavily influenced by Flaubert's description of Salammbô, but also generally reflected an Orientalizing influence.[41] According to Pierre-Louis Matthieu, "Scarcely any changes would be needed in this [i.e., Flaubert's] description of the virgin priestess of Astarte to bring it into line with the daughter of Herodias."[42] Unlike the careful attempts at historical reconstruction in Flaubert's *Salammbô* and "Hérodiade," however, Moreau's depiction of Salome dancing before Herod is all over the religious, historical, and archaeological map:

> In and around the person of Salome Moreau accumulated the tokens of the spell she cast over the old king Herod Antipas . . . the pinkish white lotus flower she holds symbolizes sensual pleasure; on her left arm is a bracelet adorned with a large eye, the Ujat of the ancient Egyptians, source of the magic fluid; opposite her is a black panther, a symbol of lust; behind the bare-breasted girl playing a lute, Herodias holds in her hand a fan made of peacock's feathers, another symbol of lust; overlooking Herod's throne is a statue of the great goddess Diana of Ephesus with her double row

38. Meltar, *Salome and the Dance of Writing*, 17–18.
39. Ibid., 18–19.
40. "Wilde French *Salomé*," para. 2.
41. Matthieu, *Gustave Moreau*, 122.
42. Ibid., 123.

of breasts, an image of fecundity; and she is flanked by two statues of Ahriman, the Persian god of evil; finally, at the far left of the picture is a large intaglio engraved with an image of the sphinx holding in its claws the body of a male victim.[43]

Moreau continued the theme of Salome's dance in a watercolor, also exhibited in the Salome of 1876, which united the dance and its consequence, the severed head of John the Baptist. In *The Apparition*, which has been described as a "dream" or "hallucination," a stripped-down Salome is confronted by her gory trophy, floating, disembodied, and haloed. Appalled, she points to the head, but none of the other figures in the painting, who are marginal to the interaction between Salome and John's head, are capable of noticing. Ary Renan has suggested that Moreau may have been influenced here by Heine's *Atta Troll*, of which Moreau had a copy in French,[44] but it seems that Salome is more terrified than enchanted by the head, and she has no contact with it.

Moreau was to return again and again to the subject of Salome: altogether he created nineteen paintings, six watercolors, and three hundred and fifty drawings on the subject.[45] For Moreau, as for later Symbolist and Decadent painters and authors, Salome "was the very image of perversity."[46] And yet, even by Moreau, the perverse, highly sexualized, but ultimately inscrutable Salome is depicted in contradictory ways. One of his Salome paintings, *Salome in the Garden*, depicts a young girl in a deep blue dress, picking up the head of the Baptist like some strange flower. Matthieu comments that "the light is so mild, the colour scheme so harmonious, Salome herself so pure and girlish, that one has some difficulty in making the scene agree with Moreau's expressed intention":

> This woman jaded, whimsical, of an animal nature, giving herself the pleasure, not a keen one for her, of seeing her enemy lying on the ground, such is her disgust with any satisfaction of her desires. This woman strolling nonchalantly in a dull and brutish way in the gardens which have just been sullied by this ghastly

---

43. Ibid., 124.

44. Renan, *Gustave Moreau (1826–1898)*, 391–92; cited in Matthieu, *Gustave Moreau*, 126.

45. *Visual Arts Encyclopedia*, "Gustave Moreau, French Symbolist Painter."

46. Matthieu, *Gustave Moreau*, 128.

murder, appalling to the executioner himself, who runs away in bewilderment.[47]

Flaubert and "Hérodiade"

Flaubert, picking up the Herodias/Salome narrative in "Hérodiade," in his *Trois Contes* (*Three Tales*, 1877), was likely influenced in his own turn by Moreau's paintings. As in *Salammbô*, Flaubert brings his historical and antiquarian interests to his writing, although he also gives them a Decadent gloss. He takes advantage of the confusion of names in the New Testament: is the dancer's name the same as that of her mother, Herodias? In Flaubert's account, it really doesn't matter, because Salome becomes Herodias—the daughter is the extension or incarnation of her mother.

Flaubert's tale begins with Herod Antipas at the palace of Machaerus, fearing an attack from the Nabataean Aretas, whose daughter he rejected because of his desire to marry Herodias. Herod is also expecting the arrival of the Roman governor of Syria, Vitellius, with his troops. He is nervous because "the Jews" are becoming intolerant of his idolatries.[48] He also thinks he can hear the cry of his prisoner, Iokanan (John the Baptist),[49] so he calls for his Samaritan servant, the giant Mannaeï, in a panic.

Herodias interrupts his musings to bring him news of her brother Agrippa's imprisonment at home; she reminds Herod that she has left even her daughter by Philip, her previous husband, hoping that she would bear Herod children. But Herodias's reminders of her sacrifice and her caresses leave Herod cold: "The love she was trying to revive was so far off now!"[50] The idea of Herodias's being repulsed by Antipas will later be a major theme in the Salome narrative, especially in Wilde's version. But Herodias goes on to relate her insults and humiliation by the prophet Herod is protecting; she is "paralyzed" and "stifled" by her fears.[51] Suddenly, "a young girl" steps onto the balcony of a nearby house, with masses of heavy hair and a "deli-

---

47. Von Holten, *L'art fantastique de Gustave Moreau*, 18, cited in Matthieu, *Gustave Moreau*, 129.

48. Flaubert, "Hérodiade," 127.

49. Flaubert's rendering of John's Hebrew name reflects his interest in historical verisimilitude and in the exotic. The spelling of the name varies in the nineteenth-century versions of the Salome narrative.

50. Flaubert, "Hérodiade," 132.

51. Ibid., 135.

cate neck."⁵² Breathing heavily, Herod watches her "lissome" movements, and asks Herodias who she is. The queen replies that she does not know, but goes away "suddenly quieted."

Preparations for the feast on Herod's birthday are being made when Vitellius and his troops arrive. The Roman general insists on a tour of the fortress's underground chambers, which are filled with weaponry and marvelous white horses. But Vitellius, like all Romans, having a "passion" to find Herod's treasure, keeps looking. In a "huge pit" he finds the imprisoned prophet Iaokanan, who denounces his entire audience and announces the coming of the true king, the "Son of David." Antipas correctly perceives this as an "insult and a threat" and commands him to be silent, but the prophet continues to "howl like a bear, like a wild ass, like a woman in her travail," saying that the royal couple has been justly punished for their "incest" by sterility.⁵³ His most intense venom is reserved for Herodias, the "Jezebel" who has stolen Herod's heart with "the creaking of thy slipper."⁵⁴ Finding no support against the prophet's railing, Herodias disappears. Herod, however, consults with an Essene named Phanuel, who warns Herod that the stars predict "the death of a man of importance, that very night, in Machaerus."⁵⁵ Ruling out Vitellius and Iaokanan, who has been turned over to the Romans, Herod concludes that it means he himself will die. Seeking consolation now from Herodias, he once more gains a glimpse of the mysterious girl's "delicious young arm" emerging from a curtain in Herodias's room. Asking her if it is her slave girl, Herodias replies it is no concern of his.⁵⁶

Herod's birthday banquet is prepared in terms of "Oriental" opulence. Herod himself has an exotic appearance, with "rouge on his cheek-bones," a "fan-shaped beard," and "blue-powdered hair."⁵⁷ The Romans at the banquet are portrayed as intolerant, gluttonous, and decadent; the Jews, especially the Pharisees, as quarrelsome, disgusting, even demonic, with "tapering skulls, stubbly beards, and weak, unpleasant hands," or with "snub-nosed faces, with big round eyes and a bull-dog air."⁵⁸ The guests' conversation about resurrection, Mithraism, and the mysterious Jesus is interrupted by

52. Ibid., 137.
53. Ibid., 134.
54. Ibid., 155.
55. Ibid., 158.
56. Ibid., 160.
57. Reminiscent of the violet-powdered hair of Salammbô.
58. Flaubert, "Hérodiade," 169.

shouted arguments and the demands of the people for "Iaokanan!" But what really stops the controversies is first the entrance of Herodias, who toasts Caesar, and then, with "a hum of admiring surprise" as a young girl enters, the mysterious girl on the balcony: "It was Herodias, just as she used to be in youth."[59] In this way, Flaubert overcomes the textual difficulties in the New Testament about the name and identity of the dancer: "It was Salome, the daughter of Herodias, whom her mother had had trained far away from Machaerus to capture the Tetrarch's heart."[60]

She draws aside her veil and begins to dance with her little feet as her body writhes and undulates and "her breasts quiver." She mimes "the passionate desire which insists on being slaked," in a repertory of exoticism: "She danced like the Indian priestesses, the Nubians of the cataracts, the Maenads of Lydia."[61] As she "opens her legs," she bends her knees so that her chin touches the floor. As she does so, "the desert-dwellers schooled in abstinence, the Roman soldiers expert in debauchery, the greedy publicans and old priests embittered by disputes all panted greedily, with their nostrils dilated."[62] She circles "frenziedly, as if in a mad round of witches" around Herod's table. He cries out "in a voice broken by sobs of passion," promising her half of his kingdom. But she is not done: she throws herself "onto her hands with her heels in the air,"[63] her skirts framing her face with its painted lips, "deep black eyebrows," and "terrifying eyes"; beads of moisture on her forehead "like a vapour on white marble."[64] As she and Herod silently look at each other, a snap of fingers from the balcony summons Salome, and, as in Mark's gospel, she goes quickly up and then down, making her request "with a childish air, lisping a little"[65]: "I want you to give me, in a dish, the head ... The head of Iaokanan!"[66] At first overwhelmed, Herod then recalls Phanuel's prediction, and realizes that if Iaokanan dies, it will not be himself, and calls Mannaeï to do the work. He comes back "in a state of

---

59. Ibid., 172.
60. Ibid., 173.
61. Ibid.
62. Ibid., 174.
63. This position, possibly that of the *jongleuresses*, is found in several medieval manuscripts, as noted in chapter 2. See also Kuryluk, *Salome and Judas*, 196.
64. Flaubert, "Hérodiade," 174.
65. Bach, *Women, Seduction, and Betrayal*, 230, agrees with Flaubert about Salome: she is "a child charming an adult audience."
66. Flaubert, "Hérodiade," 175.

collapse," even though he is a practiced executioner, because he has seen "the Great Angel of the Samaritans" in front of the pit, and must be forced to go out a second time. He brings back the head, puts it in a dish, and offers it to Salome, who takes it "nimbly" up to the balcony—and disappears, returning the head to the diners by an old female servant. The story is no longer Salome's—nor even Herodias's—but of the head, which is presented to Antipas, who weeps over it. Iaokanan's head both presages the death of Jesus and brings the tale to a close heavily in two senses: the head is "very heavy," and it ends the story.[67]

Mallarmé's "Hérodiade"

Although Salome has excited the male guests at her stepfather's banquet by her sensuous dancing, both Moreau and Flaubert depict her as self-contained, virginal, possibly unaware of, or uncaring of, her role in hastening the beheading of the prophet by provoking male sexual desire. Or her virginity and inaccessibility may themselves make her the object of that desire. In Stéphane Mallarmé's unfinished poem "Hérodiade," begun in 1864, in the first scene of a tragedy that eventually became a poem, in 1869, "the shade of a Princess," according to her old Nurse, wishes to remain untouched, and is a "sad flower that grows alone with no other passion / Than its shadow."[68] The princess Hérodiade is completely solipsistic: "Yes, it's for me, for me that I flower deserted!"[69] She loves "the horror of virginity," as she describes it, wanting to keep herself "inviolate."[70] The poem uses images of whiteness and cold: icicles, "cruel snow" (suggestive of the legendary end to which Herodias/Salome came, falling through ice), "cold and precious stones."[71] The third part of the poem, which was not published until 1913, the "Canticle of Saint John," gives the head of the Baptist the last word, as does Flaubert's "Hérodiade," when the "head leapt up" and "cuts / The old disaccords with the body."[72]

67. Ibid., 175–78.
68. Lenson, trans., "Hérodiade," 573. Other page numbers refer to this translation.
69. Ibid., 585.
70. Ibid., 586.
71. Ibid.
72. Ibid., 587.

The idea of Herodias/Salome's sexuality (the body's "disaccords" with the head) is a preoccupation of the later Decadent/Symbolist writers. Despite many definitions of Decadence and its often coterminous Symbolism, George P. Landow lists five characteristics of this style, which emerged in the late nineteenth century: an "anti-Romantic" sense of the "omnipresence of evil and the grotesque," which accompanies the "fallenness" of humankind and nature, although not in the religious sense; a mood and tone of exile, ennui, isolation, and emptiness (of meaning); imagery that relies upon dreams and "extreme artifice"; an emphasis on the "unnatural" rather than nature; "incomplete and unsuccessful attempts to escape the human condition"; and "extreme or hyperbolic juxtapositions," like those that create the jumble of images in Mallarmé's work—and even more so, the work of Jules Laforgue, who stands between "Mallarmé's symbolism and Flaubert's exoticism," particularly in regard to Salome.[73] Laforgue's phantasmagorical poem "Salomé," in his *Moralités Légendaires* (*Legendary Moralities*, 1886) envisions Salomé painting John the Baptist's head with makeup, kissing it, and then throwing it into the sea. Unfortunately, she overbalances, and falls on the rocks below, in a strange kind of recompense for John's death. But Symbolism, like Decadence, was contrary to Naturalism and the depiction of reality: it sought to make art that was "independent of moral and social concerns."[74]

SYMBOLIST SALOME: HUYSMANS'S *AGAINST THE GRAIN*

A classic example of the Decadent/Symbolist ethos is Joris-Karl (J.-K.) Huysmans's novel *À Rebours* (*Against the Grain*), whose title could also be translated *Against Nature*, written in 1884. Its protagonist is the aesthete and neurasthenic Des Esseintes, whose surrender to carnality has left him in despair, with a collapsed nervous system. Remarking that "Nature has had her day,"[75] Des Esseintes adopts a stance of antinaturalism in favor of artifice, procuring "paintings of a subtle, exquisite refinement . . . reminiscent it may be of ancient corruption." These introduce him "to an unknown world, revealing to him the traces of new possibilities, stirring the nervous

---

73. Landow, "Aesthetes and Decadents"; Silvani and Strukelj, "The Legend of Salome," 105–20.
74. Thuleen, "*Salomé*," section 5.
75. Huysmans, *Against the Grain* (*À Rebours*), 54.

system by erudite phantasies, complicated dreams of horror, visions of careless indifference and cruelty." The painter he admires above all others is Gustave Moreau, "who most ravished him with unceasing transports of pleasure."[76] And his favorite of Moreau's "masterpieces" is his *Salomé Dancing before Herod*, which has obsessed Des Esseintes for years. He finds in the painting, "going altogether beyond the meager facts supplied by the New Testament," the "weird and superhuman" Salomé of his dreams. Not merely does she, like Flaubert's "Hérodiade," destroy the energy and break the will of Herod by her "quivering bosoms, heaving belly, and tossing thighs"; she becomes "the symbolic incarnation of world-old Vice, the goddess of immortal Hysteria, the Curse of Beauty supreme about all other." With her stiff flesh and steely muscles, Salome becomes the "monstrous Beast of the Apocalypse, indifferent, irresponsible, insensible, poisoning ... all who near her, see her, touch her." No longer associated with a particular biblical tradition, not even with the Great Whore of the Apocalypse, whom Des Esseintes conflates with the Beast on which she rides, Salomé is allied with the "ancient Theogonies of the Far East," outside of time.[77]

Des Esseintes also possesses Moreau's watercolor *The Apparition*, which he describes as "even yet more troubling to the senses" than his oil painting, with a nearly naked Salomé, gazing with horror on the severed head that is visible to her alone.[78] Here she is "less majestic, less imposing, but more ensnaring to the senses" than in the other work. "Petrified and hypnotized by terror," she is no longer goddess but "mime" and "courtesan." Des Esseintes believes:

> In this, she was altogether feminine, obedient to her temperament of a passionate, cruel woman; she was active and alive, more refined and yet more savage, more hateful and yet more exquisite; she was shown awakening more powerfully the sleeping passions of man; bewitching, subjugating more surely his will, with her unholy charm as of a great flower of concupiscence, born of a sacrilegious birth, reared in a hothouse of impiety.[79]

Huysmans / Des Esseintes regards Moreau as an untutored "mystic Pagan," steeped in the mythologies of the Far East. He admires Flaubert as

---

76. Ibid., 74.
77. Ibid., 76.
78 Ibid., 77.
78. Ibid., 78.

a "great author," particularly for *Salammbô*;[80] but he idolizes Mallarmé, especially his "Hérodiade," which keeps him "in a veritable spell," as when he looks at Moreau's *Salomé*. He considers decadence "incarnate in Mallarmé in the most consummate and exquisite perfection."[81] In the end, however, Des Esseintes' nervous dyspepsia returns, and he is forced to return to Paris and to "the waves of human mediocrity."[82] The idyll, if it was one, is over. Not only is Des Esseintes defeated, but so is Salomé herself, since this Salomé cannot really exist beyond the aesthete's interpretation of a painting and watercolor that themselves are symbolic.

OSCAR WILDE AND THE DANCE OF THE SEVEN VEILS

Oscar Wilde's one-act play *Salomé* has probably been more influential than any other artistic work from the late nineteenth century to the early twenty-first century in its portrayal of the inscrutable, virginal yet seductive and monstrous young dancer. As many critics have observed, Wilde himself was well aware of earlier portrayals of Herodias/Salome, including those of Heine, Moreau, and Flaubert, whose *Salammbô*, as we have seen, he admired; Huysmans, Mallarmé, the Belgian symbolist writer Maurice Maeterlinck (whose *La Princesse Maleine* influenced the opening lines of Wilde's play), and even the American J. C. Heywood, whose dramatic poem *Salome*, was published in 1862.[83] In turn, Wilde's play is the inspiration for Richard Strauss's opera by the same title, which appears to have treated the play as a master narrative of the story.

According to Neil McKenna's biography, Wilde was "obsessed by the spirit of Salomé," who for him "had become the incarnation of decadence, mysterious, alluring, erotic, a symbol of the spectacular collusion of love and death."[84] One can see why, however, other critics might view Wilde's *Salomé* as a "Late Romantic" work, in which the image of the "woman dancer symbolizes the self wholly integrated with Nature."[85] Wilde, however, declared that he was writing "a play about a woman dancing in her

80. Ibid., 161.
81. Ibid., 175.
82. Ibid., 190.
83. Kohl, *Oscar Wilde*, 191–92; Thuleen, "*Salomé*," section 3.
84. McKenna, *The Secret Life*, 164–65.
85. Scanlon and Kerridge, "Spontaneity and Control," 32.

bare feet in the blood of a man she has craved for and slain."[86] Perhaps Wilde intended Salome to be dancing in the blood of John the Baptist in a possible victory dance, but in the end, although there is blood on the floor, it is not the Baptist's, but that of the Young Syrian Narraboth, who kills himself for unrequited love of Salomé. Love, or at any rate desire, is of prime importance in this play: Narraboth loves Salomé, who is beautiful but cold and chaste as the moon (to him); Herodias's Page loves the Young Syrian; Herodias and Herod Antipas once had adulterous love for each other that has now cooled; Herod lusts after Salomé; Salomé is enamored of Iokanaan (John the Baptist) and wishes to kiss his mouth, a kiss accomplished only in death on the lips of his severed head.

Primarily, however, Wilde's *Salomé* is a paean to "scopophilia," the power of the "penetrating gaze" that arouses and at times satisfies male heterosexual desire, leading at times to deadly consequences.[87] Men are always looking at Salomé, and always being told, "Do not look at her." At the beginning of the play, the Young Syrian signals this connection by saying, "How beautiful is the princess Salomé tonight!" Herodias's Page, who is in love with him, tells him to look instead at the moon, who is "like a woman who is dead."[88] The Young Syrian, obsessed with Salomé, can only see the moon as the object of his adoration, like a "little princess, who wears a yellow veil and whose feet are silver. She is like a princess who has little white doves for feet. You would fancy she was dancing."[89] The Page reiterates, ominously, "She is like a woman who is dead," and again cautions the Young Syrian against gazing at Salomé: "You look at her too much . . . Something terrible may happen." The soldiers standing nearby repeat the theme of the gaze: Herod the Tetrarch is "looking at someone." The Young Syrian cannot seem to tear himself away from looking at Salomé: she looks "so pale, like the shadow of a white rose in a mirror of silver,"[90] as the Page once more cautions him, "You must not look at her. You look too much at her."[91]

The soldiers continue to gaze at Herod's banquet and remark on the appearance of Herodias, whose hair is "powdered with blue dust," reminiscent of Flaubert's Herod in "Hérodiade" and of his Salammbô, whose hair

---

86. McKenna, *The Secret Life*, 164.
87. Kramer, "Culture and Musical Hermeneutics," 273.
88. Wilde, *Salomé*, 2.
89. Ibid., 1.
90. Ibid., 3.
91. Ibid., 4.

is similarly powdered, with violet dust, indications of Eastern exotica. They also discuss Herod's fondness for wine, and as in Flaubert's "Hérodiade," embark on a conversation about religion, from which we learn who the prophet Iokanaan is, and that the Tetrarch has forbidden anyone to see him.

The Young Syrian returns to the object of his obsession, "the Princess," who has hidden her face behind her fan. He compares her hands to doves and "white butterflies," while the Page warns him yet again not to look at her because "Something terrible may happen."[92] When the Young Syrian notices that Salomé has risen to leave the banquet, the Page continues to remind him not to look at her, as Salomé enters, declaring that she in turn cannot bear Herod's gaze, "with his mole's eyes under his shaking eyelids."[93] She despises the entire group of guests, "the Jews from Jerusalem, tearing themselves in pieces over their foolish ceremonies," the barbarians who "dine and drink," the Greeks from Myrna, with their "painted eyes and painted cheeks and grizzled hair curled in twisted coils," the "silent, subtle Egyptians, with long nails of jade and russet cloaks," and the "brutal and coarse" Romans with their "uncouth jargon."[94] A more Western European catalog of Orientalism cannot be matched. The irony is that Salomé herself is an exotic, though attractive, Oriental—a "princess of Judea."

When the Young Syrian asks her to be seated, the Page is alarmed; he sounds his familiar refrain: "Something terrible will happen." Salomé remarks on the moon, "cold and chaste" as an undefiled virgin, whom she admires, as Salammbô admires the moon-goddess Tanith.[95] Iokanaan's voice is heard, and Salomé questions the company about him, finding that he speaks "with a strange voice," and wants in turn to speak with him.[96] She insists that he be brought to her, although the soldiers and the Young Syrian reply that the Tetrarch has forbidden it. Testing her powers of seductive persuasion, she promises the Young Syrian, addressing him by his name, Narraboth, that if he obeys her, she will show him signs of her favor, letting fall "a little green flower,"[97] looking at him "through muslin veils," and

---

92. Ibid., 8.
93. Ibid., 10.
94. Ibid.
95. Ibid., 11.
96. Ibid., 14.
97. Chapple, "Re-envisioning Salome," 98, suggests that several critics felt that the green flower signified the theme of homosexuality, although Wilde denied it. If it were the case, it might be another indication that Wilde was not only "obsessed" with Salomé, but in some sense saw himself in her.

maybe smiling at him.[98] Compelled, the Young Syrian summons a soldier to get the prophet: "The Princess Salomé desires to see him."[99] As we know by now, the sight cannot bode good.

Once again, vision sets the mood: as the Page remarks on the moon as "the hand of a dead woman who is seeking to cover herself with a shroud," the Young Syrian compares her to a "little princess, whose eyes are of amber." Anticipating the smile of Salomé, he compares the moon to a "little princess" who smiles "through clouds of muslin." Iokanaan is brought in, and denounces Herod and Herodias, and Salomé herself as "the daughter of Babylon."[100] Although Salomé initially finds him "terrible," with his "black eyes," she is still fascinated by him, although he rejects her speech and gaze: "I will not have her look at me . . . with her golden eyes, under her gilded eyelids."[101] The prophet goes on to denounce Salomé's mother, Herodias, somewhat anachronistically, borrowing language from the book of Revelation, as the Whore of Babylon (as do Moreau and Huysmans), who "has filled the earth with the wine of her iniquities." All that Salomé hears is that his voice is "like wine." When he denounces her as "daughter of Sodom," and tells her to cover her face with a veil and scatter ashes on her head and to seek the "Son of Man," she can only reply, "Is he as beautiful as thou art?"[102]

Iokanaan tells her to "get behind" him (as Jesus bids Satan), as Salomé hears the "beating of the wings of the angel of death,"[103] the wings that Herod will later feel in a cold wind, after he swears the infamous oath to Salomé. In imagery like that of the Song of Songs, Salomé tells the prophet directly that she is "amorous" of his white body—"Nothing in the world so white as thy body"—and asks to touch it. When he refuses her, she reacts by calling his body "hideous" and "loathsome," but then turns to his hair, to praise it in similarly sensual terms,[104] asking to touch his hair. Rebuffed once more, she calls his hair "horrible," and a "knot of black serpents." Finally, climactically, she praises his mouth in even more extravagant terms than his body or his hair: ominously, she calls it "a pomegranate cut with

---

98. Wilde, *Salomé*, 16.
99. Ibid., 17.
100. Ibid., 24.
101. Ibid., 20.
102. Ibid., 21.
103. Ibid., 11.
104. Ibid., 23.

a knife of ivory."[105] Dwelling on the desirable redness of Iokanaan's mouth, she insists that she will kiss it: "I will kiss thy mouth, Iokanaan." When the Young Syrian kills himself in despair, Salomé is impervious to the death or to the news of the death, repeating, like a refrain, "I will kiss thy mouth."[106]

As the Page laments the Young Syrian's death, the soldiers drag the body away, anticipating the arrival of the Tetrarch, Herod Antipas, who has come seeking Salomé, even as Herodias chides him not to look at her: "You are always looking at her!" Herod, who seems to find symbols in everything, remarks on the "strangeness" of the moon, like mad, drunken woman "naked in the sky," seeking for lovers." Herodias tries to bring him down to earth: "The moon is like the moon: that is all."[107] She later chides his fancies: "You must not find symbols in everything you see; it makes life impossible," in what is perhaps a Wildean slap at the Symbolist aesthetic. On the terrace, Herod ominously slips in the blood of the Young Syrian and laments his death, recalling his "languorous eyes," that "looked too much at Salomé," a remark not lost on Herodias, who says that there are "others" who look too much at her. Herod ignores her, remarking that Salomé is deathly pale, giving Herodias one more chance to tell him, "I have told you not to look at her."[108]

In what is clearly an attempted seduction, Herod tempts Salomé to drink wine ("dip into it thy little red lips"), to eat ripe fruit ("I love to see in a fruit the mark of thy little teeth"), to sit on her mother's throne, figuratively replacing her. Though Herod obviously lusts after her, Salomé replies coldly, using his formal term, "Tetrarch": she is not hungry, she is not thirsty, she is not tired.[109] The scene is interrupted by the voice of Iokanaan and by a quarrel between the "Jews," the "Nazarenes," and the Roman Tigellinus about the messiah. Iokanaan continues to rail against "The wanton! The harlot! The daughter of Babylon," and calls for her to be stoned, pierced, and crushed. Herodias guesses that she is meant by his tirade, although Herod points out, rightly, that the prophet has not mentioned her name.[110]

As Herodias pleads with Herod to silence the prophet, Herod is getting drunk and talking at random: finally, he turns to Salomé, asking her

105. Ibid., 23.
106. Ibid., 24.
107. Ibid., 14.
108. Ibid., 31.
109. Ibid., 32–33.
110. Ibid., 42.

to dance for him. Both she and Herodias refuse three times. Iokanaan now turns to describe a figure seated on a throne, with a cup "full of blasphemies," again anachronistically describing the Great Whore of Revelation. Sadly, Herod once again begs Salomé to dance for him, promising her anything, "even unto the half of my kingdom."[111] Interested now, despite her mother's warnings, Salomé gets Herod to swear his infamous oath, to give her whatever she asks. But as he swears, Herod feels the beating of those great wings, choking him with heat instead of cold, and seeing the red of his rose-petal garland as blood.[112]

Salomé, triumphant, feels no such warnings. She asks her servants to bring her perfumes, her "seven veils," and to take her sandals off, leaving Herod to admire her naked feet, which are "like little white doves," like "little white flowers" images borrowed from Moreau's paintings and reminiscent of the Young Syrian's description of the moon. But then Herod remembers that she is dancing in blood, the blood of the Young Syrian, who has killed himself because of her—an evil omen.

As another evil omen, the moon has turned red as blood, a sign, as Herod believes, from the prophet, although Herodias once more mocks his belief in symbols. Iokanaan's voice sounds again, quoting ironically from the Song of Songs. Although Herodias insists and urges that her daughter not dance, Salomé says tersely and ominously, "I am ready, Tetrarch," upon which statement follow the famous but maddeningly brief stage directions, "Salomé dances the dance of the seven veils."[113] When she asks for her reward "in a silver charger," Herod thinks at first that she is "charming," but when she asks for the head of Iokanaan on it, he is appalled, although Herodias praises her: "Ah! That is well said, my daughter."[114] When Herod urges her not to listen to her mother, Salomé makes it clear that she is not doing it for Herodias: "It is not my mother's voice I heed. *It is for mine own pleasure that I ask the head of Iokanaan on a silver charger.*"[115] (Herod continues to urge Salomé not to press her request: "The head of a man that is cut from his body is ill to look upon, is it not? It is not meet that the eyes of a virgin should look upon such a thing."[116] As Herod continues to offer her various

111. Ibid., 49.
112. Ibid., 51
113. Ibid., 54.
114. Ibid., 55.
115. Ibid., 56 (italics added).
116. Ibid., 57.

exotic treasures, including the "mantle of the High Priest" and the "veil of sanctuary," at which blasphemies "the Jews" cry out, Salomé insists on her request, and he relents.[117]

Salomé leans over the cistern in which Iokanaan is imprisoned, and hearing nothing, she believes that the executioner has failed. Impatiently, she demands that the Page tell the soldiers to "bring me the thing I ask, the thing the Tetrarch promised me, the thing that is mine," because "there are not dead men enough."[118] The Page and the soldiers recoil in horror from this bloodthirsty request. Finally, according to the very explicit stage directions, unlike those about the dance:

> A huge black arm, the arm of the Executioner, comes forth from the cistern, bearing on a silver shield the head of Iokanaan. Salomé seizes it. Herod hides his face with his cloak. Herodias smiles and fans herself. The Nazarenes fall to their knees and begin to pray.[119]

Salomé announces that she will now kiss Iokanaan's mouth: "I will bite it with my teeth, as one bites a ripe fruit," as Herod urged her to do previously. She taunts his closed eyelids and the "red viper" of his tongue, gloating that although he spoke of her scornfully, she can now do with his head whatever she wants.[120] Nevertheless, she sighs, "Ah, Iokanaan, Iokanaan, thou wert the man I have loved among men! All other men were hateful to me. But thou, thou wert beautiful." She says that if he had only he had gazed on her as she on him, he would have loved her as she did him: "I love thee yet, Iokanaan . . . I am hungry for thy body. "This necrophiliac lust causes Herod to recoil, telling Herodias, "She is monstrous, thy daughter; I tell thee, she is monstrous."[121] He tells his servants to put out the torches, calling for the moon and the stars to hide, but in the darkness Salomé croons, "Ah, I have kissed thy mouth," finding the dead lips have "a bitter taste." In her exaltation, a moonbeam covers her with light, according to the stage directions. Herod cries out, "Kill that woman!" The final stage directions read, "The soldiers rush forward and crush beneath their shields Salomé, daughter of Herodias, Princess of Judea."[122]

117. Ibid., 62.
118. Ibid., 63.
119. Ibid., 64.
120. Ibid.
121. Ibid., 66.
122. Ibid., 68.

The Salome Project

WILDE EMBROIDERY:
THE SALOMES OF BEARDSLEY AND STRAUSS

Wilde wrote his *Salomé* in 1891, in terse, almost telegraphic French that has been criticized as the language of the "phrasebook"[123] but that also accomplishes the effect of making the play more visual. The audience, like the other characters, must gaze at Salomé, to get the full meaning of the drama, which is largely spectacle. In 1892, when the play was already in rehearsal, Edward Pigott, "Examiner of Plays in the Lord Chamberlain's Office," would not grant a license for its performance, ostensibly because censorship laws did not permit biblical characters to be depicted onstage. Pigott noted privately, however, that the play was "half biblical, half pornographic," and unacceptable to the British public, especially Salomé's kissing the mouth of John the Baptist's dead head "in a paroxysm of sexual despair."[124]

The play was first performed in France, in 1896, and had already been translated into English by Wilde's presumed lover, Lord Alfred Douglas, known as Bosie, in 1893. But even before that, a twenty-one-year-old artist by the name of Aubrey Beardsley had been so struck by the French version that he published an illustration of Salomé achieving the climax of her desire by kissing Iokanaan's lips—*J'ai Baisé ta Bouche, Iokanaan*—also known as *The Climax*, in the London journal the *Studio* in 1893. Wilde was so impressed by the spirit of Beardsley's interpretation of his character that he sent him a copy of the play, dedicated to Beardsley as "the only artist who, besides myself, knows what the dance of the seven veils is, and can see that invisible dance."[125] Ironically, even though Wilde asked Beardsley to illustrate the English edition of *Salomé*, and was even thinking of asking him to translate it, Beardsley never did draw the actual dance. In fact, his version of Salomé's dance is the stomach dance, and bears no resemblance to a dance with veils. Beardsley saw no reason to cleave to the text of Wilde's drama very closely, if at all. Eventually, he became repelled by Wilde, and "cruelly satirized" him in four of his original drawings for *Salomé*, most obviously in *The Woman in the Moon*, in which a slender naked young man and woman stand gazing at the moon, one of the most important objects and metaphors in the play. The moon's face, however, is that of a bloated Wilde, with half-shut eyes and droopy eyelids, wearing a flower, a parody

123. Thuleen, "Symbolism and Decadence," section 5.
124. Pigott to Spencer Ponsonby, in Gagnier, *Idylls of the Marketplace*, 170–71; McKenna, *The Secret Life*, 189.
125. Primorac, "Illustrating Wilde," 2; see also McKenna, *The Secret Life*, 261.

of some of his better-known photographs.[126] Beardsley supposedly "divined the autobiographical element in [Wilde's] Herod, and in one of his illustrations gave the Tetrarch the author's face."[127] In turn, the outcry when the illustrated English version of the work was published in 1894 caused Wilde to believe it threatened to displace his own writing as secondary to Beardsley's illustrations. (Indeed, the way I first came to know Wilde's *Salomé* was through Beardsley's grotesque and fascinating black-and-white drawings.)

Beardsley, however, was not the only artist to be as fascinated by Wilde's play as Wilde was by previous versions of Salome. Richard Strauss attended a private performance of the play in 1902 but had already begun work on an opera based on it, or rather on Hedwig Lachmann's 1896 translation, published in 1900.[128] The opera *Salome* was produced in Dresden in December 1905. According to John Williamson, "Few operas have provoked more critical discord on their first performance than *Salome*, perhaps because it was based on Wilde's 'unwholesome work.'"[129] Strauss's opera nonetheless seems to have been a success, having been performed in fifty opera houses within two years.[130]

Strauss also contributed something that had, tantalizingly, been missing from Wilde's work: the instructions, or at least the music and partial directions, for the "Dance of the Seven Veils." He composed the music for the dance after the rest of the opera, but did not actually issue any directions or "sketch a scenario" how it was to have been performed until much later, probably in the 1920s.[131] Some critics objected to the dance, because it slowed the opera down—aesthete Alma Mahler, wife of the composer Gustav, called the dance "the one weak spot in the score—just botched-up commonplace."[132] It is hard to find a reason for Mahler's judgment if one listens to the score, still less if one sees a performance, but perhaps she was thinking of the "commonplace" vaudeville versions of the Salome dance, which were starting to be all the rage on stages in Europe and the United States, and were very different from what Strauss had envisioned for his Salome. He left an interesting scenario for his version of the dance. His

---

126. McKenna, *The Secret Life*, 263, citing Stirgis, *Aubrey Beardsley*, 131–32.
127. Ellmann, "Overtures," 34.
128. Puffett, "Introduction," 4; Chapple, "Re-(en)visioning," 5.
129. Williamson, "Critical Reception," 131–32.
130. Wikipedia, "*Salome* (opera), Performance History."
131. See Puffett, "Appendix A," 165–87.
132. Gustav Mahler, in Alma Mahler, *Gustav Mahler: Memories and Letters*, 88–89, cited in Puffett, "Appendix A," 196n2.

description of Salome taking off her veils follows, in part, Moreau's painting *Salome Dancing before Herod*, with the removal of the first veil. Curiously, however, for no discernible reason, Strauss describes only the removal of the first, second, third (removed "violently"), and fifth veils. "What has happened to the fourth, sixth, and seventh veils?"[133] The composer noted that he wanted to focus on Salome's "dignity as a heroine," on her showing decorum even as she dances, "as a chaste virgin and an oriental princess." It is difficult to know, however, in view of his milieu, how Strauss managed to link together decorum and the Oriental. His restrained approach to Salome is echoed by that of Lachmann and her own chosen illustrator, Marcus Behmer, whose illustrations in black and white recall those of Beardsley, but are "more closely linked to the text," and share with Lachmann "a vision of a less tainted and wanton Salome, which their collaborative work strives to illuminate."[134] According to Craig Aysey, moreover, Strauss's version of Salome, even at the climax of the drama, does not support a view of Salome as "perverse." He asserts that Salome attempts to "fully engage with Jokanaan [sic]," but his eyes are closed to her in life as they are in death. Consequently, Aysey argues that Salome's final monologue, addressed to the head, attempts to "bring him symbolically to recognize her as an individual,"[135] although one might seriously argue that having a man beheaded is an unsuccessful way to have him recognize one's individuality.

Understandably, Strauss experienced some difficulties with the staging and performance of his opera. Most of the sopranos who sang the role of Salome balked at the necessity of having to do the Dance of the Seven Veils, which after all belonged to ballet rather than to opera, and so the dance was usually undertaken by another performer. There were also places where the opera was considered too salacious to be performed: London (unsurprisingly) until 1910, where it was banned by the Lord Chamberlain's Office; and Vienna, until 1918, despite the pleadings of Gustav Mahler.[136] The première of the opera in the United States took place at the Metropolitan Opera House on January 22, 1907, with the famed soprano Olive Fremstad and dancer Biana Froehlich performing the role of Salome. Outrage to "Anglo-Saxon minds" caused patrons to demand it not be performed again,

---

133. Puffett, "Appendix A," 164–67.
134. Chapple, "Re-(en) visioning Salome," 92.
135. Aysey, "Salome's Final Monologue," 109–11.
136. Wikipedia, "*Salome* (opera)."

and it was not, until 1934.[137] It may be that these sensibilities were offended by the Orientalism, the Decadence—not to mention the "Jewishness"—of the play and its heroine.

J. C. HEYWOOD AND THE REHABILITATION OF SALOME

American authors of the nineteenth century, however—Henry Wadsworth Longfellow, Harriet Beecher Stowe, and most of all the lesser-known J. C. (Joseph Converse) Heywood—did not see a perverse sexuality in Salome. That role they assigned to Herodias, and they produced works that tended to excuse and even rehabilitate her daughter. This rehabilitation took a turn different from the Decadent and Symbolist version of Wilde. While clearly influenced by, and even borrowing from, other authors, Wilde created a Salome that was not an amalgam but a climax, molding the story into what has become its received form. Most commentary on Wilde's influences focuses on previous Decadent and Symbolist authors, and although one certainly could include the quasi-Romantic Heine in this list, there is one influence that is barely considered: the American poet J. C. Heywood. Heywood wrote a dramatic poem called *Salome, The Daughter of Herodias* in 1862, which he later turned into a trilogy of poems: *Herodias*, *Salome*, and *Antonius* (1867).[138] There seems to have been quite a difference of opinion between Wilde, who reviewed Heywood's *Salome* in 1888, prior to writing his own play, and American critics of Heywood's work. The *American Catholic Quarterly Review* called "each of these three dramas complete in itself," but found that together they formed a "perfect whole." In *Herodias*, the reviewer found that "seldom have the passion of revenge and the terrific tortures of remorse and despair been more profoundly analyzed and presented with more power." The poem *Salome* is "superior to both the others in dramatic intensity," but "all three of these dramas are lofty in conception and abound in passages of very great beauty and strength."[139] Wilde begged to differ. Although Heywood's trilogy appeared in print before his own *Salomé*, he did not find it as "thrilling" as the American critics had. Wilde remarks acidly that "the best one can say of it is that it is a triumph

---

137. Ibid.

138. Ellmann, "Overtures," 22.

139. Unsigned review of J. C. Heywood's trilogy, *American Catholic Quarterly Review*, 13 (1888) 184–85.

of conscientious industry. From an artistic point of view, it is a very commonplace production indeed."[140]

The modern reader will most likely agree with Wilde. Yet his reading of Heywood along with his reading of other authors such as Flaubert, not only shows the widespread dissemination of the Salome legend by the end of the nineteenth century, but also demonstrates Wilde's own fascination with the character, on whom he may have projected his own sexual desire, which others found "perverse."[141] Heywood's Salome, who is unlike Wilde's, is a character developed in two long dramatic poems: *Salome, The Daughter of Herodias* (1862), and *Herodias* (1867), later combined with a related poem, *Antonius* (1867), to form a trilogy. Heywood forms part of a minor American tradition about Salome. More famous authors such as Longfellow wrote about "the Daughter of Herodias" in his *Christus: A Mystery* (1872), passages that were quoted and elaborated on by Harriet Beecher Stowe in her *Woman in Sacred History: A Series of Sketches* (1873), particularly in her section on "The Daughter of Herodias."[142] Neither Longfellow nor Stowe is inclined to blame Salome, and instead they condemn Herodias, the "haughty royal adulteress,"[143] and "the demon, the evil thing,"[144] rather than her "beautiful daughter," with her "flower-like head."[145]

Heywood also exonerates Salome, who, far from desiring John the Baptist's body, longs to receive instruction from him, and calls him, "Good Master." She brings him food and tells him that she wants to free him.[146] In a quasi-Jesus moment, John asks her if she loves him three times, and when she says she does, he bids her, "Keep my words," "Follow the Christ," and "Follow the Christ, and come whither I go."[147] After her exchange with John, Salome leaves for Herod's banquet, which she attends unwillingly, as the moon, so significant in Wilde's play, appears.

140. Wilde, Review of *Salome*, by J. C. Heywood.

141. Showalter, *Sexual Anarchy*, 157, cites a photograph in Richard Ellmann's 1969 biography of Wilde that supposedly depicts the playwright in drag as Salome, but it was later shown to be the soprano Alice Guszalewicz in Strauss's *Salome* in Dresden in 1908. See Wikipedia, "Alice Guszalewicz."

142. Stowe, *Woman in Sacred History*, 321–34. Thanks again to Amy Easton-Flake for this suggestion.

143. Ibid., 323.

144. Ibid., 330, quoting Longfellow, *Christus*.

145. Ibid., 323.

146. Heywood, *Herodias*, 25.

147. Ibid., 27.

Salome Counter Salome

At Herod's feast, one of the guests anticipates "th'alluring, dangerous depths, / Of dark, dissolving eyes, and snowy breasts,"[148] the "crowning glory" that will be "the daughter of Herodias," whom no one has yet seen (as in Flaubert's "Hérodiade"). Herodias has compelled her daughter to appear, against Salome's "purest maiden modesty," but still she dances, and Herod makes his rash vow. So far, it appears Heywood has weighed in on the side of Salome's innocence in the dance. We then find that the virginal Salome has a Roman beloved, Sextus, who loves her, and whom Salome has saved from the arena, but Herodias has sent him away to the army. Sextus returns, and Salome tells him about her dance, and that she has not chosen a "giddy woman's choice," jewelry or a tiara. She is torn between asking Herod for ennobling Sextus or releasing John as the price for her dance—but her mother has other plans. Halfway through the poem, we finally hear—and meet—Herodias. She is the one who has taught Salome to dance:

> What but my love caused thee to learn the art
> Which in itself concentrates every art
> By woman found, which flashes more than wit
> Which kindles blood more than the burning eye . . .
> Enchains the reason more than linked words.

The dance "teacheth modesty to calculate / And how conceal the least, the most display / The golden treasures of Hesperides."[149] Herodias praises Salome for having won over the king and promises to teach her, as she did the dance, her own "life-craft," at which Salome cries "Purely I'd live, / With Justice and my conscience to approve."[150] Herodias urges her instead to "exhale the power of woman, feel the joys / Of power." While Salome resists, saying that all she wants is to love and be loved, Herodias says that "to be loved is power," while loving is weakness.[151] Salome should "conquer, all that charms may win." Love is no good; power is all. Herodias invites Salome to "become a woman," with a "woman's stinging wisdom, cupped from griefs."[152]

To convince Salome, Herodias tells her own story. She loved Salome's father, but he went to war, and she yielded to Herod Antipas. In turn, he

---

148. Ibid., 33.
149. Ibid., 130.
150. Ibid.,131.
151. Ibid., 132.
152. Ibid., 145.

betrayed and mocked her. Her first husband (Antonius) returned, then fled. Pregnant and disgraced, Herodias seized her child and "strangled it." She seduced Philip, then Herod. The only thing standing in the way of her complete domination of Herod is John the Baptist, who, surprisingly, Herodias first sought to seduce, and now seeks to kill, so "no other shall love him."[153] Salome begs Herodias to remember forgiveness, as taught by John, but Herodias will have none of it. When Salome refuses to ask for the head of John the Baptist, Herodias tells her that if she does, she can marry Sextus; otherwise—Herodias has already strangled one child, and she can do it again.[154] Although Salome is willing to die, Herodias adds to her threats that she will kill Sextus unless Salome writes a note to Herod. With Herodias chanting, "Write!" Salome madly writes and then falls unconscious.

In an apocalyptic interlude, a voice cries, "Woe," and the "Prince of the Powers of the Air," with the "Prince of the Powers of the Depths," call for chaos and anarchy. This episode forms a prelude to the interview between Sextus and Salome, in which she declares she is "a murderess accursed," because she has raised her hand "against a man of God, / And ta'en away his life."[155] She tells Sextus that to save his life, she has taken John the Baptist's, and that she must "expiate my crime in holy acts / Of charity and self-denial."[156] Meanwhile, the vengeful Herodias gloats over the Baptist's head: "And thou, sweetheart, yes, thou art mine at last."[157] She kisses the blood on John's lips, and in a frenzy, weaves her fingers in his hair, strokes his temples, and fondles him as she also mocks, spits on, and spurns him.[158] But these excesses also drive her mad. Salome, on the other hand, prays for redemption and has a vision of Jesus, "of whom John spoke." She addresses him as "Lord God" and vows to follow him. In an interesting plot twist, Herodias appears to her former lover, Antonius, and he recognizes her as his "perfidious Livia," who has become possessed by a fury.[159] Herodias dies, and goes to the "blackest perdition."[160]

153. Ibid., 188.
154. Ibid., 165.
155. Ibid., 189.
156 Ibid., 200.
157 Ibid., 211.
158. Ibid., 214.
159. Ibid., 234.
160. Ibid., 249.

Salome Counter Salome

With Herodias vanquished, Heywood takes on the future fate of Salome, "daughter of Herodias, the beautiful and bad," in *Salome, The Daughter of Herodias*.[161] In this poem, Salome has become a Christian and, somewhat anachronistically, a "vestal." The poem is set in the last days of Jerusalem and the temple, during its siege by Titus, the Roman commander. Salome, through the power of Christianity and her resolute chastity, like so many other early Christian virginal heroines, has the power to cure diseases.[162] She and her companions are so chaste, modest, innocent, and beautiful that they can repel repeated attacks on their virtue, raising "the noblest feelings of the noblest man, / And gentleness create in breasts the rudest."[163] In an even more convoluted plot than that in *Herodias*, Salome tries to save her hapless lover Sextus, but is desired by the strange and powerful Jew Kaliphilus, who threatens her with her own death and that of Sextus unless she yields to him. Salome is sadder but wiser now, realizing that sacrificing John to save Sextus was wrong.[164] After several harrowing episodes, imprisonment in the same dungeon in which John the Baptist languished, and harassment from Simon, a Jewish soldier, Salome confesses that she is now a Christian and is willing to die for her faith. Intervening in a fight between Kaliphilus and Sextus, Salome is mortally wounded, and dies, saying in a martyr-like fashion, "Lord, receive my spirit."[165] From wanton to martyr, Salome is now redeemed.

MICHAEL FIELD AND SALOME'S LAST DANCE

Another version of the death of Salome appears in the early years of the twentieth century but should be included here because it belongs to the trajectory of writings, few but significant, that try to portray Salome as a sympathetic yet misunderstood character. A poetic version of the legendary death of Salome was composed by the duo of Katherine Bradley and her niece and collaborator—and probable lover—Edith Cooper, known together as the single author Michael Field. The poem, "A Dance of Death," is based on the apocryphal legend of Salome's dancing (or playing) on thin

---

161. Heywood, *Salome*, 12.
162. Ibid., 71.
163. Ibid., 73.
164. Ibid., 148.
165. Ibid., 220.

ice, falling through, and being decapitated by the shards of ice—a fitting end to the woman who caused the decapitation of John the Baptist. Oscar Wilde knew this tale, and originally called his drama *The Decapitation of Salome*, although how he was going to portray her death by ice is unclear.[166]

The death of Salome by dancing in Field's "A Dance of Death" is not portrayed as retribution or punishment. The poem appears in the volume *Poems of Adoration* (1912), one of devotional verse. As LeeAnne M. Richardson observes, Michael Field's poetry, and especially this poem, fits into the "Decadent" mode; it also significantly "troubles" the familiar categories of Decadence.[167] Using a "classic Decadent figure," Salome, with the exotic imagery familiar from Moreau, Huysmans, Wilde, and Strauss, Field instead "transgresses" the expected Decadent context to create a different Salome, one who is not a femme fatale, but instead an artist who is beautiful and tragic but not sexualized.[168] Field's poem uses a legend from Nicephorus Callistus Xanthopoulos that is also employed by the seventeenth-century poet Henry Vaughan, but as a condemnation of Salome. In "The Daughter of Herodias," Vaughan writes,

> Leave then, yong Sorceress; the Ice
> Will these coy spirits cast asleep,
> Which teach thee now to please his eyes
> Who doth thy loathsome mother keep.[169]

Field's poem begins with ice, "so motionless and still," that is yet "calling as with music to our feet."[170] The ice presents a "dare" and a "challenge" to the onlookers, but already there is a dancer on the ice, moving on tiptoe, without skates, "a lovely dancing-girl." The language seems to play upon the sensual and disreputable connotations of "dancing-girl," only to nullify them. Although the dancer dances "As she never had lost, / In lands where there is no snow, / The Orient's immeasurable glow," she is presented, not as an Oriental, but as "a dancer white," thus confusing categories of Oriental and European. Finally, as we raptly gaze at her dance, as in so many portrayals in the late nineteenth and early twentieth centuries, she

---

166. Scanlon and Kerridge, "Spontaneity and Control," 41.
167. Richardson, "Michael Field's 'A Dance of Death,'" 71.
168. Ibid., 72–74.
169. Vaughan, "The Daughter of Herodias," lines 9-12; The Works of Henry Vaughan, 103.
170. Text from "A Dance of Death" comes from poetrynook.com/.

is identified as Salome, "an exile," with Herod and Herodias, as tradition relates. She has sought to dance on the ice, and is "ecstatic," as "her spell she flings / And Winter in a rapture of delight, / Flings up and down the spangles of her light." This rapturous picture ends abruptly: "Where is the Vision by the snow adored? / The Vision is no more." Instead, "She is engulphed [sic] and all the dance is done." All that is left is a head severed by ice, but instead of being grisly, it is still a beautiful, moving, even dancing vision, "sped in dance that never stops, / It skims and hops / Across the ice that rasped it. Smooth and gay, / And void of care." Yet there is something ominous about Salome's head: her "little face" is grey; her mouth is opened in a soundless scream; her eyes are "fixed as they beheld the silver plate" that held the severed head of John the Baptist: "In the face what fear, / to what excess compelled!" Field seems to exonerate Salome for the death of the Baptist, because she is "compelled," and she scarcely deserves to end as a static severed head. Unlike the head of John the Baptist that is virtually a relic, Salome's head is still mobile:

> Salome's head is dancing on the bright
> And silver ice. O holy John, how still
> Was laid thy head upon the silver white,
> When thou hadst done God's will!

For Richardson, the poem is a conflation of the death of a martyr—that of John, having "done God's will—and that of an artist following her "artistic impulse to dance," as Michael Field followed their artistic (and religious) impulse in their poetry. Salome's head "is subjugate / To its own law," that of artistry, as John's is to God's will.[171] Moralizing is left out of the equation for Salome, yet she is not depicted as immoral: she is a dancer, and she must dance, regardless of the consequences for her and for anyone else. Did Field, like Wilde, imagine themselves as Salome, a transgressive figure? Field's work is a striking combination of

> baroque unorthodoxy and exotic Orientalism, which crosses many moral and ideological borders, tacitly deconstructs Christian conventionality, and widens the parameters of romantic love. Their women are rarely depicted as melancholy victims ... Even when women die in a Field poem, often by a 'curse' from God, their self-affirming passion is defiant and undeterred, as in 'A Dance of Death.'[172]

171. Richardson, "Michael Field's 'A Dance of Death,'" 75–76.
172. Cronin et al., eds., *Companion to Victorian Poetry*, 331.

4

Reviving Salome

SALOMANIA: SALOME AS SUBJECT AND SPECTACLE

At the end of the nineteenth century, the figure of Salome had taken over center stage from Herodias and had come closer to being represented as an exotic dancer. When Wilde wrote his stage directions in his *Salomé*, when Strauss's opera version featured a nine-minute dance, so-called Oriental dances were starting to appear on stages; could these artists have taken some of them over for their own works?[1] Conversely, it may have been that female performers knew of the role of Salome and that it included a sensuous barefoot and veiled dance, whose erotic physicality, especially in Wilde's version, posed a challenge and created a potential problem on how to get it past censors. When Sarah Bernhardt, to Wilde's great delight, agreed to play his Salomé, she would have known that the character performed the Dance of the Seven Veils. No one knows exactly how she would have performed it, however, since the play was banned when it was in rehearsal. We do know that she commissioned her own costumes, agreeing with the designer Graham Robertson that the main color should be yellow.[2] Yellow, as with many other colors in Wilde's play, was significant on several levels. According to Stanley Weintraub, it meant both dandyism (a Wildean trait)

---

1. Bentley, *Sisters of Salome*, 281. She notes that the dance, with Salomé's subsequent monologue, lasted eighteen minutes. Maybe Alma Mahler was right.
2. Stern, ed., *Salome*, by Oscar Wilde, 131.

and the color of salacious French novels.³ It was also the color of the "self-conscious degeneracy of the fin de siècle," as signified by the periodical of the Decadents, *The Yellow Book*.⁴ But, as Sander Gilman has noted, this particular color choice by Bernhardt may have been a belligerent assertion of her Jewishness, especially in her role as "Salomé, Princess of Judea"—yellow being a color associated with Jews.⁵ A black-and-white photo by Napoleon Sarony of Bernhardt in the costume of Salomé exists—one presumably taken in rehearsals—and, while partaking of the general Oriental aspect attributed to Salomé, it seems less than overtly sensuous.

Richard Strauss went out of his way to insist on Salome's chastity and virginity, and if that were not enough—after all, Wilde's Salomé was also a chaste if lustful virgin—the composer declared that he intended the dance in his opera to be performed "as if it were being done on a prayer mat,"⁶ a statement that either reflects Strauss's ignorance of the uses of prayer mats or is wildly overstating the case. On the other hand, Maria Wittich, the soprano who performed Strauss's *Salome* in its première production in 1905, refused to perform Salome's dance, stating, "I am a decent woman."⁷ It does seem odd that the person who otherwise sang about kissing the lips of the dead Iokanaan, and possibly doing it onstage, would have jibbed at performing a dance that Strauss strenuously insisted was not lascivious, unless the idea of dancing itself—of being a "dancing girl" (a euphemism for *prostitute*)—was repellent to a "respectable" actress. Calling Salomé a "*danseuse*" in Wilde's play as reproduced by Strauss reduces her "to the epitome of sexual availability."⁸

Loïe Fuller and the Salome Dancers

Although we do not know the kind of dance *la Bernhardt* would have performed, we do know of several forms of dances called "Oriental," veiled, or "Jewish," that were taking place in Paris in the late nineteenth century. Already the American Loïe Fuller, who came to Paris in 1892, had constructed a quasi-Oriental "serpentine dance," which involved a veil-like costume of

---

3. Weintraub, *The Yellow Book*, 99; cited in Stern, ed., *Salome*, 131.
4. Gilman, "Salome, Syphilis, Sara Bernhardt, and the 'Modern Jewess,'" 204.
5. Ibid.
6. Wilhelm, *Richard Strauss*, 102, cited in Bentley, *Sisters of Salome*, 35.
7. Wilhelm, *Richard Strauss*, 100; cited in Bentley, *Sisters of Salome*, 31.
8. Marcus, "Salomé!!," 1010.

yards of silk that left only her head and hands visible, and relied on colored and rotating spotlights to create various exotic mobile forms.[9] Much in the same way as Wilde admired "the divine Sarah [Bernhardt]" in a celebrated 1879 performance of *Phèdre*,[10] Stéphane Mallarmé, whose own character Hérodiade loved "the horror of virginity" (praising those who "burn with chastity"[11]) was one of the many who were enchanted with Fuller and her carefully projected onstage modesty, writing that she "acquired the virginity of undreamt-of-palaces."[12]

Fuller also staged two versions of the Salome story (not just the dance): one in 1895, and the other twelve years later, in 1907, after Fuller's fame had won her a theater under her own name at the 1900 World's Fair in Paris.[13] According to Rhonda Garelick, Fuller was riding the tide of the European fascination with "all things Oriental, particularly with the women perceived as living Salomes, the seductive, often veiled '*danseuses du ventre*' imported from the colonies."[14] The 1895 performance was a critical failure because Fuller did not "look like" Salome.[15] Indeed, one of the challenges she faced in this kind of dance performance was that her character had to live up to a preconceived idea of a nubile, sensuous Oriental princess, and both physically and chronologically, she was far from it. But even more, her interpretation of Salome ignored what was becoming the standard femme fatale depiction. She chose instead to portray "the dancing princess as a chaste and frightened child," using a costume covered with large white roses, a symbol of sexual purity, that evoked the Madonna, "the white rose without a thorn," rather than a seductive whore.[16] Perhaps it was this juxtaposition of virgin and whore that bothered audiences. According to Ewa Kuryluk, Salome is the "anti-Madonna," the "diametrical opposite" of the Virgin Mary.[17] Fuller's production recalls the works of other Americans,

---

9. Garelick, *Electric Salome*, 2–4.
10. Marcus, "Salomé!!," 104.
11. Lenson, trans., "Hérodiade," 586.
12. Garelick, *Electric Salome*, 5, quoting Mallarmé, "Les Fonds dans le ballet," 308.
13. Petzer, "Veils in Action," 243–67.
14. Garelick, *Electric Salome*, 92. It is possible that Aubrey Beardsley may have gotten his idea of "The Stomach Dance" illustration from these belly dancers.
15. Ibid., 5.
16. Ibid., 96. Pier Paolo Pasolini's film *The Gospel according to St. Matthew* similarly portrayed a sweetly adolescent Salome dancing in a simple white garment.
17. Kuryluk, *Salome and Judas*, 190–91.

Reviving Salome

J. C. Heywood and Harriet Beecher Stowe: "It is Herod who plots John's murder, while Salome worships the Baptist, and is so virtuous and proto-Christian of spirit that she offers her own life in exchange for his," dying of grief and shock after seeing his head on a platter.[18] This is not a Salome who kisses John's dead lips, nor does she please Herod, who proceeds with John's execution despite her dance and not because of it. Fuller's Salome is not the expected femme fatale, but a "would-be Christian martyr."[19] Fuller's second version of the story, *La Tragédie de Salome*, with music by French composer Florent Schmitt, employed her usual veils and colored images to make her into a literal "projection screen" as a "vampy temptress," and for a moment, she undid her usual artistic decisions to veil and conceal her body, by projecting her naked forty-five-year-old self in silhouette.[20] She thus anticipated by several decades a performance of *Salome* by the Danish Flemming Flindt ballet company, in which Vivi Flindt as Salome danced the last act entirely nude.[21]

So-called Salome dancers were appearing everywhere in 1907–1908, on American vaudeville stages and in Parisian cabarets and theaters alike. These dancers, unlike Fuller, "cooked up their own variations on a common theme: a wild, gyrating interpretive dance number" that was informed by Wilde's play, Strauss's opera, or some creative combination thereof, usually including the Dance of the Seven Veils, which supposedly symbolized "the surrender of maidenhood."[22]

Other dancers of Fuller's stature also gained fame (or notoriety) for their performances of Salome. The Russian Jewish actress Ida Rubenstein had her début as a dancer in 1908 with a private solo performance of Oscar Wilde's *Salomé*. She collaborated with the designer Léon Bakst, who also designed the costumes for her performance as Cleopatra, another "Oriental" figure, that same year, and with the choreographer Michel Fokine. Bakst, Fokine, and Rubenstein were later to achieve fame in connection with the Ballets Russes. The music for the dance was composed by Alexander Glazunov, who had denounced Strauss's opera, and tried to write music "that was devoid of sensuousness."[23] Rubenstein's performances involved

18. Garelick, *Electric Salome*, 99.
19. Ibid., 101.
20. Ibid., 95.
21. Wikipedia, "Flemming Flindt."
22. Erdman, *Blue Vaudeville*, 107–8.
23. Petzer, "Veils in Action," 248; ClassicalCDReview.com, review of *Glazunov: King of the Jews*.

veils—twelve, in the case of Cleopatra—and were emblematic of audiences' continued fascination with the *belle femme orientale* or *femme fatale orientale*, as well as with the "exoticized" *belle juive*.[24]

The Trial of Salome

The Canadian actress Maud Allan, however, was perhaps the most celebrated performer of the Salome dance. In 1902, she and Richard Strauss both attended performances of Wilde's *Salomé* in Berlin.[25] In 1905, Strauss's opera *Salome* premiered in Dresden; in 1906, Allan's *Vision of Salomé* premiered in Vienna.[26] Allan was to base her career on the Salome dance; it was also to prove the basis for a degrading and disastrous trial, recalling Wilde's own. Even though Allan's rendition of Salome's dance was openly sensuous and she appeared in a state of seminudity, having actually posed nude for the sculptor Artur Bock and the painter Franz von Stuck, she insisted, as had Fuller, that "Salome was merely an innocent child who is conned by her vengeful mother," and, going Fuller one better, declared that her dance was a form of "atonement" for her mother's sin, an interesting and original theological twist on the relationship of Salome and Herodias.[27] Allan's Salome was an outstanding success in Britain, successfully playing into the late Victorian taste for "embodying contradictions": at least for the moment Allan's appearance of respectability let her, like Loïe Fuller, be whatever she wanted to be onstage.[28]

Although she had performed to critical acclaim on British stages, Allan's tour of the United States in 1910 proved disappointing for her. The Salome craze was coming to an end, and she now had many imitators.[29] On her return to England in 1918, hoping to recoup her losses, she agreed to play Salome in Oscar Wilde's play, a role that even the divine Sarah Bernhardt had been unable to take on, thanks to the squeamishness of the Lord Chamberlain's office. It was apparent that the British prejudices against the now-dead Wilde, his play, and his sexual preferences had not died, and in fact had resurfaced in an even uglier form, one of conspiracy theory.

24. Petzer, "Veils in Action," 248–49.
25. Stern, ed., *Salome*, by Oscar Wilde, 32.
26. Ibid., 38.
27. Bentley, *Sisters of Salome*, 60–61.
28. Ibid., 70.
29. Ibid., 71.

A British member of Parliament, Noel Pemberton-Billing, published an assertion in a right-wing newsletter, the *Imperialist*, that tens of thousands of British citizens were guilty of "depraved and lecherous behavior" that betrayed Britain to the German enemy it was fighting in World War I.[30] He accused Allan, along with others, of lesbianism and treachery, for which her performance in Wilde's discredited *Salomé* was simply grist for the mill, recalling as it did Wilde's own conviction for sodomy in 1895. Understandably, but unwisely, Allan chose to sue Pemberton-Billing for libel, just as Wilde had sued the Marquess of Queensbury, and to similar disastrous effect. As Toni Bentley has noted, this is the first time that Salome was on trial, ironically on charges of lesbianism.[31] As Dr. Serrell Cooke, who testified for the defense, asserted, Wilde's Salomé also had to be a sadist, even a vampire, who could not "get any sexual excitement unless [she bites] with violence enough to draw blood, even suck it, taste it, and then . . . [has] a violent sexual orgasm."[32] The connection of Salome with vampires, lunatic as it sounds in this context, has an impact on later depictions of Salome, although it probably was not taken very seriously at the time, only as tangential to the proof that anyone playing Salome had to be so sexually perverse that anyone reporting her perversity was actually doing a service for the public good.[33] The jury apparently thought so as well, as Pemberton-Billing was acquitted of libel and Maud Allan's career was over.

African American Salome: Aïda Overton Walker

Before the waning and eventual near extinction of the Salome dance, and prior to its revival in a new form of spectacle, the cinema, an African American actress and dancer, Aïda Overton Walker, emerged, like Maud Allan, from the vaudeville stage, to create a more original, and, as she hoped, a more elevated form of the dance. Walker had premiered a form of the Salome dance in her show *Bandana Land* (1908), but apparently wanted to perform a version of the dance that would defy two stereotypes: the view that African Americans were incapable or unworthy of "higher" entertainments than comedy and ragtime, and the idea that African American

30. Ibid., 73–74.
31. Ibid., 75.
32. Ibid., 79, citing Kettle, *Salome's Last Veil*, 151.
33. Bentley, *Sisters of Salome*, 75.

women, especially actresses and dancers, were "immoral and oversexed."[34] She was treading a fine line. Even before the Allan trial, when exclusively white actresses and dancers were portraying Salome, they did not shy away from scantily clad and highly sexualized versions of her dance. Walker, on the other hand, choreographed a dance that was "very different from the titillating performances of the countless white actresses who had previously portrayed the biblical character," choosing not to highlight the erotic element. Instead, she concentrated on expressing emotion through her dance: she wanted something more artistic and perhaps more dignified, more like opera and less like vaudeville.[35] It is unclear whether she knew what Strauss had intended for his Salome and her dance, but she certainly knew about the controversy surrounding the première of his opera at the Met in 1907, and may have chosen to show audiences that Salome's dance need not be wanton or "perverted." Images of Walker costumed as Salome show that she did not succumb to the Orientalizing mode of portraying Salome as a kind of half-clad belly dancer. Instead, as the reviewer for the *New York World* comments, "she dances better than some of the Salomes that wear fewer clothes."[36]

Mallarmé, Martha Graham, and Her Herodiade[37]

With Alla Nazimova's 1923 silent movie *Salome*, the dancer and her dance went celluloid. There was, however, a version of Herodias/Salome that did not attempt the Orientalizing vaudevillian versions of "Salomania" but instead recalled the artistic interpretations of Loïe Fuller, whom Stéphane Mallarmé admired as "poésie par excellence."[38] Martha Graham's two-person modern ballet, *Herodiade* (1944),[39] with music by Paul Hindemith and a set by Graham's frequent collaborator, the designer Isamu Noguchi, represented for her a turn towards the strong and complex female mytho-

---

34. "Black Acts," 4.
35. Ibid.
36. Ibid., 8n33, citing Krasner, "Black Salome," 202.
37. For some reason, although it is based on Mallarmé's poem, Graham's *Herodiade* does not have an acute accent over the first *e*.
38. Jones, *Literature, Modernism, and Dance*, 43.
39. Chronologically, this section is a bit out of place, but Graham merits a special section, particularly in contrast to the Salome-dancers and film versions of Salome's dance.

logical characters, like Medea and Clytemnestra, who were later to be the subjects of her dances.[40]

In choreographing her *Herodiade*, Graham was departing in significant and deliberate ways from Wilde's touchstone drama *Salomé*, with its Dance of the Seven Veils, and from the Orientalist and exotic Salome dances derived from it, which may have explained her choice of Mallarmé's "Hérodiade" in the first place. By all accounts, Graham experienced "real agony" over her interpretation of Mallarmé's protagonist, "the mysterious and elusive Hérodiade—a self-absorbed young woman, who was a much a product of Mallarmé's linguistic explorations as she was a phantom from antiquity," although Mallarmé got the idea of the "Scène" between Hérodiade and the Nurse from a similar scene between Flaubert's Salammbô and her Nurse.[41] As Graham finally interpreted the poem, now set to Hindemith's sonorous score, she evoked Mallarmé's character's "agony of passion."[42] Her dance is austere, even frightening, conveying the poem's cold, untouchable heroine and the "horror of virginity" that she perversely is in love with.[43] Central to her interpretation is the stark set in black and white with Noguchi's sculptures looking like bleached bones, conveying the "white night of icicles and cruel snow" of chastity.[44] The set also featured a mirror, essential in Mallarmé's dramatic poem—one might even say a character in its own right—in which Hérodiade gazes at herself in its "idolatry."[45] There is also a dark cloak in which Hérodiade wraps herself at the conclusion of the piece.

Susan Jones notes that Graham's interpretation is decidedly intertextual: "Graham's *Herodiade* expresses . . . a curiously 'Yeatsian' interpretation of Mallarmé's poem, conveyed partly by the modernist Japanese flavor of the sets by Noguchi."[46] The reference to William Butler Yeats involves two of his final plays, *A Full Moon in March* (1935) and its complementary *The King of the Great Clock Tower* (1934), "written under the influence of Nôh drama."[47] Both of these plays are heirs to the Salome narrative as it developed from Heine to Mallarmé and Wilde, but they are "only indirectly

---

40. Bannerman, "A Dance of Transition," 1.
41. Ibid., 10; De Man, *The Post-Romantic Predicament*, 45–46.
42. Ibid., 12.
43. Lenson, trans., "Scène" from "Hérodiade," 586.
44. Ibid.
45. Ibid.
46. Jones, *Literature, Modernism, and Dance*, 43.
47. Puchner, *Stage Fright*, 135.

related to the biblical story."[48] *A Full Moon in March* takes place in an Irish setting, although the main characters are derived from a fairy tale by Hans Christian Andersen about a queen and a swineherd. He must woo the remote, virginal, and cruel queen with his song. If he fails, he will be beheaded. According to Martin Puchner, Yeats confessed "in several letters" that "this play is in fact an estranged and transposed version of the Salome story," in which Herodias and Salome become one in the person of an Irish queen who has the swineherd beheaded for insulting her and later dances with his head.[49] In *The King of the Great Clock Tower*, the queen dances with the severed head of a man called the Stroller, who has come to court demanding to look at the beautiful, mysterious queen. This time, it is the king who is insulted by the stroller's presumption and has him beheaded. When his head is brought in, the queen dances, and the head begins to sing along with the queen, who kisses its lips in a Salome-esque climax, although fortunately, unlike Wilde's Herod, the king does not have his queen executed.[50]

There are no severed heads in Graham's performance, only an enacted "dialogue" between Hérodiade and the attendant (the nurse in Mallarmé's poem). Nonetheless, Graham's version of the story ends with Hérodiade, "alone onstage, enveloped in her black cloak . . . [giving] the impression of a disembodied head."[51] The expressive body, which Hérodiade forbade the attendant to touch—by kiss, by perfumes, or even by grooming her hair—is still, even gone. As in Mallarmé's dramatic poem, evoking a princess who is a "purely imaginary creature, entirely independent of history," but not the impressions summoned up by the name and idea of the dance, Graham's performance embodies an emotional yet aloof and mysterious entity.[52] It is no accident that a mirror is an essential object in Graham's work, as it is in Mallarmé's, a place of "living potential" and also of the kind of artistic creation that is exposed and "sacrificial."[53] Here, Hérodiade, who has known "the white thrill of my nudity" from looking in the mirror[54] (585), is the creation and the sacrifice.[55]

48. Ibid.
49. Ibid.
50. Ibid., 136.
51. Jones, *Literature, Modernism, and Dance*, 43.
52. Bannerman, "Dance," 3, quoting Mallarmé and Mondor, *Correspondence, 1862–1871*, 226.
53. Ibid., 16.
54. Lenson, trans., "Hérodiade," 585.
55. A version of Graham's *Herodiade*, by the Martha Graham Dance Company, can

Reviving Salome

ALLA NAZIMOVA'S SILENT SALOME

In a rather curious novel, *Salome: An Invitation to the Dance*, Marcus Johnson invites readers to share a rainy holiday taken by the Bogweasel family, including their children, Stella, seventeen years old; Lloyd, fifteen; and Berenike, aged ten, together with Stella's boyfriend, Barry, and various friends and relatives who drop in from time to time. To entertain themselves indoors, Mr. Bogweasel, a history professor, encourages the family to explore films and novels about Salome, and to do the appropriate research to prove—or disprove—them. The result is the most complete listing of twentieth- and twenty-first-century literature and film—mainly the latter—on the subject that I have found.[56]

Johnson's research shows that three other silent films preceded the one that has the most publicity, Alla Nazimova's art film *Salomé* (1923).[57] All three were based on Wilde's play. Little is known about them other than the names, some stills, and some details of their production. The first (1906) is Oskar Messter's *Tanz der Salome*, a silent film that is little more than the Wildean dance itself, basically a striptease that reflects the "Salomania" craze.[58] *Salome (The Dance of the Seven Veils)* is an American production from 1908, starring Florence Lawrence and directed by J. Stuart Blackton, that seems to have followed the same Salomaniac theme, although with less nudity than the German production. In 1918, a silent film version of Wilde's *Salomé* was produced, now unfortunately lost except for its posters and reviews; the loss is all the more regrettable, because the film starred Theda Bara, the ultimate "Vamp," as Salome.[59] Bara, born Theodosia Goodman, took her place in a long line of Jewish actresses, "beautiful women with exotic names,"[60] often pseudonymous, who were successful by being portrayed as seductresses, "vamps," and exotic others, echoing the nineteenth-century theme of *la belle juive*. A *New York Times* review from October

---

be viewed on YouTube: http://www/youtube.com/watch?v=sRw5gv8gMYI/.

56. Johnson, *Salome*. His historical conclusions, although presented in the framework of fiction, support much of what is said in this chapter, although the book was substantially complete before I discovered Johnson's work.

57. Ibid., 79–80.

58. Ibid.; Internet Movie Data base (IMDb)'s page for *Salomé* (1922). Information about all the movies mentioned in this chapter may be obtained from IMDb. Most can be found on YouTube as well.

59. Landy, "1923—Movies and the Changing Body," 106.

60. Coulthart, "Alla Nazimova's *Salomé*."

7, 1918, is largely favorable to the film, citing the "richness and extent of pageantry, sumptuousness of setting," and praising Bara's exemplary role as "every minute the vampire."[61]

In 1923, another version of Wilde's *Salomé* was released, this time starring another Jewish actress, the bisexual Alla Nazimova, in a film that was rumored to have an "all-gay cast," or at least one of men in drag.[62] The film, which can still be seen on YouTube, has costumes and sets by Natacha Rambova, wife of Rudolf Valentino and rumored lover of Nazimova, which were based on Aubrey Beardsley's illustrations for Wilde's *Salomé*. Because Beardsley's illustrations were in black and white, they were particularly suited to the then black-and-white medium of the cinema. Because no major studio would produce this "dangerously decadent work," Nazimova's adaptation of Wilde's play was "inaugurated, produced, and even front-financed" by Nazimova herself.[63] As Sabrina Starnaman observes, Nazimova's *Salomé* is "replete with transgressive images of incest, homosexual desire, fluid gender performances, and aggressive female desire."[64] One might argue that if Nazimova sought to be faithful to Wilde's drama, that is precisely the performance one would get, although the movie was billed as a "historical fantasy." The screen adaptation, written by Peter M. Winter, did make a nod in the opening to the higher moral sensibilities that American audiences might expect from a Bible movie: "Profound was the moral darkness that enveloped the World on which the Star of Bethlehem arose." Emphasizing the corruption of Herod, Herodias, and their court, and pointing to Iokanaan as forerunner of Christ, Winter describes the "foreigners" congregating in Judea as "Rome, rotting within . . . Greece, senile and conquered; Egypt, wrapped like its own mummies in the vestments of the past."[65] Winter also emphasizes Salomé's initial innocence. Alice Bach claims that Nazimova portrays her as "trying to seduce John but not really understanding what she's doing."[66] Indeed, the Dance of the Seven Veils,

61. Unsigned review, "Theda Bara Films Orient in 'Salomé,'" Movies, *New York Times*, October 7, 1918 http://www.nytimes.com/movie/review?res=9F06E4DE1539E1 3ABC4F53DFB6678383609EDE/.

62. Brunotte, "'All Jews,'" 211.

63. Coulthart, "Alla Nazimova's *Salomé*."

64. Starnaman, "Yezierska's Salome," 1.

65. Winter (screenwriter), *Salomé* (1923, by Charles Bryant, with Alla Nazimova), public television broadcast, December 25, 2012, YouTube, http://www.youtube.com/watch?v=IYbJmD2RH68/.

66. Bach, "Calling the Shots," 122.

borrowing from Beardsley's drawings but not adhering to them too closely, creates a curiously exotic yet nonerotic scene. The dance itself has echoes of Loïe Fuller's Salome dances, more fabric and concealment than flesh. At the end of her dance, when Nazimova's Salomé receives the head, she wraps herself and the head in her cloak as if she is secretly making love to it, although we do not see either the head or the expected kiss. Despite the elaborate artistic production, with a heroine reviewed as "a character of paradox and willfulness wrapped in spectacular costumes,"[67] Nazimova's film was not a critical or financial success.

THE RETURN OF THE "JEWESS": ANZIA YEZIERSKA'S *SALOME OF THE TENEMENTS*

In the same year (1923) that Nazimova released her silent version of Wilde's *Salomé*, Anzia Yezierska's so-called immigrant novel, *Salome of the Tenements*, appeared. Two years later (1925) it too became a silent movie adapted from the novel by Sonya Levien and produced by Sidney Olcott for Paramount Pictures, with the Lasky-Zukor players, starring the Dutch-born Jewish actress, herself a famous "vamp," Jetta Goudal.[68] According to Sabrina Starnaman, it is possible that Yezierska had access to staged, and possibly filmed, versions of Wilde's play in New York City prior to writing her novel.[69] Yet it is curious how tangential Wilde's play, with his version of Salome, seems to the novel, and perhaps just as strange that the author known as the "Sweatshop Cinderella,"[70] chose to use the New Testament characters as metaphors for her tale of class and upward mobility. It is also surprising that, as far as I am aware, the secondary literature on *Salome of the Tenements*, in its preference for analysis of class conflict, marginalization, and assimilation in "Progressive-Era America," does not discuss the use of the biblical story of Salome and John the Baptist in any depth at all.[71] Further examination of the novel, however, reveals both a strong connection to Wilde's drama and also to minor strains within the stream of the Salome narrative discussed in the last chapter, particularly the artistic

---

67. Ibid.
68. IMDb's page for *Salome of the Tenements* (1925).
69. Starnaman, "Yezierska's Salome & Wilde's Salomé," 1.
70. Fishbein, "Anzia Yezierska," 137.
71. See, for example, Rottenberg, "*Salome of the Tenements*," 65–83.

striving exemplified in Michael Field's "A Dance of Death," and the relative innocence of the character as she appears in J. C. Heywood's epic poems.

The plot of the story revolves around a Russian Jewish immigrant, Sonya Vrunsky,[72] living in the Lower East Side ghetto and reporting for the *Ghetto News*. She is sent to report on the WASP millionaire philanthropist John Manning, who has decided to live among what he calls the "real people" of the East Side. Set on fire by the idea that marriage to him will save her from the poverty of her existence, Sonya persuades another Jewish immigrant, Jacky Solomon, now known as the haute couture designer Jacques Hollins, to make her a beautiful dress for free so that she can meet Manning at lunch without being ashamed of her cheap clothing. Bemused, Hollins calls her Ghetto Princess—another connection with Salome, "Princess of Judea." Charmed with her appearance, Manning asks if he can visit her at home. Shamed by her gaudily decorated yet disintegrating apartment, she entices Benjamin Rosenblat, her landlord, who believes that she is a "high-flying chorus girl,"[73] into fixing the entire building. Anxious to decorate the place appropriately—that is, in restrained Anglo-Saxon style—she charms the pawnbroker, Honest Abe, into lending her a hundred dollars on the premise that she will pay him back five hundred when she marries Manning, who is immediately attracted to her because of the "primitive fascination of the Oriental . . . the intensity of spirit of the oppressed races."[74] Yet he continues to see her as a passionate, willful child. He cannot sustain her passion, the passion of the "over-emotional Ghetto."[75] In the end, she leaves this "dead lump of self-righteousness,"[76] and strikes out on her own again, eventually earning her way into designing clothes and reconnecting with Solomon/Hollins, to sell beautiful clothes not only to upper-class matrons, but at reduced prices to Lower East Side girls like herself.

From this initial surface description, it does not seem as if there is a lot to connect Sonya Vrunsky with Salome. Yezierska's novel is in part a fictionalized recounting of her own broken romance with the American educator and philosopher John Dewey, combined with the story of her close friend, Rosa Pastor, who married the millionaire socialist Graham

---

72. Her name is changed in the film to Sonya Mendel, perhaps for greater euphony.
73. Yezierska, *Salome of the Tenements*, 52.
74. Ibid., 101.
75. Ibid., 132.
76. Ibid., 152.

Stokes, but then became disenchanted with him.[77] Throughout the novel, however, Yezierska continually insists on identifying her heroine with Salome and her object of desire with John the Baptist. She uses a particularly American understanding of their relationship, reflected in Heywood's dramatic trilogy but derived in part from Wilde's depiction of Salome's desire for Iokanaan. Her first chapter, in fact, is titled, "Salome Meets Her Saint." Sonya believes that John Manning's dedication to philanthropy and his choice to live among the "real people" will not only "burn like the fire of a new religion" but will also save her own soul from the grinding poverty she despises.[78] For her, Manning is both prophet and savior, forerunner and Messiah. Sonya believes wholeheartedly that she has found her "deliverer," but her passion and its forthrightness are somewhat embarrassing to him, and will remain so, although eventually he succumbs to it, telling her in slightly bedazzled but condescending admiration, "You have the burning fire of the Russian Jew in you."[79]

Ever since she was a child, "desire with Sonya had always been a mere prologue to attainment."[80] As Gay Wilentz notes in the introduction of the reprinted novel, "Like the biblical Salome . . . young Sonya creates an illusion to win over the man who, metaphorically, is a bloodless John the Baptist—all head and no heart."[81] As Sonya sweeps all obstacles away before her in her desire to charm Manning, she creates symbolic "veils" of illusion: on one occasion she buys an expensive literal veil she can hardly afford to cover her designer dress. Her comrade at the *Ghetto News*, the virtuous but drab Gittel, cautions her: "Nu meshugeneh Salome! We'll see where all your wild love-madness will land you—whether with all your crazy dances you'll get the head of your John the Baptist."[82] As Sonya uses the money from Honest Abe to redecorate her rooms in a "simple style" that will appeal to Manning, she cries: "To get him, I'd pluck the moonbeams out of the moon,"[83] recalling both the moon symbolism of Wilde's play—cold, virginal, and unattainable—and his Salomé's passionate desire to kiss Iokanaan's mouth.

77. Wilentz, "Introduction," xiv–xvii.
78. Yezierska, *Salome of the Tenements*, 1–2
79. Ibid., 3.
80. Ibid., 84.
81. Wilentz, "Introduction," xviii.
82. Yezierska, *Salome of the Tenements*, 58.
83. Ibid., 64.

Initially, these illusions work. Manning, already believing that the East Side ghetto represents naturalness, is charmed by what he thinks is Sonya's "beautiful" poverty and toil, "unveiled by any artifice."[84] He thinks that she will be an ideal companion to work with him in his settlement house and promote the "gospel of the Simple Life," because she has achieved "beauty without expense,"[85] while Sonya calculates just how much the expense the illusion has cost through wheedling, cajoling, and pledging her way into beguiling Manning. Attracted to the "intoxicating lure of her beauty,"[86] Manning tries to break the enchantment by keeping his distance and sending her a letter that turns her love into "crazy hate of him and his things," because he is "always at arm's length. Always encased in ice,"[87] as remote as the Baptist was to Salome. She is also wild because Honest Abe is now dunning her for a thousand dollars, because she has not yet married her millionaire. Once again, Gittel sums up Sonya's seductive ways in biblical terms:

> You stop a man in the middle of the street, and begin to call him 'Benefactor of humanity,' 'Savior of your soul,' and so he invites you to lunch . . . Then you storm a Fifth Avenue store and get another strange man to dress you up from head to toe like a Delilah; then you vamp a landlord, hypnotize a helpless Honest Abe, turn the whole world upside down to get the setting for your man. And if you didn't catch on to him . . . it's only because you're a heartless Salome and you don't care if you get your man dead or alive, as long as you get him.[88]

Sonya nonetheless suffers deeply because she cannot figure Manning out: "Did she suffer so merely because she loved a high-souled saint—a John the Baptist—a man without blood in his veins?"[89]

Manning, however, cannot stay away from her and her "Oriental" fascination. He believes that she can "interpret" to him the "oppressed races" that he longs to stoop down and help,[90] but the real reason he is attracted to her haunts him in a dream: "So tired was he that he fell asleep almost in-

---

84. Ibid., 73–74.
85. Ibid., 75.
86. Ibid., 87.
87. Ibid., 90.
88. Ibid., 95.
89. Ibid., 96.
90. Ibid., 101.

stantly to dream that he was John the Baptist loving with a self-destruction the white-fleshed loveliness of Salome, who lured and drew him with the dazzling color of her voluptuous dancing."[91] They marry, but the marriage is almost immediately a disaster. Manning is "terrified" by his own sexual desire as well as by the emotions of the "vivid exotic" he has married.[92] The first "veil of illusion" drops when her passionate intensity proves more than he needs or wants.[93] More illusions are shattered on both sides when an unwilling Sonya is forced to hold a reception after the marriage that must include Manning's "uptown" friends and relatives along with her own "gaudily-attired and loud-voiced Ghetto friends."[94] The damning judgment of Manning's "higher-up" acquaintances, which Sonya happens to overhear, focuses on her foreignness and her Jewishness, which make her a mere sexual being: "Russian Jewesses are always interesting to men ... They are mere creatures of sex."[95] Sonya flees, but Manning forces her to return to the reception, treating her "as a dog he had just punished."[96] From that point on, Sonya, like the Wildean Salomé to whom the text constantly alludes, questions, "Do I love him because I hate him so?"[97]

Yezierska depicts the failure of the marriage with heavy irony: "Sonya and Manning, tricked into matrimony, were the Oriental and the Anglo-Saxon trying to find a common language."[98] Sonya represents the "overemotional Ghetto," and "East Side savage," while Manning is "the thin air of puritan restraint" and the "strait-jacket of American civilization," in which she cannot exist. Sent to observe the settlement workers Manning employs, all Sonya can see is patronizing, misunderstanding, and disrespect for the "unworthy" poor. When Honest Abe reappears, now demanding fifteen hundred dollars or Sonya's engagement ring for her promissory pledge, she is cornered. With this consciousness of her deceit, she cannot respond to Manning's sexual advances, which are "tinged with shame."[99] As Sonya reproaches him for being a "cold fish, a high-brow, an educated hypocrite,"

91. Ibid.
92. Ibid., 106.
93. Ibid., 109.
94. Ibid., 124.
95. Ibid., 128.
96. Ibid., 129.
97. Ibid., 130.
98. Ibid., 132.
99. Ibid., 146.

The Salome Project

Manning begins to realize that she is now "tearing away [the] veils between him and reality."[100] He still feels passion for this "mystery," but Sonya again disillusions him, telling him that she owes Honest Abe fifteen hundred dollars. The shame of his name being attached to a note in the hands of "that Jew" turns his desire to crushing scorn: he forgets that Sonya is herself a Jew and never pretended to be otherwise. He tells her that he will not divorce her, but that they are "through." She denounces him as "a faking saint—bloodless higher-up," and "dead in your stony goodness as those in their graves!"[101]

Leaving Manning, realizing, as did Salomé after her rejection by the Baptist, that "all that had once been love had turned to hate,"[102] Sonya struggles as a waitress, living in a bleak women's hotel, becoming yet another biblical character—"a bruised and broken Hagar wandering in the wilderness toward an unknown goal."[103] She still loves beauty, and dreams of becoming a dress designer, saving her earnings towards that goal, when she receives a letter from Manning that makes it clear all he cares about is his "name" and avoiding a public scandal; she tears the letter into pieces and burns them.

Yet Sonya has not lost her persuasive ways. In the restaurant, she meets a man in the dress trade, Ziskind, and signs up with him as an apprentice. Designing a dress with "beautiful plainness," she rejoices over its beauty, in part because she is not using it to deceive: "They said I was a Salome wanting the heads of men, but you know I was only seeking—seeking for the feel of the beautiful."[104] Her talent leads her to work again with Jaky Solomon/Jacques Hollins, and they plan to marry. As they dine in Sonya's apartment, Manning reappears. He is now abject, having himself become "primitive," with a "savage passion," longing for the "beautiful, maddening Jewess" he has rejected.[105] Although she is tempted to feel the "triumph of her sex" in awakening his desire, Sonya realizes that Manning has become a "human being," like Christ, "suffering—wounded—despised and rejected in his hour of need . . . She was the cross on which he bled."[106] Humbled, she now

100. Ibid., 149–50.
101. Ibid., 152.
102. Ibid., 154.
103. Ibid., 156.
104. Ibid., 170.
105. Ibid., 181.
106. Ibid., 182.

knows what he represented to her: "Romance. The madness, the daring, the deathless adventure of youth," and that only love and beauty last forever.[107] This "Salome of the tenements" has much in common, ironically, with the Decadent and Symbolist Salome, in her dedication to "art for art's sake" and to beauty—at a cost.[108] Throughout the novel Sonya echoes biblical women known for their seductiveness, deception, and sexual irregularity—Esther, Delilah, Salome, Hagar—while Manning represents both the person of Christ and his forerunner, John. Like Salome in Heywood's trilogy, moreover, this Salome is also redeemed, through her love for Manning, the failed prophet, which has "ennobled" her, and enables her to rise "triumphant,"[109] although not in the destructive sense of previous Salomes. Nor has she been defeated in her desire, as in Wilde's play. Instead, her desire for beauty has been redeemed, largely through her own efforts. In the end, Sonya and Jaky, as true artists, reject "mass production and the homogenization process that goes along with it," remaining neither in the ghetto nor assimilated to the dominant "Anglo-Saxon" culture.[110]

SALOME AT THE MOVIES

It took several decades after the box office failure of Nazimova's *Salomé* for the biblical dancer to return to the screen. American novelists of the 1950s who wrote about Jesus of Nazareth, however, were unable to resist the appeal of the story of Salome. According to Marcus Johnson, Lloyd C. Douglas had included her in two of his historical novels about Jesus: *The Robe* (1943), about the tribune who helped crucify Jesus, got his robe when the soldiers cast lots for his garments (Mark 15:24), and later converted to Christianity; and *The Big Fisherman* (1949), about the apostle Peter.[111] Although Salome plays a small part in each of these novels, when both came to the big screen—*The Robe* directed by Henry Koster and starring Richard Burton as the tribune Marcellus, in 1953, and *The Big Fisherman*, directed by Frank Borsage and starring Howard Keel—she does not seem have made the cut, although "Princess Fara," an Arabian princess whose father turns

---

107. Ibid., 184
108. Zagona, *The Legend of Salome*, 11.
109. Yezierska, *Salome of the Tenements*, 184.
110. Rottenberg, "*Salome*," 79.
111. Johnson, *Salome*, 53–55.

out to be Herod Antipas, is a main character in the latter film.[112] Another American author, Henry Denker, wrote a novel, *Salome: Princess of Galilee* (1953), in which Salome falls in love with a Roman centurion, Cornelius, who is already a follower of John the Baptist. He later becomes a Christian and is blinded for it by Pontius Pilate. Salome, as in J. C. Heywood's trilogy, also becomes a Christian and leads the blind Cornelius on his missionary excursions.[113] Denker's plot has been followed to some extent, although without acknowledgement, by what is arguably the most famous—or spectacular—Salome movie of the twentieth century: Rita Hayworth's *Salome* (1953), directed by William Dieterle, with Stewart Granger as her love interest.[114] According to Margarita Landazuri, the film rode the wave of renewed interest in biblical epics in the 1950s, now appearing in Technicolor. Hayworth had previously played a glamorous femme fatale in *Gilda* (1946), but the story of Salome was revamped—or really devamped—to make the character more sympathetic.[115] She thinks she is dancing to save John the Baptist, whom she spiritually admires: instead, the Baptist is beheaded at the instigation of Herodias before Salome even finishes the dance.[116] The big box office draw, however, was the Dance of the Seven Veils, in which Hayworth wore a flesh-colored body stocking to appear nude beneath her filmy bejeweled clothing, much like the earlier Salome dancers in vaudeville. The *New York Times* review of the movie, by Bosley Crowther, acknowledged the unlikely but titillating combination of its "righteously sanctimonious air" with the "fascination of its heroine," whose dance, a "discreet striptease," is intended to make the audience, like the actor Charles Laughton, who played Herod Antipas, "pop-eyed."[117] Apart from the dance, however, there is very little to connect this film version of the Salome story with Wilde's play or any other version.

The idea of a seductive dance for Salome, usually cast as a teenaged temptress, is embedded in most Jesus movies from the 1950s on.[118] Nicholas Ray's *King of Kings* (1961), which took the unusual step for Hollywood

---

112. IMDb, page for *The Robe* (1953); IMDb, page for *The Big Fisherman* (1959).
113. Johnson, *Salome*, 55.
114. Ibid., 82; IMDb, page for *Salome* (1953).
115. Landazuri, "Salome (1953)."
116. Bach, "Calling the Shots,"117.
117. Bosley Crowther, review of *Salome*, starring Rita Hayworth, *New York Times*, March 25, 1953, Movies section.
118. Bach, "Calling the Shots," 115–16.

of having an actual actor, Jeffrey Hunter, play Jesus, instead of the usual voice or beam of light, featured an actual teenager as Salome, the actress Brigid Bazlen, who danced an erotic, midriff-baring dance that she claimed was based on a "purely Oriental-African dance movement of the period."[119] George Stevens's *The Greatest Story Ever Told* (1965), with Max von Sydow as Jesus, includes a dimly lit dance by Salome, clad in diaphanous garments for Herod alone, but the drama here is really between John the Baptist (Charlton Heston) and Herod (José Ferrer), and the actress who dances Salome is not even listed in the credits.[120] In Marcus Johnson's novel about Salome, the teenaged Lloyd Bogweasel, who has seen the film, comments petulantly: "In this movie, Herod Antipas actually decided to kill John before Salome even started her dance, and the head was off before she finished. So why she had to dance, I don't know."[121] Franco Zeffirelli's epic TV miniseries *Jesus of Nazareth* (1977), featuring Robert Powell, as Jesus, featured Isabel Mestres as Salome. (She is also featured in that role in Pedro Almodóvar's 1978 film, *Salome*.)[122] Mestres performed a vaguely Middle-Eastern dance, reminiscent of Bazlen's, in a short, spangled, see-through outfit, and finished at the feet of Herod (Christopher Plummer); both are breathing heavily, although Salome manages between breaths to demand John the Baptist's head. The sole exception to the portrayal of Salome as an exotic and erotic teenage temptress is Pier Paolo Pasolini's 1964 film *The Gospel according to Matthew*. "Pasolini steadfastly refuses to dip into the standard images . . . Salome's dance for Herodias a chaste dance that has nothing to do with veils," and is more like part of a modern dance recital, her mother encouraging her with a kiss on the cheek.[123]

Wilde and Wilder Salome

The earlier silent movies about Salome, *Tanz de Salome* (1906), *Salome*, with Florence Lawrence (1908), the lost 1918 version with Theda Bara, and Nazimova's 1923 rendition established a pattern of following Wilde's play,

---

119. Brigid Bazlen, interview with Peter S. Haigh, *ABC Film Review*, 1962, cited in Wikipedia, "Brigid Bazlen."

120. IMDb page for *The Greatest Story Ever Told* (1965).

121. Johnson, *Salome*, 49.

122. IMDb page for *Jesus of Nazareth* (TV miniseries, 1977).

123. Burton, "The Gospel according to Saint Matthew (1964)," par. 3. Again, thanks to Nancy Heisey for mentioning Pasolini's version of the dance.

The Salome Project

including its dance, either closely or loosely, but always with his *Salomé* as the paradigm.[124] Other films were either productions of Wilde's drama or embellished versions that freely departed from his script but always alluded to it. Rita Hayworth's 1953 *Salome* used the dance but departed rather substantially from Wilde's Decadent portrayal of the character. The Jesus movies of the 1960s and 1970s treated Salome as a tangential, if tantalizing, part of the larger drama.

Beginning in the 1970s, however, a number of movies appeared that put Salome at the center.[125] Carmelo Bene's 1972 film *Salome*, based on an earlier 1964 stage version, is consistently referred to in reviews as "psychedelic," and includes lurid episodes of sadomasochism and even vampires,[126] which increasingly become associated with the character of Salome until she becomes a vampire herself in the TV series *True Blood*. Bene himself plays Herod, as Al Pacino is to do in his staged and later film versions; African American supermodel Donyale Luna is Salome, the first black Salome since Aïda Overton Walker. In 1973, Clive Barker, famous for the horror film *Hellraiser*, produced a twenty-minute black-and-white movie loosely based on Wilde, with no dialogue and a dreamy, barely clothed actress, Anna Jo Ciampa, as Salome.[127] Claude d'Anna's 1986 *Salome* featured a trendy mixture of ancient, medieval, and contemporary, including Roman legionaries in World War II garb.[128]

In 1988, flamboyant director Ken Russell set his film *Salome's Last Dance* in a French brothel, where Wilde's *Salomé* is performed for his birthday by male prostitutes, as he lolls on a lush sofa, occasionally enjoying the caresses of a gilded chorus boy. Russell, known for his gothic style, seems to have out-Wilded Wilde in decadence.[129] On the other hand, Steven Berkoff's iconic 1992 filmed version of a staged performance of *Salomé* is truer to Wilde, evoking his imagery by bluish-white lighting, and to

---

124. Johnson, *Salome*, 79–81.

125. Most of these movies are catalogued in Johnson, *Salome*, 82–84.

126. Ibid., 83; IMDb, page for *Salomè* [sic] (1972); Bachman, Review of *Salomè* by Carmelo Bene," 20–23.

127. Johnson, *Salome*, 83; IMDb, page for *Salome* (1973); Coulthart, "Two Films by Clive Barker."

128. Johnson, *Salome*, 83; IMDb, page for *Salomè* [sic] (1986).

129. IMDb, page for *Salome's Last Dance* (1988).

Beardsley's drawings by costuming all his actors in black and white, and in whiteface, except for Salome's vivid red mouth.[130]

Two later films riff on the idea of a performance-within-a-performance. A little-known film starring Albert Finney, *A Man of No Importance* (1994)—its title playing on Wilde's play *A Woman of No Importance* (1893)—set in 1963, features a closeted homosexual bus driver (Finney), who directs an amateur production of Wilde's *Salomé*.[131] An unusual performance of *Salomé*, directed by Carlos Saura (2002), uses the perspective of a flamenco troupe as it rehearses and then enacts the play. In an unusual plot twist, Salomé (Aida Gomez) commits suicide by hanging because of remorse for John's death, recalling the earlier opera by Jules Massenet (1881), a setting of Flaubert's "Hérodiade" in which Salome seduces John the Baptist and then stabs herself in shame.[132]

Unlike these, *Salomé* (1978), a short, early sixteen-millimeter effort by Spanish filmmaker Pedro Almodóvar, featuring Isabel Mestres reprising her role of Salomé, and his brother Agustin as Abraham—yes, Abraham!—presents the biblical story of the patriarch's near sacrifice of his son Isaac. Anachronistically, Salomé comes into the story when she tempts Abraham into giving her anything for a dance, and he promises the head of his son Isaac. She dances like a matador, to the accompaniment of bull ring music, although the opening credits begin with Paul Anka's "Dance On, Little Girl." No critic seems to know exactly what Almodóvar is up to here in his odd reinterpretation by juxtaposition of two biblical stories, but perhaps he wants to use familiarity with the story of Salome as presented by Wilde to shock viewers out of their expectations about another familiar religious story and its outcome.[133] Recent representations of Salome on stage and screen have not taken as great liberties with Wilde's script as Almodóvar did, and still regard Wilde's *Salomé* as a point of departure. In 2006, actor-director Al Pacino staged Wilde's play in both New York and Los Angeles. He then filmed the play and later coupled it with a documentary (2011) that shows the interaction between the play's staging and Wilde's own story, leading the actor to a variety of places associated with the playwright, and several interviews about Wilde with people from Bono to Gore Vidal. According to the producer of *Wilde Salomé*, Barry Navidi, Pacino had been

---

130. Johnson, *Salome*, 84; Coulthart, "Steven Berkhoff's *Salomé*."
131. IMDb, page for *A Man of No Importance* (1994).
132. Johnson, *Salome*, 84; IMDb, page for *Salomé* (2002).
133. IMDb, page for *Salomé* (1978).

interested in Wilde's play for more than twenty years, beginning with "Steven Berkoff's landmark *Salomé* on stage in London."[134] In an interview, Pacino relates his "crazy," layered production of the play, the movie about the play, and the documentary about the playwright to whom the play was so "personal."[135] Pacino's production is more of a gangster-cum-vampire movie—Herod wears gold chains and has a New York City street accent; Salomé's mouth drips with blood after kissing Iokanaan's dead lips—but it preserves the dialogue of Wilde's play virtually intact.

A very recent staging of Wilde's play by South African director, adapter, and playwright Yaël Farber pushes the boundaries of the play and the biblical story into contemporary Middle Eastern politics. Originally staged for the Women's Voices Theater Festival, presented by the Shakespeare Theater Company from October 6 through November 8, 2015, and then in a revised production in London at the National Theatre, from May 3 through July 6, 2017, the play took the framework of Wilde's play, but not his dialogue or premise. Farber, whose adaptation of August Strindberg's *Miss Julie* as the racially charged South African *Mies Julie*, also employed a political theme, understood "Salomé's encounter with Iokanaan [as] the opposite of Wilde": "In the Wilde, she desires him sexually, [with him] calling her whore of Babylon, invoking the Book of Revelation. We're using the Song of Solomon," ostensibly to demonstrate that "sensuality is not anathema to holiness," although Wilde also alluded to the Song of Solomon, albeit with different intent. As Farber envisions Salomé's dance, it is not the "Dance of Death," but a "Dance of Life."[136]

Farber also plays on the name Salomé, as meaning "peace," but also on the actual namelessness of the biblical character. Her production begins with a white-haired woman, robed in white, called the Nameless Woman, played by Olwen Fouéré, who played Salomé in Steven Berkoff's famous production of Wilde's play in 1988. She intones, "You don't remember me—the girl you left for dead . . . You do not know my name." She represents not only the older Salomé, but also the nameless women involved in political struggles who are erased from the history in which they participate. In Farber's retelling of the story, Salomé is "an ally of the doomed prophet," Iokanaan, and helps to promote his execution, which neither Herod nor his

---

134. Gallagher, "Al Pacino Goes Wilde."

135. Pacino, *Wilde Salomé* interview.

136. Farber," Walking in the World of Salomé," 10–11. See also Streete, "Salome as History and Fetish," 14–19.

Roman masters want, to "spur the Jewish people to insurrection," and act for which she is imprisoned and tortured by Pontius Pilate.[137] The identification of Ioakanaan with an occupied people is reinforced by the fact that he speaks Arabic, not the Aramaic that he possibly would have spoken; Ioakanaan's Arabic thus evokes present-day occupied Palestine. The famous dance of Salomé is not the Dance of the Seven Veils: instead, it is part of her baptism by Iokanaan, in which she sheds jewels and clothes until she is "naked before God," in yet another version of Salomé-as-convert.[138]

VAMPIRE SALOME

In the early twentieth century, beginning with silent film, a new type of femme fatale, the Vamp, emerges. The vampire figure is associated with Salome and other femmes fatales by the late nineteenth century, thanks to the popularity of Bram Stoker's novel *Dracula* (1897), which appeared approximately at the same time as Wilde's *Salomé*, and, like the play, was influenced by exotic and Oriental dancers such as Ida Rubenstein in her solo performance of the Dance of the Seven Veils in 1908. Already by 1900, "the vampire had come to represent woman as the personification of everything negative that linked sex, ownership, and money . . . the eternal polyandrous prostitute"; this was true especially in film, giving rise to the verb "vamping" and the noun "vamp."[139] The link of sexual predation with death, however, had already been made by the early nineteenth century. Associated with the term *vampire*, the vamp is "the beauty who uses her feminine wiles to undermine a moral and upright man, for evil purposes," and is sexually attractive but evil.[140] One of the first vamps of cinema, known simply as "The Vamp," Theda Bara, began her vampish career in 1915, in a film called *A Fool There Was*, and later starred in one of the early silent versions of Wilde's *Salomé*, in 1918.[141] Anzia Yezierska's *Salome of the Tenements* echoes this construction of the vamp when the embittered Gittel

---

137. Marks, "Salome, We Hardly Knew Ye." See also Bowie-Sell, "Yaël Farber."
138. Marks, "Salome, We Hardly Knew Ye."
139. Dijkstra, *Idols of Perversity*, 348–51; Petzer, "Veils in Action," 248.
140. See "The Vamp" on the *TV Tropes* website (http://tvtropes.org/pmwiki/pmwiki.php/Main/TheVamp/).
141. Wasserman, "Theda Bara (1890–1955)," para. 4.

charges Sonya, "And what's your 'work' but to vamp men? Didn't you kill Lipkin [the poet], make mush of your Anglo-Saxon saint?"[142]

Calling female seductresses "vamps" or "vampires" apparently derives from their ability to suck the blood literally or figuratively from their victims, draining their vitality. Legends of vampires long existed in folk traditions, particularly in the Balkans, but the emergence of the vampire in English literature, particularly Romantic literature as it shades into the Gothic, appears with John Polidori's *The Vampyre* in 1819. Polidori was Lord Byron's personal physician, and the novel, sometimes attributed to Byron, was the product of a challenge involving the poet, Polidori, Percy Bysshe Shelley, Mary Godwin (later Mary Shelley), and Claire Clairmont, Mary's stepsister, to write ghost stories inspired by the Gothic horror tales they had been reading while staying in Geneva in the Villa Diodati during an extraordinarily wet and gloomy June. While Mary Shelley's *Frankenstein* is inarguably the most famous novel to come out of that group, and Stoker's *Dracula* is better known, Polidori was the first writer in English literature to create the elegant figure of the undead character who preys physically (including sexually) upon the innocent and unaware.[143] Polidori's Lord Ruthven, a true Byronic vampire, is not, of course, female. That honor belongs to Sheridan LeFanu's lesbian vampire *Carmilla* (1872), who preys not upon men but upon women because she is their mirror image, the image of innate sexual evil.[144] It is probable that this character was the source of the extraordinary and fanciful connection between lesbianism, vampires, and Salome—a connection made by Dr. Cooke in the trial of Maud Allan's libel suit.

Vampire lore seems to have come to the United States from Eastern European immigrants, but substantial literary interest in vampires in America does not emerge until the series known as *The Vampire Chronicles* (1976–2016) by New Orleans author Anne Rice. Another series, *The Southern Vampire Mysteries* (2001–2013), by Charlaine Harris, is also set in the South, in a fictional Louisiana community called Bon Temps, and centers on the relationship between a telepathic waitress, Sookie Stackhouse, and a "gentleman vampire," Bill Compton. A television series, *True Blood*, created by Alan Ball and based on Harris's novels, ran for seven seasons, from 2008

---

142. Yezierska, *Salome of the Tenements*, 158.
143. Barroso de Sant' Anna, *The Vampire*, 32.
144. Dijkstra, *Idols of Perversity*, 341–42; Wikipedia, "Sheridan LeFanu."

to 2014, on HBO.[145] One of the vampires who appeared in and often dominated the fifth season of the show was a two-thousand-year-old vampire, Salome Agrippa, who the series takes pains to establish as *the* (i.e., biblical) Salome. Salome in the series is a true vamp: when she is introduced in the second episode of season 5, she assists in interrogating vampires Bill Compton and Eric Northman, suspected of disloyalty to the Authority, the vampire council that insists on regarding humans merely as prey for the purist blood-sucking "Sanguinistas."[146] In episode 3, she seduces both Bill and Eric, with a view to finding out their secrets. When they realize what she has done, they acknowledge that she is the type of woman who "usually gets what she wants." In the same episode, she also beds her lover, the leader of the Authority, a five-hundred-year-old vampire named Roman Zimojic, who dismisses her concerns for his safety in a possible uprising: "With you as my secret weapon, how could I lose?"

The series often has "origin stories," told either through flashbacks or as straight narration. Salome tells Bill that she was just a girl when she was "delivered" by her mother to her stepfather's bed in a "kind of dance" (i.e., intercourse).[147] Consequently, Salome seems compelled to satisfy her desires through sexual wiles. She is also associated with another biblical—or extrabiblical—character, another sexual predator, Lilith, the legendary first wife of Adam who refused to submit to him and was expelled from paradise, in order to appear forever as a succubus. In *True Blood*, however, she is the "Mother," the Progenitor of the vampire race, created by God in God's image. Adam and Eve were created as prey to feed her. Lilith, however, has suffered the "True Death" by being exposed to the sun, but is still manifested in her blood, kept in a crystal vial revered by Salome. In episode 12 of season 5, Salome says that she regards herself as the "new vessel" for Lilith and her power. She also claims, "I understand a little more about John the Baptist, the first man I killed," admiring him for his "true devotion" to his faith. In the end, however, it is her devotion to Lilith and her blood, together with her "monumental narcissism," that leads to her own "True Death." Believing that she is drinking Lilith's blood and so becoming her "vessel," Salome is tricked by Bill into drinking blood laced with electrolyzed silver

---

145. IMDb, page for *True Blood* (TV Series 2008–2014). Wikipedia, "*True Blood*, https://enwikpedia.org/wiki/True_Blood/.

146. All episodes available on YouTube. Complete information on the series can be found on the *True Blood* Wiki, trueblood.wiki.com/wiki/True_Blood_Wiki/.

147. Lee, "The Dance of Seduction," 6–8.

(a vampire deterrent), and is so debilitated by poisoning that, in a parody of the sex act, Bill is able to drive a stake through her. So, Salome dies, in a much more gruesome (and perhaps in the logic of the series), more fitting way than being crushed to death under Herod's soldiers' shields or falling through ice. In a sense, she is punished for her flagrant exercise of unrepentant and rapacious female sexuality.

QUEERING SALOME IN HARLEM: THE ART OF RICHARD BRUCE NUGENT

Richard Bruce Nugent (1906–1987), artist and writer, an openly and vocally gay member of the cultural élite of the Harlem Renaissance, found in the character of Salome, especially as constructed theatrically by Oscar Wilde and visually by Aubrey Beardsley, a way to express the "fluidity" and "conjectural" nature of gender in the club scene of his day, in a Harlem conflicted between creative transgression and the perceived necessity for racial uplift. According to Ellen McBreen, Nugent's art deliberately evokes Wilde's and Beardsley's Salome, the character's "sexual deviance," and, especially, Wilde's association with homoeroticism. She observes that "unlike the exclusively misogynist representations dominating Symbolist art and literature, the gay subtext of Wilde's play," as interpreted by Nugent, "transforms Salome into a queer heroine."[148] For Nugent, and other, less "out" homosexuals, Salome "distills the loaded tensions between racial and sexual identities in the Harlem Renaissance."[149]

Nugent played with ideas of racial as well as gender performance in a series of drawings from 1930 that he referred to as the "Salome" series, "incorporating biblical themes in which unexpected juxtapositions of color, strongly idiosyncratic stylistic elements, and unconventional composition . . . contrive to stunning effect."[150] His visualizations range from the two Beardsleyesque black-and-white line drawings of *Salome Dancing* (1925–1930), which show a slender Salome, apparently dancing the Dance of the Seven Veils nearly nude: in one, she appears to cast off one of the veils, with her head down; in the other, her head is thrown back and the veil looks like a giant scimitar, nearly bisecting her, perhaps in a reference to John the Baptist's gruesome end. In other drawings, Nugent plays with color—not

148. McBreen, "Biblical Gender Bending," 26.
149. Ibid., 23.
150. Wirth, "Richard Bruce Nugent."

with racial black and white, but with various somewhat unnatural "dyes commonly used to colorize black-and-white photographs."[151] *Untitled* (Salome series, 1930), a drawing typical of many of his female nudes, depicts a woman with pinkish flesh, green pubic hair, a yellowish vagina, and exaggerated breasts with erect nipples. In the same series, Mary Magdalene is depicted with exaggerated sexual characteristics, huge half-lidded eyes, and flowing hair.

Nugent's male nudes, "homoeroticized white male bodies," are less "hyperbolized" in their sexuality, less predatory than objects of predation.[152] Nugent's *Untitled* male nude in this series, usually assumed to be John the Baptist,[153] exhibits "the saint's hesitant masculinity (the flaccid penis?)," as the object of "Salome's forbidden desire,"[154] looking rather pensive and very Caucasian with yellow hair, beard, and pubic hair. An armlet of thorns pierces his arm, which is dripping blood—a possible reference to his death. Like the paired drawings of Salome in her dance, this drawing seems to be paired with another in the series, *Lucifer*, which replicates the coloration of *Untitled*, but with an erect penis, red hair, and the red blood replaced by two red horns on Lucifer's forehead.[155] With these works Nugent recovers Wilde's identification with the transgressive sexuality his Salome represents, and puts it into a gendered, racialized, and drag context.

GLOBALIZING SALOME

Perhaps it remains for a global Salome to have the final word, although the final word, in terms of chronology, may be the German symphonic metal band Xandria's album *Salomé—The Seventh Veil*, even though only the fifth cut on the album specifically refers to Salome. She herself is the "seventh veil," as "both villain and prey," shedding the veils of illusion, innocence, and pride along the way.[156] Another way of looking at a globalized Salome comes from composer Terry Riley, who created a musical piece originally conceived of as a ballet; like Farber's Salome, it belongs to the interpretation

151. McBreen, "Biblical Gender-Bending," 27.
152. Ibid., 25.
153. Smith, "Cultural Studies," 194.
154. McBreen, "Biblical Gender-Bending," 25.
155. Nugent, *Gay Rebel*, 231.
156. Xandria, "Salomé," in *Salomé—The Seventh Veil*, released May 20, 2007. Lyrics from http://www.darklyrics.com/lyrics/Xandria/salometheseventhveil.html/.

of her name as "peace." In his composition *Salome Dances for Peace*, Riley explains that his point of departure is the biblical Salome, "the legendary seductress in King Herod's court who called for the head of John the Baptist to be brought to her on a plate in return for removing her seven veils during a lewd dance." All of that sounds pretty standard, but Riley re-creates Salome's narrative thus: "Peace has been stolen from the earth by dark forces and Salome is chosen to win it back." Salome is summoned back to earth by the Great Spirit, "who sees in her the embodiment of the feminine force." As Riley sees it, "Salome in this case becomes like a goddess who—drawn out of antiquity, having done evil kinds of deeds—reincarnates . . . as a shaman. Riley's music consists of six parts or acts that embrace "jazz, blues, North Indian raga, Middle Easter scales, Minimalist patterns and traditional Western art music."[157]

In part 1, "Anthem of the Great Spirit," Salome is led by sages in a "Peace Dance," in which she receives the "gift of innocence" and develops the discipline to confront and defeat the Wild Talker, representing sexual temptation. She then becomes a warrior, initiated by the shaman Half Wolf. Together, they descend to the Underworld. Their descent may be a nod to the putative origins of the Dance of the Seven Veils, in which the Babylonian goddess Ishtar (Sumerian Inanna) travels to the Underworld to redeem her lover, Tammuz, from the goddess of the dead, her sister Ereshkigal. In this descent, she must remove on every level an item of clothing or jewelry, until she is as naked as the dead.[158] Part 2, "Conquest of the War Demons," depicts a battle in the Underworld, in which "all its fantastic beings" are elevated into the Realm of Light. In part 3, "The Gift," Salome dances around the world. Finally, she is given another mission, "to attract the attention of the world's most powerful leaders." Showing shades of the biblical Salome, she must seduce Bear Father (Russia) and the Great White Father (the United States), leading to the latter's emotional breakdown and a final epiphany in part 4, "The Ecstasy," in which Salome finally succeeds in winning world peace. The final section, part 5, ends with "The Good Medicine Dance," which is a "return to old wisdom and teachings, with the counsel to become guileless, and to pursue self-knowledge." We could say that in Riley's vision, Salome's redemption of the world is ultimately redemption of herself, to fulfill the meaning of her name—peace.

---

157. Riley, interview with Mark Swed, *Salome Dances for Peace*, liner notes.
158. Bentley, *Sisters of Salome*, 30–36.

Reviving Salome

Farewell, Salome. Essentially, you remain an enigma now, as you have for two thousand years. From your first appearance you have puzzled, beguiled, and tempted us to make you in our own image. And yet you still elude us.

Bibliography

Albin, Tania. "Woman at Fin de Siècle: The Creation of the Femme Fatale." English/History of Art 151, Brown University. *The Victorian Web*. http://www.victorianweb.org/gender/albin/1.html/.
Ambrose, Saint, Bishop of Milan. *Select Works and Letters*. NPNF[2] 10. Grand Rapids: Eerdmans, 1955.
American Catholic Quarterly Review. Unsigned review of *Herodias: A Dramatic Poem*, by J. C. Heywood. 13 (1888) 184–85.
"Amy." "Dancing Seductress: Salome—A Literary Adventure in Art History." In *carravagista.com*, November 18, 2011. http://caravaggista.com/2011/11//dancing-seductress-salome/.
Anderson, Janice Capel. "Feminist Criticism: The Dancing Daughter." In *Mark & Method: New Approaches in Biblical Studies*, edited by Janice Anderson Capel and Stephen D. Moore, 111–43. 2nd ed. Minneapolis: Fortress, 2008.
Anselm, Saint. *The Prayers and Meditations of St. Anselm*. With the *Proslogion*. Translated, and with an introduction by Sister Benedicta Ward, SLG. Foreword by R. W. Southern. Penguin Classics. London: Penguin, 1973.
Aristotle. *Generation of Animals*. Translated by A. L. Peck. LCL. Cambridge: Harvard University Press, 1942.
———. *Aristotle. The Politics*. Translated by H. Rackham. LCL 264. London: Heinemann, 1932.
Art, the Bible & the Big Apple. Curated by the staff of the Museum of Biblical Art, New York. "Spotlight: Salome." http://artthebibleandthebigapple.org/2012/09/25/spotlight-salome/.
Atlas Obscura. "The Head of John the Baptist at Amiens Cathedral." https://www.atlasobscura.com/places/the-head-of-st-john-the-baptist-at-amiens-cathedral/.
Ava, of Melk. *Ava's New Testament Narratives: "When the Old Law Passed Away."* Introduction, translation, and notes by James A. Rushing Jr. Medieval German Texts in Bilingual Editions 2. Kalamazoo: Medieval Institute Publications, 2003.
Aysey, Craig. "Salome's Final Monologue." In *Richard Strauss, Salome*, edited by Derrick Puffett, 109–30. Cambridge Opera Handbooks. Cambridge: Cambridge University Press, 1989.
Bach, Alice. "Calling the Shots: Directing Salome's Dance of Death." *Semeia* 74 (1996) 103–26.

Bibliography

———. *Women, Seduction, and Betrayal in Biblical Narrative*. Cambridge: Cambridge University Press, 1997.
Bachman, Gideon. Review of *Salomè*, by Carmelo Bene. *Film Quarterly* 2 (1972–1973) 20–23.
Baert, Barbara. "The Dancing Daughter and the Head of John the Baptist (Mark 6:14–29) Revisited: An Interdisciplinary Approach." *LS* 38 (2014) 5–29.
Bannerman, Henrietta. "A Dance of Transition: Martha Graham's *Herodiade* (1944)." *Dance Research* 24/1 (2006) 1–20.
Barroso de Sant'Anna, Ariel. *The Vampire in Nineteenth-Century English Fiction: The Various Faces of the Other*. PhD diss., Universidade do Estado do Rio de Janeiro, 2005. Livròs Gratis, 2005. http://www.livrosgratis.com.br/.
Becker-Leckrone, Megan. "Salome: The Fetishization of a Textual Corpus." *New Literary History* 26/2 (1995) 239–60.
Bentley, Toni. *Sisters of Salome*. Lincoln: University of Nebraska Press, 2002.
Bernard of Clairvaux, Saint. *Apology*. In *Internet History Sourcebook*. https://sourcebooks.fordham.edu/source/bernard1.asp/.
Bielski, Sarah. "The Femme Fatale as Seen in the Work of J. K. Huysmans, Felicien Rops, and Aubrey Beardsley." *Art Criticism* 1711 (2001) 47–54.
"Black Acts: The Later Years of Aïda Overton Walker (1911–1914)." Yale University Digital Commons Exhibits. http://blackacts.commons.yale.edu/exhibits/show/blackacts/walker/.
Boccaccini. "Category: Salome." In *4 Enoch: The Online Encyclopedia of Second Temple Judaism and Christian Origins*. http://www.4enoch.org/wiki4/index.php?title=Category:Salome_(subject)/.
———. "Erodiade (Herodias/1832 Pellico), play." In *4 Enoch: The Online Encyclopedia of Second Temple Judaism and Christian Origins*. http://www.4enoch.org/wiki4/index.php?title=Erodiade_(Herodias_/_1832_Pellico),_play/.
Bornay, Erika. *Mujeres de la Biblia en la pintura del Barroco: Imágines de la ambiguëdad*. Madrid: Cátedra, 1998.
Bowie-Sell, Daisy. "Yaël Farber: The Director Re-writing the Story of Salome." *WhatsOnStage*. London, West End, 3 May 2017. http://www.whatsonstage.com/london-theatre/news/yael-farber-salome-women-redefining-national-theatre_43487.html/.
Browne, Clare, et al., eds. *English Medieval Embroidery: Opus Anglicanum*. New Haven: Yale University Press, in association with the Victoria and Albert Museum, 2016.
Bruce, F. F. "Herod Antipas, Tetrarch of Galilee and Peraea." *ALUOS* 5 (1963–1965) 6–23.
Brunotte, Ulrike. "'All Jews Are Womanly, but No Women Are Jews': The Femininity Game of Deception; Female Jew, *femme fatale Orientale*, and *belle Juive*." In *Orientalism, Gender, and the Jews: Literary and Artistic Transformations of European National Discourses*, edited by Ulrika Brunotte et al., 195–220. Europäisch-jüdische Studien Beitrage 23. Berlin: de Gruyter Oldenbourg, 2015.
Bryant, Charles, dir. *Salomé*. 1923. Written by Peter M. Winter. Starring Alla Nazimova. PBS broadcast, December 25, 2012. YouTube. https://www.youtube.com/watch?v=lYbJmDzRH68/.
Burton, Nick. "The Gospel according to Saint Matthew (1964)." *Pif Magazine* 20 (Feb. 1999). http://www.pifmagazine.com/1999/02/the-gospel-accordingto-saint-matthew-1964/.
Calvin, John. *Commentary on Matthew, Mark, and Luke*. CCEL 1. https://www.ccel.org/ccel/calvin/calcom31.html/.

Bibliography

———. *Institutes of the Christian Religion*. CCEL. https://www.ccel.org/ccel/calvin/institutes/.
Carnaval. "Roman Dance." http://www.carnaval.com/italy/dance/roman_dance.htm/.
Cavafy, Constantine P. *Before Time Could Change Them: The Complete Poems of Constantine P. Cavafy*. Translated with an introduction and notes by Theoharis Constantine Theoharis. With a foreword by Gore Vidal. New York: Harcourt, 2001.
Chapple, Norma. "Re-(en)visioning Salome: The Salomes of Hedwig Lachmann, Marcus Behmer, and Richard Strauss." MA thesis, University of Waterloo, 2006.
Cicero. *On Old Age, On Friendship, On Divination*. Translated by William Armistead Falconer. LCL. Cambridge: Harvard University Press, 1923.
Classical CD Review.com. Review by R. E. B. *Glazunov: King of the Jews*. http://www.classicalcdreview.com/glazunovking.htm/.
Cobb, L. Stephanie. *Divine Deliverance: Pain and Painlessness in Early Christian Martyr Texts*. The Joan Palevsky Imprint in Classical Literature. Oakland: University of California Press, 2017.
Collins, Adela Yarbro. *Mark: A Commentary*. Hermeneia. Minneapolis: Fortress, 2007.
Colwin, Laurie. *More Home Cooking*. New York: HarperPerennial, 1993.
Corley, Kathleen E. *Private Women, Public Meals: Social Conflict and Women in the Synoptic Tradition*. Peabody, MA: Hendrickson, 1993.
Cotter, Wendy. "The Parable of the Children in the Market-Place, Q (Luke 7:31–35): An Examination of the Parable's Image and Significance." *NovT* 29 (1987) 289–304.
Coulthart, John. "Alla Nazimova's *Salomé*." *Feuilleton* (April 20, 2007). http://www.johncoulthart.com/feuilleton/2007/04/20/alla-nazimovas-salome/.
———. "Steven Berkhoff's *Salomé*." *Feuilleton* (May 17, 2010). http://www.johncoulthart.com/feuilleton/2010/05/17/steven-berkoffs-salome/.
———. "Two Films by Clive Barker." *Feuilleton* (July 14, 2011). http://www.johncoulthart.com/feuilleton/2013/11/14/two-films-by-clive-barker-the-forbidden-and-salome/.
Crawford, Sidnie Ann White. "Esther." In *Women's Bible Commentary*, edited by Carol A. Newsom and Sharon H. Ringe, 131–37. Expanded ed. Louisville: Westminster John Knox, 1998.
Cronin, Richard, et al., eds. *A Companion to Victorian Poetry*. Blackwell Companions to Literature and Culture 15. Oxford: Blackwell, 2002.
Crowther, Bosley. "*Salome* at Rivoli, Stars Rita Hayworth as Enchantress of Biblical Story." *New York Times*, March 25, 1953. Movies section. http://www.nytimes.com/movie/review?res=9804E7D81F3AE23BBC4D51DFB5668388649ED.
Currit, Travis. "*Wilde French Salomé: Une Lange Étrange*; A Strange Tongue; The Francophilie and Francophonie of Oscar Wilde's *Salomé*." http://home.utah.edu/~u0286091/Flaubert.html/.
Décaudin, Michel. "Un Mythe 'fin de siècle: Salomé." *Comparative Literature Studies* 4 (1967) 109–17.
De Man, Paul. *The Post-Romantic Predicament*. Edited by Martin McQuillan. The Frontiers of Theory. Edinburgh: Edinburgh University Press, 2012.
Derrett, J. Duncan M. *The Making of Mark: The Scriptural Bases of the Earliest Gospel*. 2 vols. Shipston-on-Stour: Drinkwater, 1985.
Dewey, Joanna. "The Gospel of Mark." In *Searching the Scriptures*, edited by Elisabeth Schüssler Fiorenza, 470–509. A Feminist Commentary on the Bible 2. New York: Crossroad, 1994.

Bibliography

Dijkstra, Bram. *Idols of Perversity: Fantasies of Feminine Evil in Fin-de-Siècle Culture.* New York: Oxford University Press, 1986.

Dronke, Peter, trans. and ed. *Nine Medieval Latin Plays.* Cambridge Medieval Classics 1. Cambridge: Cambridge University Press, 1994.

Earl, Martin. "John Keats: 'La Belle Dame sans Merci': Beyond Self-Expression." Poem Guide. In *Poetry Foundation,* https://www.poetryfoundation.org/articles/69748/john-keats-la-belle-dame-sans-merci/.

Easton-Flake, Amy. "Harriet Beecher Stowe's Popular Exegesis." Paper presented at the Annual Meeting of the AAR–SBL, Atlanta, GA, November 21, 2005.

Ellmann, Richard. "Overtures to Wilde's *Salomé.*" In *Richard Strauss, Salome,* edited by Derrick Puffett, 21–35. Cambridge Opera Handbooks. Cambridge: Cambridge University Press, 1989.

Erdman, Andrew L. *Blue Vaudeville: Sex, Morals, and the Mass Marketing of Amusement, 1895–1915.* Jefferson, NC: McFarland, 2004.

Eusebius. *Life of Constantine the Great.* In NPNF² 1. New York: Scribner, 1925.

Farber, Yaël. "Walking in the World of Salomé." Directors Word. *Asides,* issue 1 (2015/2016) 9–13. http://www.shakespearetheatre.org/_pdf/asides/Salome.pdf/.

Fewell, Danna Nolan. "Judges." *Women's Bible Commentary,* edited by Carol A. Newsom and Sharon H. Ringe, 73–83. Expanded ed. Louisville: Westminster John Knox, 1998.

Fewell, Danna, and David M. Gunn. "Controlling Perspectives: Women, Men, and the Authority of Violence in Judges 4 and 5." *JAAR* 58 (1990) 389–411.

Ferrebee, Wayne. "Cranach's Obsession with Severed Heads." *Ferrebeekeeper* (blog), June 9, 2011. https://ferrebeekeeper.wordpress.com/2011/06/09/cranachs-obsession-with-severed-heads/.

Field, Michael. "A Dance of Death." In *Poems of Adoration.* 67–70. Edinburgh: Sands, 1912.

Fishbein, Leslie. "Anzia Yezierska, the Sweatshop Cinderella, and the Invented Life." *Studies in American Jewish Literature* 17 (1988) 137–41.

Flaubert, Gustave. *Greatest Works: Madame Bovary, Sentimental Education, November, A Simple Heart, Herodias, and More.* Translated by Eleanor Marx-Aveling. [Cork]: e-artnow e-books, 2015.

———. "Hérodiade." In *Three Tales.* Translated by Arthur McDowall. Introduction by Harry Levin. 124–78. The New Classics. Norfolk, CT: New Directions, 1924.

Friesländer, Elisabet. "The Mantle Dancer in the Hellenistic Period: Glorification of the Himation." In art_book2001.pdf. 1–23. Tel Aviv: Department of Art History, Tel Aviv University, 2001.

Gagnier, Regina A. *Idylls of the Marketplace: Oscar Wilde and the Victorian Public.* Stanford: Stanford University Press, 1986.

Gallagher, Lauren. "Al Pacino Goes Wilde." *San Francisco Examiner,* March 16, 2012. https://archives.sfexaminer.com/sanfrancisco/al-pacino-goes-wilde/Content?oid=2196402/.

Garelick, Rhonda K. *Electric Salome: Loïe Fuller's Performance of Modernism.* Princeton: Princeton University Press, 2007.

Gilman, Sander L. "Salome, Syphilis, Sarah Bernhardt, and the 'Modern Jewess.'" *German Quarterly* 66/2 (1993) 195–211.

Ginzberg, Lewis. *The Legends of the Jews.* 7 vols. Translated by Henrietta Szold. Philadelphia: Jewish Publication Society of America, 1968.

Bibliography

Girard, René. "Scandal and the Dance: Salome in the Gospel of Mark." *New Literary History* 15/2 (1984) 311–24.
Glancy, Jennifer. "Unveiling Masculinity: The Construction of Gender in Mark 6:17–29." *BibInt* 2/1 (1994) 34–50.
Guy, Josephine, and Ian Small. *Studying Oscar Wilde: History, Criticism and Myth. 1880–1920* British Authors Series 22. Greensboro, NC: ELT Press, 2006.
Griffin, Robert. *The Rape of the Lock: Flaubert's Mythic Realism*. French Forum Monographs 70. Lexington, KY: French Forum, 1988.
Haigh, Peter S. "Interview with Brigid Bazlen." *ABC Film Review* (UK). 1962/2.
Hall, Edith, and Rosie Wylos, eds. *New Directions in Ancient Pantomime*. Oxford: Oxford University Press, 2008.
Hanson, K. C. "The Herodians and Mediterranean Kinship. Part 1: Genealogy and Descent." *Biblical Theology Bulletin* 19 (1989) 75–84.
———. "The Herodians and Mediterranean Kinship. Part 2: Marriage and Divorce." *Biblical Theology Bulletin* 19 (1989) 142–51.
Heine, Heinrich. *Atta Troll: A Midsummer Night's Dream*. English translation. http://davidsbuendlerfreehostia.com/troll.htm/
———. "Poem: Donna Clara." In *Poetry Nook*. https://www.poetrynook.com/poem/donna-clara/.
Henzen, Guilelmus, and Iohannes Baptista de Rosi, eds. *Inscriptiones urbis Romae Latinae*. Corpus Inscriptionum Latinarum 6. Berlin: Reinerum, 1876.
Heywood, J. C. *Antonius: A Dramatic Poem*. New York: Hurd & Houghton, 1867.
———. *Herodias: A Dramatic Poem*. New York: Hurd & Houghton, 1867.
———. *Salome, The Daughter of Herodias: A Dramatic Poem*. New York: Putnam, 1862.
Hoffeditz, David M., and Gary E. Yates, "Femme Fatale Redux: Intertextual Connection to the Elijah/Jezebel Narratives in Mark 6:14–29." *BBR* 15 (2003) 199–221.
Holten, Ragnar von. *L'art fantastique de Gustave Moreau*. Paris: Pauvert, 1960.
Huysmans, Joris-Karl. *Against the Grain (À Rebours)*. Translated by John Howard. New York: Three Sirens Press, 1931. With an Introduction by Havelock Ellis and a 1903 Preface by J.-K. Huysmans. Unabridged republication by Rosings Digital Publications, 2013.
Ibn Kathir, Al-Imam. "Prophet Yahya." In *Stories of the Prophets*, 27. Translated by Muhammad Mustapha Beme'ah, Al-Ashar. http://www.islamawareness.net/Prophets/zaraiyah.html/.
Ilan, Tal. "Dance and Gender in Ancient Jewish Sources." *Near Eastern Archaeology* 66 (2003) 135–36.
Jackson, William E. *Reinmar's Women: A Study of the Woman's Song ("Frauenlied" and "Frauentrophe") of Reinmar der Alte*. German Literature and Language Monographs 9. Amsterdam: Benjamins, 1981.
Jacobus de Voragine. *The Golden Legend or Lives of the Saints*. 1st ed., 1470. Translated by William Caxton. 1st ed., 1483. In *Internet Medieval Source Book*, https://sourcebooks.fordham.edu/basis/goldenlegend/.
Janes, Regina. *Losing Our Heads: Beheadings in Literature and Culture*. New York: New York University Press, 2005.
———. "Why the Daughter of Herodias Must Dance." *JSNT* 28/4 (2006) 443–67.
Jerome, Saint. *Against Rufinus*. NPNF[2] 4. Grand Rapids: Eerdmans, 1953.
———. *Letters*. NPNF[2] 6. New York: Scribner, 1912.

BIBLIOGRAPHY

John Chrysostom Saint. *Homilies on the Gospel of St. Matthew.* NPNF[1] 10. Buffalo: Christian Literature, 1888.
Johnson, Marcus. *Salome: An Invitation to the Dance.* Houston: Strategic, 2012.
Jones, Susan. *Literature, Modernism, and Dance.* Oxford: Oxford University Press, 2013.
Josephus, Flavius. *Antiquities of the Jews.* In *The Life and Works of Flavius Josephus.* Translated by William Whiston. Philadelphia: John C. Whiston [1737].
Kadari, Tamar. "Vashti: Midrash and Aggadah." In *Jewish Women's Archive / Jewish Women: A Comprehensive Historical Encyclopedia.* https://jwa.org/encyclopedia/author/kadari-tamar/.
Kazan, George. "The Head of John the Baptist: The Early Evidence. Paper presented at St. John's College, University of Oxford, June 24, 2011.
Keats, John. *Keats' Kingdom.* http://www.keatsian.co.uk/.
———. *Poems by John Keats (1795–1821).* http://www.john.keats.com/.
Kettle, Michael. *Salome's Last Veil: The Libel Trial of the Century.* London: Granada, 1977
King, Phillip J. "The Marzēah: Textual and Archaeological Evidence." *Eretz Israel: Yigal Yadin Memorial Volume* 20 (1989) 98–106.
Kohl, Norbert. *Oscar Wilde: The Works of a Conformist Rebel.* European Studies in English Literature. Cambridge: Cambridge University Press, 2011.
Kraemer, Ross S. "Implicating Herodias and Her Daughter in the Death of John the Baptizer: A (Christian) Theological Strategy?" *JBL* 125/2 (2006) 321–49.
Kramer, Lawrence. "Culture and Musical Hermeneutics: The Salome Complex." *Cambridge Opera Journal* 2/3 (1990) 269–94.
Krasner, David. "Black Salome: Exoticism, Dance, and Racial Myths." In *African American Performance in Theater History: A Critical Reader,* edited by Harry J. Elam Jr. and David Krasner, 192–211. New York: Oxford University Press, 2001.
Kristeva, Julia. *The Severed Head: Capital Visions.* Translated by Jody Gladding. European Perspectives. New York: Columbia University Press, 2011.
Kuryluk, Ewa. *Salome and Judas in the Cave of Sex: The Grotesque: Origins, Iconography, Techniques.* Evanston, IL: Northwestern University Press, 1987.
Kuspit, Donald. *The Dialectic of Decadence: Between Advance and Decline in Art.* 1993. New York: Allworth, 2000.
Laforgue, Jules. *Moralités Légendaires.* Paris: Revue Indépendante, 1887.
Landazuri, Margarita. "Salome (1953)." *TCM (Turner Classic Movies)* Film Article. http://www.tcm.com/this-month/article/156455%7Co/Salome.html/.
Landow, George P. "Aesthetes and Decadents of the 1890s—Points of Departure." In "British and European Aesthetes, Decadents, and Symbolists." *The Victorian Web.* http://www.victorianweb.org/decadence/decadence.html/.
Landy, Marcia. "1923—Movies and the Changing Body of Cinema." In *American Cinema of the 1920s: Themes and Variations,* edited by Lucy Fischer, 95–119. Screen Decades. New Brunswick, NJ: Rutgers University Press, 2009.
Latham, Jackie E. M. "The Bradleys of Birmingham: The Unorthodox Family of Michael Field." *History Workshop Journal* 55/1 (2003) 189–91.
Latimer, Tirza True. "Aubrey Beardsley's *Salomé*: The Daughter of Too Many Mothers' Sons." *Rutgers Art Review* 19 (2001) 25–36.
Lee, Wen-Juenn. "The Dance of Seduction: The Power of Popular Culture in Shaping the Portrayal of Mark's Dancing Daughter in the Bible." *Auckland Theology & Religious Studies* (2016) 1–9.

Bibliography

Lenson, David, trans. "Hérodiade," by Stéphane Mallarmé. *Massachusetts Review* 30 (1989) 573–88.

The Letter of Herod to Pilate. In *The Apocryphal New Testament: A Collection of Apocryphal Christian Literature in an English Translation*, edited by J. K. Elliott, 223–24. Oxford: Clarendon, 1993.

Levine, Amy-Jill. "Matthew." In *Woman's Bible Commentary*, edited by Carol A. Newsom and Sharon H. Ringe, 339–49. Expanded ed. Louisville: Westminster John Knox, 1998.

Lilie, W. "Salome or Herodias?" *ExpT* 65 (1953–1954) 251.

Livy. *The History of Rome (Ab urbe condita)*. Books 38–39. Summaries. With an English translation by Evan T. Sage. LCL. Cambridge: Harvard University Press, 1936.

Longfellow, Henry Wadsworth. *Christus, a Mystery*. Boston: Osgood, 1872.

Lowe, Lisa. "The Orient as Woman in Flaubert's *Salammbô* and "Voyage en Orient." *Comparative Literature Studies* 23/1 (1986) 44–58.

Luther, Martin. "4th Sunday in Advent." In *Sermons on Gospel Texts for Advent, Christmas, and Epiphany*, edited by John Nicholas Lenker, 110–28. Translated by John Nicholas Lenker et al. The Sermons of Martin Luther 1. 1905. Reprint, Grand Rapids: Baker, 1983.

———. "Table Talk." In *LW* 54. Edited and translated by Theodore G. Lappeth. Philadelphia: Fortress 1967.

Luxford, Julian. "Out of the Wilderness: A Fourteenth-Century Drawing of John the Baptist." *Gesta* 49/2 (2010) 137–50.

Luz, Ulrich. *Matthew 8-20: A Commentary*. Translated by James E. Crouch. Hermeneia. Minneapolis: Fortress, 2001.

Magliocco, Sabina. "Who Was Aradia? The History and Development of a Legend." *Pomegranate: The Journal of Pagan Studies* 18 (Feb 2002) 1–14. http://www.jesterbear.com/Aradia/WhoWasAradia.html/.

Mahler, Alma. *Gustav Mahler: Memories and Letters*. Translated by Basil Creighton. Edited by Donald Mitchell. 3rd ed., further enlarged with a new appendix and chronology. London: Murray, 1973.

Mallarmé, Stéphane. "Les fonds dans le ballet." In *Oeuvres completes*, 179–82. Paris: Gallimard, 1979.

Mallarmé, Stéphane, and Henri Mondor. *Correspondence, 1862–1871*. Paris: Gallimard, 1959–1969.

Marcus, Sharon. "Salomé!! Sarah Bernhardt, Oscar Wilde, and the Drama of Celebrity." *Publications of the Modern Language Association* 126/4 (2011) 999–1021.

Marks, Peter. "Salome, We Hardly Knew Ye." Review of Yaël Farber's *Salomé*. *Washington Post* (Oct 14, 2015) Style section. https://www.washingtonpost.com/lifestyle/style/salome-we-hardly-knew-ye/2015/10/14/4af703a4-7221-11e5-9cbb-790369643cf9_story.html?utm_term=.600ada50a744/.

Marshall, Alex. "Donna Clara—Heinrich Heine's Bad Romance." *Oxford German Network* (blog), June 12, 2016. https://oxfordgermannetwork.wordpress.com/2016/06/12/donna-clara-heinrich-heines-bad-romance/.

Matthieu, Pierre-Louis. *Gustave Moreau*. Translated by James Emmons. Boston: New York Graphic Society, 1976.

McBreen, Ellen. "Biblical Gender Bending in Harlem: The Queer Performance of Nugent's *Salome*." *Art Journal* 57/3 (1998) 22–28

Bibliography

McKenna, Neil. *The Secret Life of Oscar Wilde: An Intimate Biography*. New York: Basic Books, 2005.
Meltar, Françoise. *Salome and the Dance of Writing: Portraits of Mimesis in Literature*. Chicago: University of Chicago Press, 1987.
Melz, Detlef. *Das protestantische Drama: evangelisches Theatre in der Reformationzeit und im konfessionellen Zeitalter*. Cologne: Böhlau, 2013.
Meyers, Carol. "Women with Hand-Drums, Dancing." *Jewish Women's Archive / Jewish Women: A Comprehensive Historical Encyclopedia*. https://jwa.org/encyclopedia/article/women-with-hand-drums-dancing-bible/.
Murray, M. A. "Ancient and Modern Ritual Dances in the Near East." *Folklore* 26/4 (1955) 401–9.
Museo Nacional del Prado, Madrid. "Salome—Collections—Titian." https://www.museodelprado.es/en/the-collection/art-work/salome/0f359b90-2055-4326-bbbe-775dbfa7c504/.
Neginsky, Rosina. *Salome: The Image of a Woman Who Never Was; Salome: Nymph, Seducer, Destroyer*. Newcastle, UK: Cambridge Scholars, 2013.
Newsom, Carol A., and Sharon H. Ringe, eds. *Women's Bible Commentary*. Expanded ed. Louisville: Westminster John Knox, 1998.
Nicephorus Callistus Xanthopoulos. *Ecclesiastical History*. Patrologia Graeca 145. Edited by J.-P. Migne. Paris: Migne, 1857–1886.
Niditch, Susan. "Eroticism and Death in the Tale of Jael." In *Gender and Difference in Ancient Israel*, edited by Peggy L. Day. 43–57. Minneapolis: Fortress, 1989.
Nugent, Richard Bruce. *Gay Rebel of the Harlem Renaissance; Selections from the Works of Richard Bruce Nugent*. Edited with an introduction by Thomas H. Wirth and a foreword by Henry Louis Gates, Jr. Durham: Duke University Press, 2002.
Oates, Joyce Carol. "The Mystery of JonBenét Ramsey." *New York Review of Books*, June 24, 1999. http://www/nybooks.com/articles/.
Olaf, Linton. "Parable of the Children's Game." *NTS* 22 (1976) 159–79.
Pacino, Al, dir. and writer. *Wilde Salomé*. Produced by Barry Navidi. Produced by Stonelock Pictures, Salome Productions, and Sneaky Pete Productions, 2011.
———. *Wilde Salomé* interview. Uploaded by pacinolove. July 25, 2012. http://www.youtube.com/watch?v=7CFaPWqPFL2A/.
Passolini, Pier Paolo, dir. *The Gospel according to St. Matthew*. An Arco Film. Produced by Lux Compagnie Cinématographique de France. Distributed by Titanus Distribuzione, 1964. 1 DVD released July 2008 by Legend Films.
Petzer, Tatiana. "Veils in Action: The 'Oriental Other' and Its Performative Deconstruction in Modern Fashion and Art." In *Orientalism, Gender, and the Jews: Literary and Artistic Transformations of European National Discourses*, edited by Ulrike Brunotte et al., 243–67. Europäisch-jüdische Studien 23. Berlin: de Gruyter Oldenbourg, 2015.
Phelan, Anthony. *Reading Heinrich Heine*. Cambridge Studies in German. Cambridge: Cambridge University Press, 2007.
Plaskow, Judith. "The Wife/Sister Stories: Dilemmas of the Jewish Feminist." In *Speaking of Faith: Global Perspectives on Women, Religion and Social Change*, edited by Diana Eck and Devaki Jain, 122–29. Philadelphia: New Society, 1986.
Plutarch. *Titus Flamininus*. In *Plutarch's Lives*, 10:322–87. With an English translation by Bernadette Perrin. 11 vols. LCL. Cambridge: Harvard University Press, 1921.
Poplin, Jeff. "Post-Biblical Traditions on John the Baptizer." Class website for James D. Tabor, *The Jewish Roman World of Jesus*, University of North Carolina–Charlotte, 1998.

Bibliography

https://clas-pages.uncc.edu/james-tabor/christian-origins-and-the-new-testament/post-biblical-traditions-on-john-the-baptizer/

Praz, Mario. *The Romantic Agony*. With a new foreword by Frank Kermode. Oxford Paperbacks. 2nd ed. London: Oxford University Press, 1970.

Primorac, Yelena. "Illustrating Wilde: An Examination of Aubrey Beardsley's Interpretation of Salomé." *The Victorian Web*. http://www.victorianweb.org/art/illustration/beardsley/primorac.html/.

Procopius of Caesarea. *The Secret History*. Translated by Richard Atwater. Chicago: Covici, 1927. Reprinted, Ann Arbor: University of Michigan Press, 1962. In *Medieval Sourcebook: Procopius: Secret History*. https://sourcebooks.fordham.edu/basis/procop-anec/.

Pseudo-Jerome. *Expositions of the Four Gospels*. PL 30. Edited by J.-P. Migne. Paris: 1844–1864.

Puchner, Martin. *Stage Fright: Modernism, Anti-theatricality, and Drama*. Baltimore: Johns Hopkins University Press, 2002.

Puffett, Derrick. "Appendix A." In *Richard Strauss, Salome*, edited by Derrick Puffett, 165–67. Cambridge Opera Handbooks. Cambridge: Cambridge University Press, 1989.

———. "Introduction." In *Richard Strauss, Salome*, edited by Derrick Puffett, 1–10. Cambridge Opera Handbooks. Cambridge: Cambridge University Press, 1989.

———, ed. *Richard Strauss, Salome*. Cambridge Opera Handbooks. Cambridge: Cambridge University Press, 1989.

Pym, Anthony. "The Importance of Salome: Approaches to a Fin-de-Siècle Theme." *French Forum* 14/3 (1989) 311–22.

Réau, Louis. *Iconografía del arte Cristiano, Iconografía de la Biblia*. 2 vols. Barcelona: Serbal, 1996.

Reed, Victoria S. "Rogier van der Weyden's 'Saint John Triptych' for Miraflores and a Reconsideration of Salome." *Oud Holland* 115 (2001–2002) 1–14.

Renan, Ary. *Gustave Moreau (1826–1898)*. Paris: Gazette des Beaux-Arts, 1900.

Richardson, LeeAnne. "Michael Field's 'A Dance of Death.'" *Nordlit* 28 (2011) 70–77.

Riley, Terry. *Salome Dances for Peace*. Performed by the Kronos Quartet. Recorded August 1988. 2 CD's. Liner notes by Terry Riley and Mark Swed. 79217-1 Elektra Nonesuch. New York: Elektra Nonesuch, 1989.

Rodney, Nanette B. "Salome." *Metropolitan Museum of Art Bulletin* 11/7 (1953) 190–200.

Ross, Leslie. *Medieval Art: A Topical Dictionary*. Westport, CT: Greenwood, 1996.

Rottenberg, Catherine. "*Salome of the Tenements*, the American Dream, and Class Performativity." *American Studies* 45/1 (2004) 65–83.

Sacred Destinations. "The Great Mosque of Damascus." http://www.sacred-destinations.com/syria/damascus-umayyad-mosque/.

Said, Edward W. *Orientalism*. 25th ann. ed., with a new preface by the author. New York: Vintage, 1979.

Salamensky, S. I. "Oscar Wilde's 'Jewish Problem': Salomé, the Ancient Hebrew and the Modern Jewess." *Modern Drama* 55/2 (2012) 197–215.

Sammons, Jeffrey L. *Heinrich Heine: A Modern Biography*. Princeton: Princeton University Press, 1979.

Saura Atarés, Carlos, dir. and writer. *Salomé*. Distributed by Prestige Films, 2002.

Scanlon, Joan, and Richard Kerridge. "Spontaneity and Control: The Uses of Dance in Late Romantic Literature." *Journal of the Society for Dance Research* 6/1 (1988) 30–44.

Bibliography

Schüssler Fiorenza, Elisabeth, ed. *But She Said: Feminist Practices of Biblical Interpretation.* Boston: Beacon, 1992.
Seidel, Linda. "Salome and the Canons." *Women's Studies* 11/1–2 (1984) 29–66.
Showalter, Elaine. *Sexual Anarchy: Gender and Culture at the Fin de Siècle.* New York: Viking, 1990.
Silvani, Giovanna, and Vanja Strukelj. "The Legend of Salome in Nineteenth-Century Literature and Art." In *Depicting Desire: Gender, Sexuality, and the Family in Nineteenth-Century Europe; Literary and Artistic Perspectives,* edited by Rachel Langford, 105–20. European Connections 21. Bern: Lang, 2005.
Skaggs, Carmen Trammell. "Modernity's Revision of the Dancing Daughter: The Salome Narrative of Wilde and Strauss." *College Literature* 29 (2002) 124–39.
Smith, Abraham. "Cultural Studies: Making Mark." In *Mark & Method: New Approaches in Biblical Studies,* edited by Janice Capel Anderson and Stephen Moore, 181–209. 2nd ed. Minneapolis: Fortress, 2008.
Smith, Geoffrey Chipps. *The Northern Renaissance.* London: Phaidon, 2004.
Socrates Scholasticus. *Church History* 305–419. In *Socrates and Sozomenius: Ecclesiastical Histories.* NPNF². Buffalo: Christian Literature, 1890.
Sozomen. *Church History, from A.D. 323—425.* In *Socrates and Sozomenius: Ecclesiastical Histories.* NPNF² 2. Buffalo: Christian Literature Publishing, 1890.
Spencer, F. Scott. *Dancing Girls, Loose Ladies, and Women of the Cloth: The Women in Jesus' Life.* New York: Continuum, 2004.
Starnaman, Sabrina. "Yezierska's Salome and Wilde's Salomé: Yezierska's Salome of the Tenements and Wilde's Salomé." October 7, 2009. http://sabrinastarnaman.com/2009/10/07/salome-and-yezierskas-salome-of-the-tenements/
Stern, Kimberly Jo, ed. *Salome,* by Oscar Wilde. Broadview Editions. Peterborough, ON: Broadview, 2015.
Stevens, Jennifer. "The Fifth Gospel of Oscar Wilde." In *The Historical Jesus and the Literary Imagination, 1860–1920,* 139–79. English Association Studies 3. Liverpool: Liverpool University Press, 2010.
Stirgis, Matthew. *Aubrey Beardsley: A Biography.* London: Overlook, 1998.
Stocker, Margaret. *Judith, Sexual Warrior: Women, and Power in Western Culture.* New Haven: Yale University Press, 1998.
Stowe, Harriet Beecher. *Woman in Sacred History: A Series of Sketches Drawn from Scriptural, Historical, and Legendary Sources.* New York: Ford, 1873.
Streete, Gail P. "Herodias' Daughter's Dance Recital." Paper presented at the Society of Biblical Literature Annual Meeting, Atlanta, GA, Nov. 21, 2015.
———. *Redeemed Bodies: Women Martyrs in Early Christianity.* Louisville: Westminster John Knox, 2009.
———. "Salomé as History and Fetish." *Asides,* issue 1 (2015/2016) 14–17. http://www.shakespearetheatre.org/_pdf/asides/Salome.pdf/.
———. *The Strange Woman: Power and Sex in the Bible.* Louisville: Westminster John Knox, 1997.
Tertullian. *Apology. De Spectaculis.* Translated by T. R. Glover. LCL. London: Heinemann, 1931.
Than, Ker. "John the Baptist's Bones Found?" *National Geographic,* June 18, 2012. https://news.nationalgeographic.com/news/2012/06/120618-john-the-baptist-bones-jesus-christ-bible-bulgaria-science-higham/.

BIBLIOGRAPHY

Thuleen, Nancy. "*Salomé*: A Wildean Symbolist Drama." Website article, December 19, 1995. http://www.nthuleen.com/papers/947paperprint.html/.
True Blood Wiki. http://www.trueblood//wikia.com/wiki/TrueBlood_Wiki/.
Vander Stichele, Caroline, and Todd Penner. *Contextualizing Gender in Early Christian Discourse: Thinking beyond Thecla.* London: T. & T. Clark, 2009.
Vaughan, Henry. *Silex scintillans.* In *The Works of Henry Vaughan*, vol. 2. Edited by Leonard Cyril Martin. Oxford: Clarendon, 1914.
Visual Arts Encyclopedia. "Gustave Moreau, French Symbolist Painter: Salomé Paintings." http://www.visual-arts-cork.com/famous-artists/gustave-moreau.htm#Salomé/.
Voyer, Cécile. "Le corps du péché. La répresentation de Salomé au Moyen Âge." In *La rumeur Salomé*, edited by David Hamidovic, 69–100. Histoire. Paris: Cerf, 2013.
Wailes, Stephen L. "Hans Sachs, John the Baptist, and the Dark Days in Nuremberg, ca. 1548." *German Life and Letters* 52 (1999) 399–411. http://onlinelibrary.wiley.com/wo11/doi/10.1111/14680483.00142.
Walker Vadillo, Mónica Ann. "Salomé: La joven que baila." *Revista Digital de Iconografia Medieval* 8 (2016) 88–107. https://www.academia.edu/26777702/Salomé._La_joven_que_baila. English version, mawalko1@ghis.ucm.es
Walsh, Carey Ellen. "Under the Influence: Trust and Risk in Biblical Drinking." *JSOT* 90 (2000) 13–29.
Wasserman, Suzanne. "Theda Bara (1890–1955)." In *Jewish Women's Archive / Jewish Women: A Comprehensive Historical Encyclopedia*, http://jwa.org//encyclopedia//article/bara-theda/.
Webb, Ruth. "Dance in the Ancient Mediterranean: Roman Period, Part Two." In The Raqs Sharqi Society Newsletter *Events* (May–Aug 2002) 1-2. http://www.raqssharqisociety.org/Dance%20in%20the%20Ancient%20Med%20Part%20Two.pdf/.
———. *Demons and Dancers: Performance in Late Antiquity.* Cambridge: Harvard University Press, 2008.
Weintraub, Stanley, ed. *The Yellow Book, Quintessence of the Nineties.* Garden City, NY: Doubleday, 1964.
Wikipedia. "Alice Guszalewicz." http://en.wikipedia.org/wiki/Alice_Guszalewicz/.
———. "Brigid Bazlen." http://en.wikipedia.org/wiki/Brigid_Bazlen/.
———. "Flemming Flindt." https://en.wikipedia,org./wiki/Flemming_Flindt/.
———. "Heinrich Heine." http://enwikipedia.org/wiki/Heinrich_Heine/.
———. "Judith Slaying Holofernes (Artemisa Gentileschi)." https://en/wikipedia.org/wiki/Judith_Slaying_Holofernes_(Artemisia_Gentileschi)/.
———. "Salome." https://en.wikipedia.org/wiki/Salome/.
———. "*Salome* (opera)." http://en.wikipedia.org/wiki/Salome(opera)/.
———. "*Salome* (opera), Performance History." https://en.wikipedia.org/wiki/Salome_(opera)#performance_history/.
———. "Sheridan LeFanu." https://enwikipedia.org/wiki/Sheridan_Le_Fanu/.
———. "*True Blood*." https://enwikpedia.org/wiki/True_Blood/.
———. "The Whore of Babylon." http://en/kikipedia.org/wiki/Whore_of_Babylon/.
Wilde, Oscar. *Salomé: A Tragedy in One Act.* London: Matthews & Lane, 1894.
———. Review of *Salome*, by J. C. Heywood. The Poet's Corner. *Pall Mall Gazette*, February 19, 1888. London: Methuen, 1908.
Wilentz, Gay. "Introduction." In *Salome of the Tenements*, by Anna Yezierska, ix–xxvi. Urbana: University of Illinois Press, 1995.
Wilhelm, Kurt. *Richard Strauss: An Intimate Portrait.* New York: Rizzoli, 1989.

BIBLIOGRAPHY

Williamson, John. "Critical Reception." In *Richard Strauss, Salome*, edited by Derrick Puffett, 131–44. Cambridge Opera Handbooks. Cambridge: Cambridge University Press, 1989.

Wirth, Thomas H. "Richard Bruce Nugent—Harlem Butterfly." http://www.brucenugent.com/About%20Frameset.htm/.

Xandria. *Salomé—The Seventh Veil*. Drakkar Entertainment. Released May 20, 2007. CD.

Yezierska, Anna. *Salome of the Tenements*. Introduction by Gay Wilentz. 1923. Urbana: University of Illinois Press, 1995.

Zagona, Helen G. *The Legend of Salome and the Principle of Art for Art's Sake*. Geneva: Droz, 1960.

Index

Readers Note: Herodias's daughter, unnamed in the original Gospel narratives, is indexed under "Salome/Herodias's daughter". She is referred to as Salome in the subentries.

Abbey of St-Jean-sur-la-Celle, Amiens, missal from, 2n2, 49
adultery
   by Herod and Herodias, 5–6, 21, 26, 35–36, 44, 58, 66, 90
   and the "outsider" woman stereotype, 35
   as theme in Wilde's *Salome*, 80
African American actresses/dancers
   in Bene's *Salome*, 116
   in Walker's *Bandana Land*, 101–2
Agnes (saint), virginity of, 44
Ahab, 33–35. *See also* Jezebel
Ahasuerus, 18, 26–28. *See also* Esther
Allan, Maud
   accusations of lesbianism against, 101
   interpretations of Salome's dance, 100
   lawsuit against Pemberton-Billing, 101
   and linking of vampish behavior with lesbianism, 120
   United States tour with *Vision of Salomé*, 100
allegory
   in Heine's "Sommernachstraum," 65–66
   in the Littlemore manuscript sword dance illustration, 50–51
   and prefiguration, 55–56
   and Pseudo-Jerome's interpretation of the Johns beheading, 57–58
   and Renaissance interpretations of the Scriptures, 55–56
Almodóvar, Agustin, 117
Almodóvar, Pedro, 115, 117
Ambrose, Saint, 44
American Catholic Quarterly Review, review of Heywood's poems from *Salome*, 89
Amiens Cathedral, France, fragment of John the Baptist's head in, 39
Amnon-Absalom story, 25–26
Anderson, Janice Capel
   on interconnections between Esther, Judith, Salome and Jezebel, 33n51
   on Salome as a male invention, 10
Anka, Paul, 117
Anselm, Saint (*Prayers and Meditations*), 49–51
"Anthem of the Great Spirit" (Riley; musical composition), 124
The Antiquities of the Jews (Josephus), 13

Index

anti-Semitism, 67. *See also* Jews, Jewish traditions
Antoninus (Heywood), 8, 89
Apocryphal Acts of John, Jesus's circle dance in, 21
apocryphal literature (New Testament), sources and intentions, 53
Apology (Bernard of Clairvaux), 47
Apology against Rufinus (Jerome), 42
The Apparition (Moreau; drawing)
  description, 71–72
  as theme in Huysmans's *À Rebours*, 77–79
Arcadia, as a Romantic concept, 63
À Rebours (Against the Grain, Huysmans; novel)
  homages to Decadent/Symbolic writers in, 78–79
  Moreau's Salome drawings as theme in, 77–79
  sexualized Salome in, 7
Aretas, Herod's war with, Herod's war with, 14–15, 20–21, 41, 73
Aristotle, 41
art
  dedication to, as theme, 93–95, 102, 107–8, 112–13
  as didactic, Lutheran view, 58
asceticism, 38, 44, 52
Atta Troll (Heine; poem)
  conflation of folklore and folk deities with the story of John the Baptist, 64
  culturally European male perspective in, 67–68
  Herodias's love for John in, 42
  linking of eroticism and death in, 65
  Orientalized description of Salome, 66
  sexualized Salome in, 7
Augustinian Order, 47
Ava of Melk, 48–49
Aysey, Craig, 88

Bach, Alice, 10, 19–20, 75n65
Bakst, Léon, 99
Ball, Alan, 120–21
Ballets Russes, 99
Bandana Land (Walker; dance), 101–2
banquets. *See also specific works of art and literature*
  beheadings associated with in Rome, 23–24
  Biblical depictions, 25
  drunken, sexual entertainment at, 44
  Esther's, parallels to Herod's, 26–28
  exclusion of non-slave women from, 23
  Greco-Roman, as decadent, 22–25
  Herod's, 22, 25, 45–46, 46n27, 74
  Jael's, 30
  Judith's, 32
  Roman customs surrounding, 22–23
Bara, Theda (Theodosia Goodman)
  career as "The Vamp," 119
  in silent film version of Wilde's *Salomé*, 105–6, 115
Barker, Clive, 116
Basilica of San Marco, Venice, 52–53
Bazlen, Brigid, 115
Beardsley, Aubrey
  illustrations for *Salomé*, 86–87
  influence on Rambova, 106
  J'ai Baisé ta Bouche, Iokanaan (The Climax), 86
beheading, John the Baptist's. *See also* head, John the Baptist's
  allegorical interpretation, 57–58
  in Flaubert's "Hérodiade," 75–76
  as focus of Renaissance portrayals, 56
  historical context, 37
  as presentiment of the Eucharist, 57
  Pseudo-Jerome's symbolic interpretation, 57–59

Index

purposeful blaming of Herod for, 40–41
Salome's repentance for, in Heywood's portrayal, 93
Salome's turning away from, in Renaissance portrayals, 56
scriptural accounts of, 1–2, 5–6, 15
stage directions for, in Wilde's *Salomé*, 84–85
as subversion of male "headship," 41
as symbol of John's difference from Jesus, 40
as theme in Josephus's *Antiquities*, 14
as way of making him distinct from Jesus, 40
and Yeats's use of beheading theme, 104
beheading, Salome's
 apocryphal legends about, 93–94
 Field's portrayal of, 94
 in Xanthopoulos's narrative, 54, 94
The Beheading of John (Sachs; play), 60
The Beheading of Saint John the Baptist (Dürer; drawing), 59
Behmer, Marcus, 88
Bene, Carmelo, 116
Bentley, Toni
 on Allan's lawsuit, 101
 on the female body as powerful and guilt-free, 11
 on length of dance in Strauss's opera, 96n1
 on Salome's "artistic hibernation," 62
Berkoff, Steven, 116–17
Bernard of Clairvaux, 47
Bernhardt, Sarah, 96–97
the Bible, Scripture. *See also specific books and narratives*
 allegorical reading of, during the Renaissance, 55–56
 apocryphal material, 53

banquets in, 25
and the beheading of John the Baptist, 1–2
dance/dancing in, 20
portrayal of religious differences, 35
the story of Esther, 26–27
the story of Jael, 30
the story of Jezebel, 33–34
the story of Judith, 29–32
warnings about excessive drinking, 25–27, 25n35
The Big Fisherman (Douglas; movie), 113–14
Blackton, J. Stuart, 105
Boccaccini, Gabriele, 4n7
Bock, Artur, 100
Borsage, Frank, 113
Bradley, Katherine. *See* Field, Michael
Bruce, F. F., 19
Burgkemair, Hans the Elder, 60
Burton, Richard, 113

Calvin, John, 60
camel's hair, association with John the Baptist, 51
"Canticle of Saint John" (Mallarmé; poem), 76
Carmilla (LeFanu; novel), 120
Cathedral of Rouen, Salome bas-relief, 49
Cathedral of Saint Étienne, chapter-room, Toulouse, Salome sculptures, 47–48
Cavafy, Constantine, 11
Chartier, Alain, 64
Chartres, France, illumination depicting Herod's banquet, 46, 46n27
child/innocent, Salome as
 in Allan's portrayal, 100
 Bach's view, 10, 19–20, 75n65
 Bruce's view, 19
 Chrysostom's view, 18
 Corley's view, 19

Index

child/innocent, Salome as (cont.)
   eroticizing of, and JonBenet Ramsey, 3–4
   in Flaubert's portrayal, 75, 75n65
   in Fuller's portrayal, 98, 100
   in the Gospels of Mark and Matthew, 6, 17–18n6, 17–20
   in Mallarmé's portrayal, 76
   in Moreau's portrayal, 72–73
children in the marketplace parable, 19
Christ
   emphasis on, in Heywood's poetry, 90–91
   John as forerunner of, 15, 38, 40, 106, 113
   and physical suffering as mark of faith, 38
   promise of, as transcending Jewish law, 41
Christian martyr, Salome as
   in Farber's portrayal, 118–19
   in Fuller's portrayal, 99–100
   in Heywood's portrayal, 8, 54, 58, 90, 93
   in Longfellow's poem, 90
   in Yezierska's portrayal, 112–13
Christus: A Mystery (Longfellow; poem), 90
Chrysostom, John, 18, 42n15, 43–44
Church History (Sozomen), 39
Church of the Holy Apostles, Thessaloniki, fresco showing Salome's dance, 52
Church of the Holy Sepulcher, Jerusalem, relics at, 39
Cianma, Anna Jo, 116
Cicero, 23–24
Cistercian Order, 47
Collins, Adela Yarbro, 10–11n29
Colwin, Laurie, 4
Confessions (Heine; autobiography), 67
Constantine, 37
Constantinople, John's head in, 39, 46
Cooke, Serrell, 101, 120
Cooper, Edith. *See* Field, Michael

1 Corinthians 11:3, 41
Corley, Kathleen, 19
corruption/decadence theme. *See also* Decadence/Symbolism
   and decadence in Huysmans's *À Rebours*, 77–78
   in Nazimova's *Salomé*, 106
Counter-Reformation, portrayals of Salome during, 59
courtship dances, 22
Cranach, Lucas the Elder, 58–59
Crowther, Bosley, 114

dance, dancing
   as art, and the imperative to dance, 93–95
   decadent, in the Esther commentaries, 27
   and *jongleuresses/jongleresses* (street dancers), 2, 2n2, 48–50, 75n63.
   naked, 64, 99
   and *saltatriculae*, 23n28
   by sexual slaves/prostitutes, 23, 44–45, 97
   types of, in the ancient world, 20–22
   victory dances, 20, 52–53
dance by Salome/Herodias's daughter. *See also* Salome/Herodias's daughter; veils *and specific works of art and literature*
   as acrobatic, 48–49, 75, 75n65
   ambiguity of, 19–20
   as baptismal "Dance of Life," 118–19
   depictions of, in the Basilica of San Marcos, 52–53
   early Christian/Medieval portrayals, 46–47, 46n27, 21n21, 49–52, 52n49
   fatality of, 21
   Flamenco/Spanish versions, 117
   as innocent, non-erotic, 10, 18–19

Index

as lustful/decadent, 44,
mantle dance, 21–22
movie portrayals, 113–15
Orientalizing/eroticizing of
 ("Dance of the Seven Veils"),
 2–3, 20, 50, 68
original celebratory setting for,
 20–23, 36
Renaissance and Reformation
 portrayals, 56–59, 61
and Riley's *Salome Dances for
 Peace*, 123–24
Rubenstein's version, 99–100
and "Salomania," 8
semi-nude/nude performances,
 99
in Strauss's *Salomé*, 7, 87–88,
 96n1
vaudeville and cabaret versions,
 87, 99–100
in Wilde's *Salomé*, 3, 7, 84
"A Dance of Death" (Field; poem)
 description of Salome's daughter's
  death, 53n55
 influence of, in *Salome of the
  Tenements*, 108
 portrayal of a repentant Salome,
  54
 Salome's death by decapitation
  in, 9
 as sympathetic portrayal, 93–94
Dance of Salome (bas relief, Rouen
 Cathedral), 49
The Dance of the Seven Veils. *See*
 dance by Salome/Herodias's
 daughter; veils
"Dance on Little Girl" (Anka; song),
 117
d'Anna, Claude, 116
"The Daughter of Herodias" (Stowe;
 biographical sketch), 8–9,
 54n57, 90
"The Daughter of Herodias" (Vaughn;
 poem), 9, 54n57, 94
Decadence/Symbolism. *See also
 Salomé* (Wilde)
 characteristics, 72, 77, 79

in Field's "A Dance of Death," 94
in Flaubert's "Hérodiade," 73
in Huysmans's *À Rebours*, 78–79
in Laforgue's "Salomé," 77
preoccupation with Salome's
 sexuality, 72, 76
in Russell's *Salome's Last Dance*,
 116–17
in Strauss's *Salomé*, 88–89
The Decapitation of Salome (Wilde;
 play), 93–94
defiance, in Field's "A Dance of
 Death," 95
Denker, Henry, 114
De Senectute (*On Old Age*, Cicero;
 essay), 23–24
desert monastics, 38
Des Esseintes (character in
 Huysmans's *À Rebours*),
 77–79
desire, conquered/thwarted. *See also*
 the femme fatale
 as focus of Wilde's *Salomé*, 79–80
 Keats's emphasis on, 64–65
 by the Lingfield John the Baptist,
  51–52
 links with death, 65, 77, 79, 86,
  119
 as theme in *Atta Troll*, 66
de Voragine, Jacobus, 39n7
Dewey, Joanna, 10, 25
Dewey, John, 108
Diana (goddess), linking with
 Herodias, 42, 63–65, 71
Dietrich, Veit, 60
Dijksra, Bram
 on Pell's painting of Salome as
  feminist, 11
 on Salome as the "idol of
  perversity," 7
dinner parties, aristocratic (*deipnon*),
 sexual entertainment at, 23.
 See also banquets
disjecta membra (body parts of
 martyrs), veneration of, 38
disobedience, Vashti's, 26–27
Douglas, Lloyd C., 113

143

Index

Douglas, Lord Alfred, 86
Dracula (Stoker; novel), 119–20
drinking, drunkenness, 25–27, 25n35, 32, 36, 43–44, 83
Dürer, Albrecht, 59

Easter pageants, 1–2
Edict of Tolerance, 37
Elijah, parallels with John the Baptist, 33–34. *See also* Jezebel narrative
Ellman, Richard, 90n141
Ephesians 5:25–33, 41
Erodiade (*Herodias*; Pellico), 62–63
eroticism, erotic desire. *See also* Decadence/Symbolism; Orientalism, Orientalizing; Romanticism; Salomé (Wilde)
  and John the Baptist's hair, 56, 82
  homoeroticism, 122–23
  linking desire with death, 65, 106, 119
  linking with innocence, 3–4
  as powerful/positive force, 11
  Salome's, 7–8, 33, 44, 46–47, 56, 65, 67, 79, 96, 101
Esther, story of, as precursor to Salome's story, 18, 26–28
Esther 1:8–9, 18n10, 26–27
Esther 2:3, 18
Esther 2:9, 25–27
Esther 2:18–23, 27
Esther 5:5, 28–29
Esther 7:4, 28
Esther Rabbah, Vashti's disobedience in, 26–27
Eucharist, 45, 51, 57
Eudoxia, Chrysostom's conflicts with, 43
"The Eve of St. Martin" (Keats; poem), 65
exile
  Herod's and Herodias's, 41, 41n11
  as isolation, emptiness theme in Symbolism, 77
  as theme in Field's poem, 95
  as theme in Sach's tragedy, 60–61
Exodus 15:20–22, 20

faeries, 64
Farber, Yaël, 8, 118–19
The Feast of Herod (Rubens; painting), 56–59
females/women. *See also* the femme fatale
  chastity as power, 93
  Galilean vs. Herodian, 40
  mystical power, 69, 121
  outsider women, 35
  Orientalized, *la belle juive*, 50, 66, 64, 68–70, 100, 105–6
  and the power of the female body, 10–11, 21n23, 28–29, 35, 41, 61, 78, 81, 91
  sexual slaves, 23, 45, 44–45, 97
feminist analysis
  and inherent misogyny on the Gospel texts, 10
  interpretation of the Esther story, 28
the femme fatale. *See also la belle juive* (the "beautiful Jewess"); the dance; the Vamp (vampire)
  and the conflation of desire and death, 65, 79, 86, 119
  Esther as, 26, 31
  the "fatal attraction" theme, 67
  foreign women as, in the Hebrew Bible, 35
  as glamorous, in film versions, 98, 114
  Jael as, 30–31
  Judith as, 32–33
  la belle dame sans merci, 64
  importance of the veil, 68–69
  and the Orientalized Jewish seductress, 50, 64, 66, 68–70, 98, 100

Index

Salome's development into, 7–8, 36, 63, 65, 98, 114–15
and sexual predation, 43–44, 77, 119, 121
and seduction as form of power, 10, 21n23, 28–29, 35, 78, 81, 91
Fey Aboundia/Domina Abundia, 64
Field, Michael (Katherine Bradley and Edith Cooper)
"A Dance of Death," 9, 53n55, 54, 108
and the dignity of the passionate artist, 93–95
sympathetic portrayal of Salome, 8–9, 93–94
Finney, Albert, 117
Flamininus, Lucius Quinctius, 23–24
Flaubert, Gustave
"Hérodiade," 73–74
Huysmans's admiration for, 78–79
influence on Moreau's depictions of Salome, 71
influence on Wilde, 68
interest in historical verisimilitude, 73n49
Salammbô as precursor for, 70
sexualized portrayal of Salome, 7
travels in the Middle East, understanding of veils and veiling, 69
use of Decadent themes in, 73
Flavius Josephus. *See* Josephus
Flindt, Vivi, 99
Fokine, Michael, 99
folklore, Romantic interest in, 63–64
A Fool There Was (silent movie), 119
Fouéré, Olwen, 118
From the Founding of the City (Livy), 24
Fourth Crusade, retrieval of relics during, 46
Frankenstein (Shelley; novel), 120
Fremstad, Olive, 88–89
Friesländer, Elisabet, 21–22
Froehlich, Biana, 88–89

Fuller, Loïe, 97–99
A Full Moon in March (Yeats; play), 103–4

Galatians 6:17, 38
Galilean women reputed fidelity of, 40
Garelick, Rhonda, 98
Gentileschi, Artemisia (*Judith Beheading Holofernes* painting), 57
Gilabertus (sculptures in Toulouse), 47
Gilman, Sander, 96–97
Girard, René, 36
Gittel (character in *Salome of the Tenements*), 109–10, 119
Glancy, Jennifer
on the ambiguity of Salome's dance, 19–20
on Salome as a male invention, 10
Glazunov, Alexander, 99
God
as the head of Christ, 41
Jezebel's and Herodias' refusal to accept word of, 34
The Golden Legend (de Voragine)
descriptions of Salome's death, 54
on the distribution of John's the Baptist's bones, 39n7
on retribution inflicted by John's severed head, 42n15
Gomez, Aida, 117
The Gospel according to Matthew (Pasolini; movie), 19, 98n16, 115
Goudal, Jetta, 107
Graham, Martha, 102–4, 102n37
The Greatest Story Ever Told (Stevens; movie), 115
Great Mosque of Damascus (Umayyad Mosque), head of John the Baptist at, 55n61
Great Whore of Revelation, 59–60

Index

Greece, ancient
    culture of, influence at Herod's court, 22
    and male as head, female as body, 41
green flower, in Wilde's *Salome*, 81, 81n97
Guszalewicz, Alice, 90n141

hair
    blue powdered, as Oriental, 74, 80–81
    flowing, as symbol of wanton sexuality, 44–45, 47, 70, 73, 123
    John the Baptist's, eroticizing of, 56, 82
"half of my kingdom" language
    in Esther, 27–29
    in the Gospel of Mark, 6, 16, 29
    in Wilde's *Salomé*, 84
Haman, in the story of Esther, 27–28
Harlem Renaissance, 122
Harris, Charlaine, 120
Hayworth, Rita, 114–16
head, John the Baptist's. *See also* beheading, Salome's *and specific works of art and literature*
    allusion to, in Graham's dance, 104
    bloodlessness, as metaphor in *Salome of the Tenements*, 109
    desecration/mistreatment of, 42, 77
    disposition of, following death, 39, 55n61
    in Flaubert's "Hérodiade," 76
    as forerunner of the Eucharist, 57
    in Mallarmé's "Canticle of Saint John," 76
    in Moreau's *The Apparition*, 71–72
    platter/plate imagery associated with, 6, 16–17, 23, 53, 53n54, 57, 59, 124

physicality of, in Renaissance and Reformation portrayals, 62
as a relic, object of worship, 11, 39–42, 46
retribution inflicted by, 42, 42n15
Salome's sexual desire for, 52–53, 66–67, 84
as symbol of male authority, 41
The Head of John the Baptist Brought to Herodias (Dürer; woodcut), 59
the Hebrew Bible. *See also* Esther, story of; Jael; Jews, Jewish traditions; Jezebel, story of
    and the ending of Hebrew law John's imprisonment as symbol of, 57–58
    portrayal of "outsider" women, 35
    as prefiguring the New Testament, 55–56
    and triumphs against Israel's enemies, 30–31
Hecate, linking with Herodias, 64
Heine, Heinrich. *See also Atta Troll* (Heine)
    ambivalence toward Judaism, 67
    folklore and folk deities, 64
    on Herodias's love for John, 42
    linking of desire and death, 65
    sexualized portrayal of Salome, 7, 67
    works featuring "Moorish" characters, 67
Helena (Constantine's mother), pilgrimage to the Holy Land, 39
Herod Antipas. *See also specific works of art*
    adoption of Greek-Roman culture, 22
    as an adulterer, 5–6, 14, 21, 26, 35–36, 44, 58, 66, 90
    consequences of John's beheading, 41
    exile, exculpation, 53, 95
    fear of John, 1–2, 5–7, 14–17, 73
    in Islamic tradition, 55

Index

Pacino's portrayals, 8, 116
 as protector of John, 73–74
 war with Aretas, 14–15, 20–21, 41, 73
 as weak, manipulable, inebriated, 22–23, 36, 43–44, 81, 83–84
 in Wilde's *Salomé*, 81, 83–84
"Hérodiade" (Flaubert; short story)
 influence on Moreaus painting, 71
 influence of in Saura's film, 117
 plot and major themes, 73–76
 Salammbô as precursor for, 70
 sexualized Salome in, 7
Herodiade (Graham; dance), 102–4, 102n37
"Hérodiade" (Mallarmé; poem)
 characterization of egotistical princess Hérodiade, 76
 Graham's dance based on, 102, 102n37
 influence of Yeats on, 103–4
Herodias. *See also specific works of art and literature*
 as an adulteress, 5–6, 21, 26, 35–36, 44, 58, 66, 90
 conflation/confusion with unnamed/same-named daughter, 6, 8–9, 13, 17, 17n5, 36, 63, 73–75
 exile, 41n11, 60–61, 95
 and failure to recognize John's truth, 34
 as jealous, spurned lover, 73–74
 linking with Diana/Hecate, 63–64
 as manipulative, evil, femme fatale, 5–8, 10, 18–19, 21n23, 34–36, 42, 65–66, 73–75, 89–92
 parallels with Jezebel, 33–34
 and the subversion of male headship, 41
 as a witch, otherworldly, 42, 65
Herodias (Heywood; poem)
 apologetic portrayal of Salome, 8
 portrayal of Salome in, 89–91
 Salome's redemption in, 90–92
 Salome as a trained seductress in, 21n23
Heywood, J. C.
 Antonius (Heywood), 8
 conversion of Salome into a Christian martyr, 8, 58
 echoes of in *Salome of the Tenements*, 108–9
 Herodias (Heywood), 8
 influence on Wilde, 89
 portrayal of a repentant Salome, 54
 Salome, The Daughter of Herodias (Heywood), 89
 Salome as a trained seductress in, 21n23
 Salome as victim in, 8
 Wilde's awareness of, 79
Hindemith, Paul, 102
Holofernes, Judith's murder of, 32
Homily on Matthew (Chrysostom; essay), 43
homoeroticism. *See eroticism, erotic desire*
Hunter, Jeffrey, 115
Huysmans, Joris-Karl (J.-K.)
 admiration for Flaubert, 78–79
 reference to Moreau's painting of Salome in, 71
 reverence for Mallarmé, 79
 Symbolist portrayal of a fantasy Salome, 7, 77–79

Iaokanan. *See John the Baptist*
Ibn Kathir, Ismail, 55
ice imagery, 54, 94–95
idols, idolatry, 15n4
the *Imperialist*, on Pemberton-Billing's accusations, 100–101
the *Inventio* (the finding), 39
Iokanaan. *See John the Baptist*
"Isabella" (Keats; poem), 65
Islam, Muslim traditions
 "daggers dance," 49–50
 Heine's fascination with, 67
 portrayals of Salome, 55

Index

Jackson, William E., 48–49
Jael, murder of Sisera, 30–31
J'ai Baisé ta Bouche, Iokanaan (*The Climax*, Beardsley; drawing), 86
Jairus's daughter, 18–20
Jephthah's daughter, 20, 27
Jerome, Saint
 on Herodias's mistreatment of John's severed head, 42
 on John the Baptist's tomb in Sebaste, 39
Jesus of Nazareth (TV miniseries), 115
Jews, Jewish traditions. *See also* the Hebrew Bible
 association of the color yellow with, 97
 and the Orientalized Jewish seductress, 63, 74
 as outsiders in Gentile society, 67
 persecution of, Heine's interest in, 67
 survival stories, 35, 55
Jezebel, story of (Book of Kings), 33–34, 33n52, 74
"Johannes" (Ava of Melk; poem), 48–49
John 1–3, 15
John 1:6–8, 40
John Manning (character in *Salome of the Tenements*), 108–13
John of Dumbleton manuscript, 51–52
John of Lingfield manuscript, 51
Johnson, Marcus
 catalog of literature and film based on the Salome story, 105, 105n56, 113, 125n127
 on *The Greatest Story Ever Told*, 115
 on *The Robe*, 113
John the Baptist (Iaokanan, Iokanaan). *See also* beheading, John the Baptist's; head, John the Baptist's *and* specific works of art and literature
 as Arab-speaking, in Farber's *Salomé*, 119
 Ava of Melk poem about, 48–49
 as blessed martyr, 50–51
 as forerunner of Christ, 1–2, 15, 38, 40, 106, 113
 Herod's fear of, 1–2, 5–7, 14–16, 73
 importance in Christian theology, 36, 38, 46, 60
 Josephus's description of, 14
 in manuscript illumination, 49–52
 as Nabi Yahya in Muslim traditions, 55
 other names for, 5n10
 relics associated with, 11, 39–42
 Salome's lust for/fatal attraction to, 9, 67, 82–84, 92, 121
 Salome's reverence for as a teacher/savior, 8, 90–91, 109–11
 as symbol of the triumph of the spiritual over the flesh, 51, 55, 123
 and theme of betrayal of the Jewish man, 35
 as a true prophet, 74–76
Jones, Susan, 103–4
jongleuresses/jongleresses (female street dancers), 48, 50, 75n63. *See also* acrobatic skill
Josephus
 background and writings, 13–14
 description of John the Baptist, 14
 expansion of the Salome narrative, 14–15, 41
 on the expulsion of the Jews, 15n4
 on Herod's fear of John, 16
 on Herod's war with Aretas, 14
 love for gossip, 15, 15n4
 naming of Salome, 7, 7n15, 14
Judges 4–5, 30
Judges 11:34, 20

Index

Judges 21:19–21, 22
Judith, story of, 28–33, 57
Judith 8–9, 31
Judith 12–13, 32
Judith 16:9, 32
Julian the Apostate, destruction of John's remains, 39, 39n7

Keats, John
 "La Belle Dame sans Merci: A Ballad," 64
 and the linking of desire and death, 65
Keel, Howard, 113
King, Philip J., 28n42
King of Kings (Ray; movie), 114–15
The King of the Great Clock Tower (Yeats; play), 103
2 Kings 1:8, 34
2 Kings 9:21–23, 34
2 Kings 9:30, 33n52
2 Kings 9:30–37, 34
2 Kings 9:32, 33
2 Kings 16–21, 34
2 Kings 16:31–34, 34
2 Kings 19:3, 34
2 Kings 21:1–14, 34
2 Kings 21:20–24, 34
korasion (girl, maiden), 17–18, 17–18n6. See also child/innocent, Salome as
Koster, Henry, 113
Kraemer, Ross S.
 apologetic perspective on Herodias and her daughter, 10, 10–11n29
 on link between Aretas and John the Baptist, 14
 on the purposes for the story of John's beheading, 40
Kuryluk, Ewa, 98

la belle dame sans merci. See *la belle juive* (the "beautiful Jewess"); the femme fatale
"La Belle Dame sans Merci: A Ballad" (Keats; poem), 64
la belle juive (the "beautiful Jewess"), 63, 69, 100, 105–6
Lachmann, Hedwig, 87–88
Laforgue, Jules, 11, 77
"Lamia" (Keats), 65–66
Landow, George P., 77
La Tragédie de Salome (Fuller), 99
Laughton, Charles, 114
law, Jewish, transcending of by Christ's offer of redemption, 58
Lawrence, Florence, 105
LeFanu, Sheridan, 120
lesbianism
 charges against Maud Allen, 101
 and LeFanu's female vampire, 120
Letter of Herod to Pilate, description of Salome's exile and death in, 41n11, 53–54
Levien, Sonya, 107
Levine, A.-J. 19
Leviticus 18:16, 5, 15
Licinius, 37
Lilith (character in *True Blood*), 121–22
Livy, 24
Longfellow, Henry Wadsworth, 90
Longinus (centurion), exculpation of, 53
Lord Ruthven (character in *The Vampyre*), 120
Lowe, Lisa, 69–70
Lucifer series (Nugent; drawings), 123
Luke 2:35, 51
Luke 9:7–9, 15
Luke 13:32, 41
Luke 16:16, 57
Luke 23:6–12, 6
Luna, Donyale, 116
Luther, Martin, 58–59
Luxford, Julian, 52, 52n49

Index

Machaerus, Herod's palace at, 23
Maeterlinck, Maurice, 79
Mahler, Alma, 87
males
    association with the head, 41
    sexual dominance by women, 35
Mallarmé, Stéphane, admiration for
    Fuller's dance, 98
Mallarme, Stéphane, "Herodiade,"
    102, 102n37
Mallarmé, Stéphane
    "Hérodiade," 76
    Huysmans's reverence for, 79
A Man of No Importance (movie), 117
mantle dance, 21–22
Mark, Gospel of
    absence of clarity about "Salome," 17
    account of the beheading of John the Baptist, 16
    ambiguities and translation difficulties, 17, 17n5
    as the first canonical gospel, 16
    lack of sympathy for Herodias or Salome, 35
    parallel between Ahab–Jezebel–Elijah and Herod–Herodias–John narrative, 34
    on reasons for Herod's fear of John, 16–17
    Salome narrative in, 5–7
    Mark 1:6, 34, 54
    Mark 5:35–45, 18
    Mark 5:42, 18
    Mark 6:7–29, 10
    Mark 6:14–16, 1–2, 16
    Mark 6:21, 22
    Mark 6:22, 10
    Mark 6:22–29, 1, 19–20
    Mark 6:23, 27–28
    Mark 6:29, 39
    Mark 8:15, 6, 40
    Mark 15:24, 113
    Mark 1:6, 34, 54
    Mark 5:35–45, 18
    Mark 5:42, 18
    Mark 6:7–29, 10

Mark 6:14–16, 1–2, 16
Mark 6:21, 22
Mark 6:22, 10
Mark 6:22–29, 1, 19–20
Mark 6:23, 27–28
Mark 6:29, 39
Mark 8:15, 6, 40
Mark 15:24, 113
martyrs, Christian
    body parts (*disjecta membra*), veneration, 38
    martyrdom as theme in Reformation tragedies, 60
    meaning of word "martyr," 38
    Salome's, 95
    veneration of, shrines to, 38–39
    virgin martyrs, 44, 93
Mary/Virgin Mary, links with Salome, 51, 98
Massenet, Jules, 117
Matthew, Gospel of
    Matthew 11:16–18, 19
    Matthew 14:1–2, 1–2
    Matthew 14:1–12, 1, 45–46
    Matthew 14:6, 17, 22
    Matthew 14:7, 27–28
    Matthew 14:8, 23
    Matthew 14:12, 39
    Matthew 16:6, 40
    parallel between Ahab–Jezebel–Elijah and Herod–Herodias–John narrative, 34
    Salome narrative in, 5–7
Matthieu, Pierre-Louis, 71–73
McBreen, Ellen, 122
McKenna, Neil, 79
Messter, Oskar, 105
Mestres, Isabel, 115, 117
Middle Ages
    and the Dance of Salome, 49
    emphasis on the acrobat aspects of Salome's dance, 47–48
    portrayals of the Dance of Salome, instructional purpose, 49
    Salome as flesh, contrasted with John's spirit, 49

Index

sharp divide between female/body and male/mind, 56
midrashim (interpretive retellings), and interpretations of the Salome story, 4, 4n7
Mies Julie (Farber; play), 118
Miriam, victory dance in Exodus, 20
Miss Julie (Strindberg; play), 118
moon symbolism
   in Beardsley's *The Woman in the Moon*, 86
   in Flaubert's *Salammbô*, 70
   in Heywood's *Herodias*, 90
   in *Salome of the Tenements*, 109
   in Wilde's *Salomé*, 71, 80–85
the Moors. *See* Islam, Muslim traditions; Orientalizing
Moralités Légendaires (*Legendary Moralities*, Laforgue), "Salomé," 11, 77
Mordecai, role in the story of Esther, 27–28
Moreau, Gustave
   color symbolism, 72
   contradictions in portrayals of Salome, 72–73
   Flaubert's influence on, 70–71
   influence on Huysmans, 71, 77–79
   Salome Dancing Before Herod, 88
   sexualized Salome in, 7
   volume of work focused on Salome, 72
Mount of Olives, John the Baptist's head at, 39
Mystery plays, Dance of Salome in, 49

Naboth in the Jezebel story, 34
Nameless Woman (character in Faber's *Salome*), 118
Narraboth (character in Wilde's *Salomé*), 80
Navidi, Barry, 117–18
Nazimova, Alla
   influence of Wilde's *Salomé* on, 115
   Salomé (silent film), 102, 105
   self-funding, 106
New Testament, apocryphal material, 53. *See also specific books of the Bible*
New York Times
   review of Bara's Salome, 105–6
   review of Hayworth in *Salome* movie, 114
New York World, review of Walker's Salome dance, 102
Noguchi, Isamu, 102n37
Notre-Dame la Daurade (Benedictine), Toulouse, 47–48
Nugent, Richard Bruce, 122–23
Nurse
   as character in Graham's *Heroidiade*, 103–4
   as character in Mallarmé's "Hérodiade", 76

Oates, Joyce Carol, 3–4
Olcott, Sidney, 107
Old Testament, Apocrypha, 28–29. *See also* the Hebrew Bible
Orientalism, Orientalizing. *See also la belle juive* (the "beautiful Jewess"); the veil
   definition and history of, 68
   eroticization and feminization associated with, 69
   in Flaubert's "Hérodiade," 73–75
   and Hesse's description of Herodias, 66
   and Orientalized women as objects of desire, 69–70
   of Salome's dance, precursors, 50
   in Wilde's *Salomé*, 81
orthodox Christianity, and the elevation of John the Baptist, 38
Osiander, Andreas, 60

Index

outsider women, 35

Pacino, Al, 8, 116–18
Palestinian struggles, referencing of in Farber's *Salomé*, 118–19
Paris, France, Orientalizing fad in, 97
Parker, Rosie, 108–9
Pasolini, Pier Paolo, 98n16, 115
peace, as meaning of the name "Salome," 118, 124
Pell, Ella Ferris, 11
Pellico, Silvio, 62–63
Pemberton-Billing, Noel, 100–101
"Persian," as synonym for decadence, 25–27
Petzer, Tatiana, 69
Piggott, Edward, 86
pilgrimages, and reverence for martyrs, 38. *See also* relics
platter image. *See* head, John the Baptist's
Poems of Adoration, "A Dance of Death" (Field), 9, 94
Polidori, John, 120
Pontius Pilate, 53, 114, 119
Powell, Robert, 115
Prayers and Meditations (Anselm), 49–51
Praz, Mario, 65, 68
"Princess Fara" (character in *The Big Fisherman*), 113–14
prostitutes
 "dancing girls" as euphemism for, 97
 and Jezebel's self-adornment, 33–34, 33n52
Protestant Reformation
 and Cranach's Lutheran iconography, 58–59
 Dürer's portrayals of Salome, 59
 and the Great Whore of Revelation, 59–60
 revival of tragedy during, 60
 and the theme of martyrdom, 60
Proverbs 31:4–5, 25n35

Pseudo-Jerome, 57
Puchner, Martin, 103–4
purple/blue, symbolism of, 15n4, 27, 45, 70, 74, 80
Pym, Anthony, 7

The Rabbi of Bacharach (Heine; novel), 67
racial tensions, in Nugent's art, 122
Rambova, Natacha, 106
Ramsey, JonBenét, 3–4, 19
Ray, Nicholas, 114–15
redemption
 in Riley's reconstruction of Salome narrative, 124
 of Salome as Christian convert/martyr, 8, 90, 119
 Salome's and Herodias's, in Pseudo-Jerome's interpretation, 58
 through love, as theme in Heywood's trilogy, 113
 through suffering, as theme in *Salome of the Tenements*, 112–13
Regnault, Henri, 71
relics
 John's head as, 39–42
 traffic in, during the Crusades, 46
 veneration of, during the fourth century, 38
Renaissance
 changing interpretations of Scripture, 55–56
 greater melding of mind and body, 56
 humanized portrayals of Salome, 56–61
 portrayals of Judith with Holofernes head, 57
 retributive deaths ascribed to, *The Antiquities of the Jews*, 13
Revelation 17:5, 59
Rice, Anne, 120
Richardson, LeeAnn M., 94–95

Index

Riley, Terry, 123–24
The Robe (Douglas; movie), 113
Robertson, Graham, 96n1
Romanesque art, eroticism in depictions of Salome, 46–47
Romans 9–11, on the acceptance of Jesus by non-Jews, 58
The Romantic Agony (Praz), 68
Romantic era, Romanticism. *See also* the femme fatale; the Vamp
    context and characteristics, 63
    Decadence/Symbolism as a response to, 77
    emergence of the vampire theme, 120
    emphasis on fantasy, imagination, 63
    and the mingling of desire and death, 63–65
    Orientalizing, 68–69
Rome, ancient
    beheading example, 23–24
    and dancing by sexual slaves, 23, 45, 44–45, 97
    exculpation of, by Christian apologists, 40
    and official recognition of Christianity, 37
royal lineage, Salome's
    emphasis of in *Atta Troll*, 66
    indicators of in Medieval portrayals, 46
    indicators of in Renaissance and Reformation painting, 56–59
    and interpretations of her dance before Herod, 19
Rubens, Peter Paul
    depiction of the desecration of John' head, 42
    portrayals of Salome, 59
Rubenstein, Ida, 99
Russell, Ken, 116

Sachs, Hans, 60
Said, Edward, 68

Saint Sylvester in Capite, Rome, 39
Saint Zeno church, Verona, bas relief showing Salome, 49
Salammbô (Flaubert; novel)
    chaînette image, 70–71
    goddess Tanith in, 69–70
    influence on Moreau, 70–71
    influence on Wilde, 68, 71
    Salammbô as object of desire, 69–70
    veils in, 69
"Salomania" craze, 8, 105
Salome (Almodóvar; movie), 115
Salome (Bene; movie), 116
Salome (d'Anna; movie), 116
Salome (Dieterle; movie), 114
Salome (Heywood; poem)
    apologetic portrayal of Salome, 8
    Emerson's positive response to, 8
    review in the *American Catholic Quarterly Review*, 89
    Wilde's negative review of, 8, 8n20
"Salomé" (Laforgue; poem), 77
Salomé (Nazimova; silent movie), 102, 105–6
Salome (Pell; painting), 10–11n29, 11
Salomé (Strauss; opera)
    Dance of the Seven Veils in, 7, 96–97, 96n1
    emphasis on Salome's chastity, 97
    first United States performance, 88–89
    opening of, discordant response to, 87
    performance challenges and delays, 88–89
    Wilde's play as basis for, 79
Salome (*The Dance of the Seven Veils*, Blackton; silent movie), 105
Salome (unattributed; silent movie), 115
Salomé (Wilde; play)
    banning of, 86, 88, 96
    Berkoff's staging of, 116–17
    color symbolism in, 96–97

Index

Salomé (Wilde; play) (*continued*)
   and the Dance of the Seven Veils, 3, 7, 84
   English translation, 86
   Farber's reinterpretation, 118–19
   German translation, 87
   importance, influence, 3, 79, 63, 89, 109, 115–17
   Orientalizing language in, 66
   original French version, 86
   Pacino's productions, 8, 116–18
   plot, major themes, 80–85
   Rubenstein-Baskt performance, 99
   scopophilia (penetrating gaze) theme in, 80–82
   silent films based on, 105, 119
   Strauss's opera based on, 100
   unrequited passion theme in, 9, 80, 82–84
Salome, The Daughter of Herodias (Heywood), 89–90, 93
Salome Agrippa (character in *True Blood*), 120–22
Salome: An Invitation to the Dance (Johnson), 105, 105n56
The Salome Dance (vaudeville), 49, 87, 99, 114
Salome Dances for Peace (Riley; musical composition), 123–24
Salome Dancing (Nugent; drawing), 122
Salome Dancing before Herod (Moreau; painting), 71–72, 88
Salome/Herodias's daughter, 118. *See also specific works of art and literature*
   apologetic, exculpatory portrayals, 8–9, 36, 88–91, 93–94, 97, 115
   atonement and remorse/martyrdom, 8, 54, 57–58, 90, 93, 99–100, 112–13, 117–19
   conflation/confusion with mother, 6, 8–9, 13, 36, 63, 73–75
   conflation with the story of Abraham, 117
   as culturally popular theme, 4, 7, 62n3
   and the dedicated artist theme, 95, 102, 112–13
   desire of, portrayal of as holy, life-affirming, 118
   as erotic, wanton, sexual, 3–4, 7–8, 33, 44, 46–47, 56, 67, 96, 101
   as evil, diabolical, perverse, 4, 11, 17, 35, 43–44, 55, 59, 72, 77
   exile, subjugation, and death, 9, 14, 41n11, 51–54, 53n55, 85, 121–22
   first visual representation, 45–46
   globalized/politicized portrayals, 107, 118–19, 123–24
   introduction of, in the Gospels of Mark and Matthew, 5–7
   humanized portrayals, 14, 56–59, 61, 66, 71
   as an innocent/sexually immature, 8–9, 18–19, 54n57, 62–63, 90, 98, 100, 124
   and love/desire for John, 66, 82, 121
   link with Mary, 51
   as male, temptress, femme fatale, 5, 7–8, 10, 30, 43, 47, 55–56, 114–15
   as mysterious, otherworldly, 9, 42, 71–72, 103–4, 116
   namelessness/naming of, 5–7, 7n15, 14, 118
   spelling variants, 1n1
   as victim of mother's manipulation, 7–8, 10, 18–19, 21n23, 36, 42, 65–66, 73–75, 92
   waning interest in after the Reformation, 62, 62n3
Salome in the Garden (Moreau), 72
Salome of the Tenements (Yezierska; novel)

Index

echoes of the biblical narrative in, 9, 107–9
echoes of the vamp character in, 119–20
focus on class conflict and assimilation, 107
plot, 108–10
redemption of Salome in, 112–13
and the theme of artistic striving, 107–8
Salome: Princess of Galilee (Denker; novel), 114
"The Salome Project," origins and development, 1–4, 105, 105n56
"Salome" series (Nugent; drawings), 122
Salome's Last Dance (Russell; movie), decadent portrayal of Wilde and Salome in, 116
Salomé -- The Seventh Veil (Xandria; record album), 123
saltatrices (leaping dancers), 23n28, 45, 48
saltatriculae (little leaping dancers), 23n28, 45
2 Samuel 13:7–19, 25
San Vitale, Ravenna, portrayals of Theodora in, 45
San Zeno, Verona, portrayal of Salome at, 2n2
Sarony, Napoleon, 97
Saura, Carlos, 117
Schmitt, Florent, 99
scopophilia (penetrating gaze), in Wilde's *Salomé*, 80–81
Sebaste, Samaria, 39
seduction
　connection to murder, story of Jael, 30–31
　and the story of Jezebel, 33
　the veil as symbol of, 69
　connection to murder, story of Judith, 31–32
Seidel, Linda, 47
Shelley, Mary Godwin, *Frankenstein*, 120

Shlomit. *See* Salome/Herodias's daughter
Showalter, Elaine, 11
silent movies
　based on Wilde's *Salomé*, 105
　influence of Wilde's *Salomé* on, 115
Simeon, prophecy to Mary, sword imagery in, 51
Sinope, illuminated manuscript from, 45–46
Sisera, Jael's murder of, 30–31
Sisters of Salome (Bentley), 11, 62, 96
Skaggs, Carmen Trammell, 4
"Sommernachstraum" ("Midsummer Night's Dream," Hesse; poem), 65–66
Song of Songs
　echoes of in Wilde's *Salomé*, 82
　echoes of in Hesse's description of Herodias, 66
　and the holiness of desire, emphasis on in Farber's *Salomé*, 118
Songs 6:13, 21
Sonya Vrunsky (character in *Salome of the Tenements*), 108–13
The Southern Vampire Mysteries (Harris; novels), 120
Sozomen, on relics of Saint John in Constantinople, 39
Starnaman, Sabrina, 106
Stevens, George, 115
Stocker, Margaret, 32–33
Stoker, Graham, 120
Stokes, Bram, 108–9
Stowe, Harriet Beecher, 8–9, 54n57, 90
Strauss, Richard
　the Dance of the Seven Veils, 87–88
　eroticism, erotic desire in, 65
　influence of Wilde on, 79
　Salomé opera, 87
Summa logiae et philosophiae naturalis (John of Dumbleton), 51–52

Index

Sveti Ivan (Saint John) monastery, Bulgaria, bone fragments, 39–40
sword imagery/sword dance
    depiction of Salome performing, 21n21
    in the Littlemore manuscript, 21n21, 49–51
    in Simeon's prophecy to Mary, 51

Tanith (goddess, as character in Flaubert's *Salammbô*), 70
Tanz der Salome (Messter; silent movie), 105, 115
Tertullian, 38, 44
Thecla, 44
Theodora, 45
Theodosius I, 37, 39
Tiberius, 14
Titian, 56
tragedy, revival during the Reformation, 60
Trois Contes (*Three Tales*, Flaubert; short stories), 73
True Blood (Ball; TV series), 116, 120–22
True Cross, fragments of (*Inventio*), 39

Untitled (Nugent; drawing), 123

the Vamp (vampire). *See also* the *femme fatale*
    Bara as, 119
    folk legends around, 119–20
    portrayals of Salome as, 119–21
    as sexual predator, 63, 119–20
The Vampire Chronicles (Rice; novel series), 120
The Vampyre (Polidori; novel), 120
van der Weyden, Rogier, 42, 56
Vashti, disobedience of, 26–27

vaudeville, popularity of Salome's dance, 49, 87, 99, 114
Vaughn, Henry, 9, 54n57, 94
veils, veil imagery
    in Beardleys drawing's, 86
    Flaubert's understanding and thematic use of," 69, 75
    in Fuller's dance, 99
    of illusion, in *Salome of the Tenements*, 109–12
    in Moreau's painting, 88
    in Nugent's drawings, 122
    in Rubenstein's Salome, 99–100
    in Strauss's *Salomé*, 87–88
    symbolism of, in nineteenth century art, 68–69
    in Wilde's *Salomé*, 81–82, 84
victim dance, ring dance, 20–21
victory dances, 20, 52–53
Villa Romana del Casale, fresco with leaping dancers, 45
On Virginity (Ambrose; essay), 44
virgins
    good vs. bad, in Ambrose's writings, 44
    Salome as, in Heywood's portrayal, 93
Vision of Salomé (Allan; dance), 100
Vitellius, role in the destruction of Herod's army, 14
von Stuck, Franz, 100
Voyer, Cécile, 49–51

Walker, Aïda Overton, 101–2, 116
Wallon der Sarton, Canon, 46
war dances, 21
Weintraub, Stanley, 96–97
Wilde, Oscar. *See also Salomé* (Wilde)
    British condemnation of, 100–101
    color symbolism, 96–97
    homoeroticism, 123
    as identifying with Salome, 81n97
    influences on, 63, 68

Index

rejection of idea of a repentant Salome, 54–55
review of Heywood's *Salome* trilogy, 8, 8n20, 89–90
Wilde Salomé (Pacino; movie), 8, 116–18
Wilentz, Gay, 109
William, Bishop of Orléans, 49
Williamson, John, 87
Winter, Peter M., 106
Wittich, Maria, 97
Woman in Sacred History (Stowe; biographical sketches), 8–9, 90
Women's Voices Theater Festival, production of Farber's *Salomé*, 118

Xandria, 123
Xanthopoulos, Nicephorus Callistus, 54, 94

Yeats, William Butler, 103–4
yellow, symbolism of, 96–97
Yezierska, Anzia, 9, 107–9

Zagona, Helen Grace, 11, 62